CW00346953

1 MONTH OF
FREE
READING

at

www.ForgottenBooks.com

By purchasing this book you are eligible for one month membership to ForgottenBooks.com, giving you unlimited access to our entire collection of over 1,000,000 titles via our web site and mobile apps.

To claim your free month visit:

www.forgottenbooks.com/free6227

ISBN 978-0-483-42071-7

PIBN 10006227

This book is a reproduction of an important historical work. Forgotten Books uses
state-of-the-art technology to digitally reconstruct the work, preserving the original format
whilst repairing imperfections present in the aged copy. In rare cases, an imperfection in
the original, such as a blemish or missing page, may be replicated in our edition. We do,
however, repair the vast majority of imperfections successfully; any imperfections that
remain are intentionally left to preserve the state of such historical works.

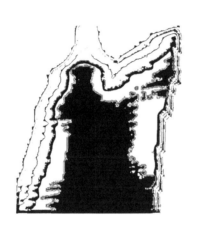

HISTORY OF THE UNITED STATES

VOL. III

1751 — JAMES MADISON — 1836.

By Asher Brown Durand, 1832.

From the original portrait in the New York Historical Society.

HISTORY

OF THE

UNITED STATES OF AMERICA

BY

HENRY WILLIAM ELSON

AUTHOR OF "SIDE LIGHTS ON AMERICAN HISTORY," ETC.

With Two Hundred Illustrations Selected and
Edited by Charles Henry Hart

·VOLUME III

New York
THE MACMILLAN COMPANY
1908

Norwood Press:
Berwick & Smith Co., Norwood, Mass., U.S.A.

CONTENTS

CONTENTS

ANNOTATED INDEX TO ILLUSTRATIONS

VOLUME III

Portraits

ANNOTATED INDEX

This very characteristic silhouette of Randolph, in riding costume with whip and spurs, was taken at Richmond, Va., June 28, 1830, as he was embarking for Russia. For an account of Brown and his remarkable work, see the writer's "The Last of the Silhouettists," in *Outlook* for Oct. 6, 1900.

When the great Seneca chief sat to Weir for this painting, he went to the studio accompanied by his interpreter and a number of braves, all of whom showed uncommon interest in the progress of the work. The medal he wears was given to him by Washington, and he was never without it even when clothed in only nature's garb.

Stuart painted for Boydell portraits of a number of painters and engravers, his contemporaries, as also this portrait of himself, which passed to Henry Graves, of London, the successor of Boydell, and on the disposal of the Graves collection, it was acquired by the National Gallery. Stuart painted an earlier portrait of himself, which is in the Redwood Library at Newport, and a self-sketch, in oil, is in the Museum of Fine Arts, Boston.

XXXIX. VAN BUREN, MARTIN (1782–1862). By Henry Inman ‑ ‑ ‑

There is a whole length of Van Buren, by Inman, in the City Hall, New York.

XL. WEBSTER, DANIEL (1782–1852). By Joseph Ames .

This is the last portrait of Webster painted from life, and was done at the same time that Ames was painting the whole length in fishing rig; that is, they were both on the easel at the same time.

Miscellaneous

XLI. CARICATURE OF RESIGNATION OF JACKSON'S CABINET, 1831

This was the first and is the only time that an entire cabinet resigned in the middle of an administration, and what is more extraordinary, it was caused by a woman. The "rats" bear the faces of "the four busy B's" in the cabinet, — Berrien, Branch, Van Buren, and Barry.

LIST OF MAPS

FULL-PAGE COLORED MAPS

MAPS IN THE TEXT

HISTORY OF THE UNITED STATES

CHAPTER XXI

THE WAR OF 1812

NOTWITHSTANDING the decline in Jefferson's popularity, many of the state legislatures invited him to stand for a third election. But he declined; not on the ground taken by Washington twelve years before, but because, as he claimed, it was well to establish a precedent for the future. He was the author, therefore, of our unwritten law that no man serve more than eight years in the presidency. He was one of our two or three Presidents who, having served two terms, might have been elected for a third; yet many believed that his embargo would have rendered his election doubtful had he desired a third term. But he did the next thing—he practically chose his successor. It was mainly through Jefferson's influence that his secretary of state was preferred before the other two aspirants, James Monroe and George Clinton. A week after the inauguration Jefferson left the Capital City on horseback "for the elysium of domestic affections." He reached Monticello, March 15, and in the remaining seventeen years of his life he never again passed beyond the bounds of his native state.[1]

[1] Jefferson's poularity soon rose to its normal standard, and as long as he lived he was the chief adviser of his party, being in constant

I

The little man of quiet, simple manners, who now stood before ten thousand people and read his inaugural address in a "scarcely audible tone," had been a leading figure in public life for many years, and was by training eminently equipped for the great office.   James Madison as a framer of the Constitution had done more than any other man in making that instrument what it is; he had been a leader in Congress under Washington, and had now just completed his eight years as chief in the Cabinet of Jefferson.   Certainly he knew the inner workings of the government as few could know them.   Moreover, next to his retiring chief, Madison was the ablest man in the country, save one, Albert Gallatin.

The new President's trouble began from the day of his installation.   He sincerely desired to make Gallatin secretary of state; but there was a faction of Democrats in the Senate, headed by Senators William B. Giles of Virginia, Samuel Smith of Maryland, and Michael Lieb of Pennsylvania, who hated Gallatin and determined to prevent his confirmation.   This faction, encouraged by George Clinton, who was again Vice President, and aided by the Federalists, could control the Senate, and Madison had to yield.   Gallatin remained in the Treasury, and Robert Smith, a brother of Senator Smith from Maryland, was made secretary of state.   The arrangement was humiliating to the President, who was thus forced to accept for the chief place in his Cabinet a man wholly incompetent, a man in sympathy with

correspondence with Presidents Madison and Monroe. After 1812 he became reconciled to his old friend and rival, John Adams, and the two were friendly correspondents as long as they lived, though they never met again. Both died on the national holiday, July 4, 1826, but few hours apart.

1761 — ALBERT GALLATIN — 1849.

By Gilbert Stuart, 1803.

From the original portrait in possession of Frederick W. Stevens, Esq.,
New York.

a faction that used its power to weaken the administration. For two years this arrangement dragged on, when at last the patient Gallatin lost patience and threatened to resign from the Cabinet. This awakened the slow-moving Madison, and led him for once to play the master. He defied the Senate faction by dismissing Robert Smith and choosing James Monroe as secretary of state. The country and even the Senate sustained him, and a signal victory was gained for the administration.

DRIFTING TOWARD WAR

There was a delicious ray of sunshine that brought joy to many at the beginning of the Madison administration. Mr. Erskine, the English minister at Washington, receiving instructions from Canning, the British foreign secretary, announced that the Orders in Council would be withdrawn on June 10, on condition that the President remove the non-intercourse restriction, in as far as it concerned England. Whereupon Madison made a proclamation suspending the non-intercourse act with England. Great was the rejoicing on all sides. The eastern ports became beehives of industry. Vessels were quickly laden with the long-accumulated produce, and in a few weeks a thousand had launched upon the sea for foreign ports. Madison enjoyed a moment of intoxicating popularity; but it was only a moment. The bubble soon burst. The overzealous Erskine had exceeded his instructions, and he was disavowed and recalled. When the news reached America that the Orders in Council were still in force, the President issued a new proclamation, reviving the non-intercourse act with Great Britain.

Francis James Jackson was then sent to replace Erskine.

Jackson was a man of much pride and little tact, who boasted an acquaintance with "most of the sovereigns of Europe," and felt that he had come to treat with a lot of "savage Democrats, half of them sold to France." He began by accusing the administration of deception in treating with Erskine in the knowledge that he was exceeding his instructions. Madison informed him that such insinuations were inadmissible from a foreign minister dealing "with a government that understands what it owes to itself." In the face of this warning, Jackson, with incredible effrontery, repeated his accusation, and was informed that no further communications would be received from him. Thus ingloriously ended his diplomatic career in America.

Meanwhile our relations with France were approaching another crisis. In the spring of 1810 the American Congress removed the restrictions on foreign commerce, but forbade intercourse with England or France if either continued hostile to our trade. This has been pronounced the most disgraceful act on the American statute book. "When Great Britain and France were raining upon us blows such as no powerful nation had ever submitted to before, we folded our hands and bowed our heads with no word of protest, except to say that if either one of them would cease its outrages, we should resent the insults of the other."[2] Napoleon had issued his Rambouillet Decree, confiscating all American ships found in French waters. But on learning of this act of Congress, he offered to revoke his Berlin and Milan decrees. This was only a contemptible trick by which to draw more of our vessels into his trap, and all that were entrapped were seized in accordance with a secret order.

[2] Gordy, Vol. 11, p. 72 (Revised Ed.).

While our foreign relations continued in this strained condition, an event in the Northwest recalled the attention of the people to important matters at home. The Indians of the Northwest had given little trouble for several years after their defeat by Wayne in 1794. But in recent years they had again become hostile, owing chiefly to the ambition of a great leader, Tecumthe or Tecumseh, who belonged to the Shawnee tribe. Tecumseh's ambition was to unite all the tribes of that region into one great Indian nation, and through it to restrict all further encroachments of the white man. He was a man of remarkable eloquence and powers of leadership, and he was assisted in his plans by his twin brother, known as the Prophet.

The governor of Indiana Territory was William Henry Harrison, a future President of the United States. He was a son of Benjamin Harrison, a signer of the Declaration of Independence, a governor of Virginia, and an intimate friend of Washington. At the time of St. Clair's defeat by the Indians in Ohio, young Harrison, a boy of nineteen years, was a medical student in Philadelphia. At the advice of both Washington and Jefferson, he left his studies and went to the West to aid in the war against the Indians. With a brave heart he set out to win glory for himself and honor for his country. In 1801 he become governor of Indiana and superintendent of Indian affairs. In September, 1809, Harrison made a treaty at Fort Wayne with the Delaware, Miami, Kickapoo, and other tribes, by which three million acres on the upper Wabash were ceded to the United States. The twin brothers were not present, nor had the tribe to which they belonged any part in the ownership or sale of the lands. But when they heard of the cession, they were wroth, and declared that the land belonged to all the tribes, and that a part had no right to sell without the consent of all. They pronounced the treaty void and threatened to kill every chief that had signed it. A year passed, and the Indians, while professing friendship for the whites, kept up a series of outrages on the frontier. Harrison advised them that the depredations must be stopped; but they continued, and he prepared for an attack.

With some nine hundred men, General Harrison marched into the Indian country in the autumn of 1811. Tecumseh was absent in the South. His brother, the Prophet, occupied the town of Tippecanoe on the Wabash. Harrison marched on and encamped near the town. The Prophet sent word that he wished a conference with the American general on the morrow. Harrison, suspecting treachery, had his men sleep on their arms, and an hour before day next morning about five hundred Indians, with fearful yells, emerged from the underbrush and made an attack. The soldiers seized their guns, and a desperate struggle raged for two hours, when the Indians broke and fled. They abandoned their village, which the Americans burned, and then hastened back to the white settlements. The battle of Tippecanoe did not belong to the war with England that was soon to come, nor had the British much, if anything, to do with inspiring it; but it gave Harrison an excellent military reputation, and it prepared the people for the greater events that were to follow.

The prophetic words of Benjamin Franklin were destined to come true—that the war ending with the surrender of Cornwallis was simply the war of Revolution, and that the war of Independence was yet to be fought. Two events in 1811 hastened the crisis with England,—the withdrawal of our minister from London, and an impromptu duel between

1771 — JOHN RODGERS — 1838.

By Charles Willson Peale, 1816.

From the original portrait in the old State House, Philadelphia, Pa.

two vessels at sea. William Pinckney, one of the ablest diplomats ever sent to a foreign court by the United States, after laboring and struggling in vain for five years with the British ministry, took "inamicable leave." This event had stirred the ministry a little. It had led them to hasten in appointing a minister to Washington, Augustus John Foster, the first since the inglorious failure of Jackson a year and a half before. While Foster was on the sea en route for his new field of duty, the other event occurred.

On the partial reopening of our trade with France, British armed vessels were again sent to blockade New York, and they amused themselves capturing vessels bound for France and impressing American seamen. One of these ships, the *Guerrière,* was said to have impressed a man named Diggio, and the secretary of the navy sent the *President,* a 44-gun frigate under Captain John Rodgers, not only to rescue Diggio and other unfortunates, but to "protect American commerce," to "vindicate the injured honor of our navy," and to support the honor of the flag "at any risk and cost." This was a new spirit for the nation that had suffered twenty years of the impressment business and had defended itself with protests alone. Rodgers was under full sail from Annapolis to New York, when he sighted a vessel which he believed to be the *Guerrière*; but she showed no colors, and he was not sure. He gave chase, and eight hours later, at nightfall, the *President* was within hailing distance. Rodgers shouted through his trumpet, "What ship is that?" The answer from the stranger was an echo of his own words, and Rodgers asked again, when instantly a flame of fire leaped from the dark hull of the strange vessel, and a shot was lodged in the mainmast of the *President.*[1]

[1] This account was given under oath by Rodgers and all his crew;

The lesson of the *Chesapeake* had not been thrown away; the *President* was prepared. In a moment both vessels were throwing broadsides. In fifteen minutes the strange vessel was silenced and disabled. At daybreak next morning Rodgers discovered that he had been fighting the *Little Belt,* a British corvette of twenty guns and about half the force of the *President.* Her encounter with the *President* proved disastrous. Twelve men lay dead and twenty-one wounded on her decks; "all the rigging and sails cut to pieces, not a brace nor a bowline left," [4] while one boy was wounded on the President. This incident was hailed with delight by the American people as the avenging of the outrage on the *Chesapeake.*

Meantime Foster arrived. Pinckney, while yet in London, had asked the significant question, What was Foster to do when he arrived in Washington? Foster had no power to promise a repeal of the Orders in Council, and the administration would treat with him on no other ground. He offered to settle the *Chesapeake* affair without even demanding reparation for the greater disaster to the *Little Belt*; but even this made no impression. Every subject brought up by the British minister received the same answer, The Orders in Council must be repealed. If America was in earnest, all signs pointed to the same thing, namely, that the United States had at last taken a stand—that if the Orders in Council were not repealed, there would be war. Foster wrote this to his government, but the British Cabinet, led by the short-sighted Spencer Perceval, refused to be moved.

but Captain Bingham of the *Little Belt* gave a different account, claiming to have been fired on first.

[4] From Captain Bingham's report.

The Twelfth Congress met in December, 1811. It differed greatly from its immediate predecessors. No longer do we find the temporizing spirit; no longer was Congress dominated by the fathers of the Revolution. A new generation had arisen to take charge of public affairs. Especially in the House did this spirit of the rising generation manifest itself. Here were half a dozen young leaders, war Democrats, as they were called, who took control of the House and shaped legislation for years to come. The leaders of this new school were Henry Clay of Kentucky and John C. Calhoun of South Carolina, both destined to spend nearly half a century in the forefront of national life. And these were ably seconded by Felix Grundy of Tennessee, and Langdon Cheeves and William Lowndes of South Carolina; and closely associated with them was the aged John Sevier, whom last we saw, a third of a century ago, directing the battle at King's Mountain. Henry Clay was elected speaker the first day he entered the House,[5] and this position he continued to hold as long as he was a member of that body. Born in the "slashes" of Virginia, Clay was left fatherless and penniless in childhood. He read law, and afterward migrated westward and made his home in the new state of Kentucky, where he soon rose to fame as a member of the bar. Now he began his remarkable career as a party manager that has few parallels in American history. Under his leadership the Twelfth Congress set itself to restore the sullied honor of the country, and to do this there was no alternative but war.

President Madison still hesitated. He was almost as fondly devoted to peace as had been the great Democrat

[5] He had served a short time in the Senate by appointment, but this was his first entrance into the House.

who preceded him.   But a new election was drawing near,
and the young leaders in Congress gave the President to
understand that he could not have their support for re-
election unless he was willing to declare war.   Madison
yielded.   During the winter Congress sounded the war
trumpet; it voted to raise the regular army from ten thousand to thirty-five thousand men, and authorized a loan of
$11,000,000.   But these measures were not passed without
much debate and strong opposition.[*]   Early in April an
embargo of ninety days was laid, as a preliminary to a declaration of war.   A little later Congress authorized the President to call out one hundred thousand militia for six months.
On June 1 the President sent his war message to Congress,
urging an immediate declaration of war.   The primary
reasons given were four in number: the impressment of our
seamen; British cruisers harassing our shipping along the
American coast; pretended blockades of the European coast,
by which American ships had been plundered on every sea;
and the Orders in Council.

As to this declaration, two things are notable: first, there
had been equal *casus belli* constantly for five years, and at
certain times greater cause than at this moment; second,
France during the same period had offended equally with
England, or nearly so.   Why declare war now? and why

---

[*] In the spring of 1812, one John Henry, an Irish adventurer, sold
to the administration for $50,000 certain "disclosures," showing that
he had been employed by Governor Craig of Canada three years before
(during Jefferson's embargo) as a secret agent to New England to
connive with the Federalists with a view of separating that section from
the rest of the Union.   Madison, believing that these letters proved the
British government to have attempted to break up the Union, and that
this would be a good war card, purchased them.   But there was little
in them not before known.

1784 — WINFIELD SCOTT — 1866.

By Minor K. Kellogg, 1858.

From the original portrait in the City Hall, New York.

against England and not against France? The first question is answered by our account of the change in party leadership. As to the second, it would have been suicidal to fight both England and France. England was the mother country, and it was more irritating to receive from her such unrelenting harshness than from the free lance, Napoleon, who made little pretense of observing international custom. Another cause of this decision was that France presented no vulnerable point. She possessed no territory to invade on this side of the water, and her navies had been destroyed and her commerce swept from the seas. Yet the war might have been averted. The British ministry was slowly yielding. England did not want war, and would have yielded sooner had she seen that America was in earnest. Even now the yielding process was slow owing to the obstinacy of Premier Spencer Perceval; but on May 11 Perceval was shot dead in the House of Commons by a lunatic, and the Orders in Council were repealed June 23. But five days before this, and weeks before the news of the repeal had reached America, Madison had set his hand to the declaration of war. The repeal came too late.

HOSTILITIES ON THE GREAT LAKES

The country was ill prepared for war in 1812. The ten old regiments, scarcely half filled, were scattered through the West in garrisons of scarcely a hundred in a place. Detroit, the scene of the desperate and vain efforts of the great Pontiac; Fort Dearborn, where was to rise in the next generation the city of Chicago; Fort Wayne, Fort Harrison on the Wabash, and other posts were each held by a handful of men who could ill be spared, for the Indians were sure to cast their lot with the British. The seacoast was unguarded. The raising of armies was exceedingly slow work, and the eleven million loan was only a little more than half taken by the first of July. Henry Dearborn, a former member of Jefferson's Cabinet, was made senior major general and commander in chief. The other major general was Thomas Pinckney, who was to command the southern department. The brigadier generals appointed were James Wilkinson, formerly connected with Burr's conspiracy, Joseph Bloomfield, ten years governor of New Jersey, Wade Hampton of South Carolina, James Winchester of Tennessee, William Polk of North Carolina, and William Hull, governor of Michigan. These were all elderly men, all had seen service in the Revolution, none had ever commanded a regiment in battle, and most of them had "sunk into sloth, ignorance, or intemperance."[7] But worst of all, the people were not united. The Federalists constituted an anti-war party, and did everything to hamper the administration. They were also gaining at this moment; they had won in the recent elections in New York and Massachusetts, and even in Congress the Democrats lost one fourth of their strength in the final vote on the declaration of war. Had the vote been deferred a month, as the Federalists urged, the news of the repeal of the Orders in Council would have reached America, and the war might have been averted. After the declaration had been passed, a number of the New England Federalists issued a protest, declaring that the war was a party and not a national war, and disclaiming all responsibility for it.[8] When Madison called upon the states for militia, the governors of Massachusetts, Connecticut, and Rhode Island flatly refused to send their quota. Thus

[7] Scott's "Autobiography."
[8] "Niles's Register," Vol. II, p. 309.

at the outset the administration was greatly handicapped by the want of unanimity among the states.[*]

Our navy consisted of six first-class frigates, built in old Federalist days, and twice as many smaller vessels, while England boasted nearly a thousand war ships. Such was the deplorable condition of the United States at the opening of war with the British Empire. But there were a few advantages: England was engaged in European wars; her navy was scattered over the seas of the world; our little navy was in the hands of young and able men; Canada was open to invasion.

At the opening of this war occurred what is considered the most disgraceful event in American history,—the surrender of Michigan Territory without a battle. The invasion of Canada was the first and chief aim of the administration. To this end Dearborn was to coöperate from the Niagara frontier with an army from Michigan. But Dearborn was incapable of grasping the situation. He spent the summer in Boston and Albany getting ready and doing nothing. William Hull was governor of Michigan. Detroit contained some eight hundred people and a fort, a square inclosure of two acres. Receiving orders to invade Canada from the west, Hull crossed the Detroit River and prepared to besiege Fort Malden, a few miles below. Meantime he wrote Mr. Eustis, the secretary of war, that coöperation from Niagara was absolutely necessary to success; but Dearborn was still loitering at Boston and undecided what to do. The British began to strengthen their fort, and in

[*] There was also some disaffection on the British side. There was armed resistance at Montreal, which was soon put down; 367 Canadians joined Hull, 9 were executed for treason in 1814. See "Cambridge Modern History," Vol. VII, p. 337.

quick succession news reached Hull of the fall of Michili-
mackinac, and that a large body of Indians were moving
toward Detroit, that his supply train from Ohio had been cut
off by Tecumseh, and that a force of British had passed
Niagara en route to Detroit. Hull was disheartened. He
gave up the siege of Malden and returned to Detroit.

The British forces in Upper Canada had the good fortune
at this time to be commanded by a man of remarkable energy
and military ability,—General Isaac Brock. When Hull re-
crossed the river, Brock, with a few hundred men, was
hastening with all speed toward Detroit. Reaching Malden,
he moved up the river and sent to Hull a summons to surrender the fort, with a threat of Indian massacre in case of
refusal. The demand was refused, and next morning Brock
crossed the river with about seven hundred regulars and
militia and six hundred Indians, and moved upon the fort
for an attack. Hull was vacillating and utterly discouraged. As the enemy approached, he was greatly agitated;
he sat on an old tent with his back against the rampart,
moody and uncommunicative. Yet he might have made an
immortal name that day. He had two 24-pounders planted
so as to cover the road on which the enemy was advancing,
and his army almost equaled that of Brock.[10] But Hull
imagined the forest swarming with savages, and he thought
of the women and children in the fort, among whom was
his daughter. His supplies would last but a month, and
then at the inevitable surrender, woe to those who remained
alive! Hull's former bravery now forsook him utterly, and
to the astonishment of friend and foe he surrendered the
fort and his army without a struggle—and all Michigan

[10] Rossiter Johnson gives Hull's force at one thousand, "War of
1812," p. 35.

1769 — SIR ISAAC BROCK, K.B. — 1812.

BY J. HUDSON, 1806.

From the original miniature portrait in possession of Miss Sara Mickle, Toronto, Canada.

Territory. On the same day Fort Dearborn (Chicago) was burned to the ground by a horde of savages, the garrison having been massacred, the day before, to the last man.

Hull was afterward tried by court-martial and sentenced to death, but was pardoned by the President in consideration of his services in the Revolution. Hull did not play the man on that day at Detroit, and cowardice in a soldier is a crime. But Hull was not alone at fault. He was not properly supported, and part of the blame should have been borne by General Dearborn, by Secretary Eustis, and by President Madison.[11]

But one week elapsed after the capture of Detroit when the energetic Brock reached Fort George, at the mouth of the Niagara, with his prisoners. The British government, on repealing the Orders in Council, had requested an armistice between the two countries in the hope of settling the other differences without war. The news of this had not reached Brock when he captured Detroit. But now on his return both sides hesitated for some days—until it was seen that the armistice would come to naught. American troops were meanwhile hastening to the lake region from Pennsylvania, New York and New England. Commodore Chauncey was building a fleet on Lake Ontario. General Stephen Van Rensselaer commanded the New York militia, and was stationed at Lewiston. General Alexander Smyth was at Buffalo with sixteen hundred men. But these two commanders were each independent of the other, and a rivalry prevented their coöperation. Van Rensselaer then deter-

[11] Henry Adams goes back still farther and holds Jefferson chiefly responsible for this disaster, as he was the author of the system by which the country was left unprepared for war. See Vol. VII, Chap. XVI.

mined to act alone.   He would cross the river and attack
the enemy on the heights above Queenstown.

Long before the dawn of October 13 several hundred men,
under Colonel Christie, embarked in thirteen boats upon the
rushing Niagara, and silently rowed for the Canadian shore.
Three of the boats lost their way and returned.   In one of
these was Christie, and the command fell on Captain John

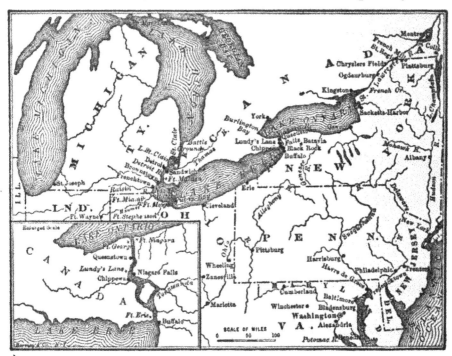

E. Wool, who landed safely with the other ten.   Up an unguarded path Wool led his men, and at daybreak he attacked
an English battery near which stood General Brock, who
barely escaped capture by flight.   Brock then made an attack on Wool; but an American bullet penetrated his breast,
and he fell dead.   The British loss in the death of this young
and gallant leader was irreparable.

Wool was painfully wounded, but for some hours he held

the ground he had won, when Colonel Winfield Scott came and took command. Six hundred American troops now occupied the heights, when early in the afternoon they saw in the distance a large force of the British advancing from Fort George, under General Sheaffe, who had succeeded Brock. Van Rensselaer, who had also crossed the river, now hastened back to Lewiston to bring over the militia, but they refused to cross. The general rode among them and urged them to go to the rescue of their brethren on the hill, but all his efforts were fruitless. The men gave as their reason for not crossing the fact, as they understood it, that they were engaged in a defensive war, and were not obliged to leave the soil of the United States. The true reason was cowardice. The noble six hundred on the heights beyond the river were attacked by more than twice their number, driven back, down the hill, over the precipice to the brink of the river. Here they found no boats, and nothing was left but to surrender. Nine hundred, including many who had not ascended the heights, were taken prisoners. Though the British won a clear victory this day, their loss in the death of General Brock was far more serious than that of the Americans. General Van Rensselaer now resigned from the army in disgust.

The chief figure in the next scene of the drama was General Smyth. Succeeding Van Rensselaer, he made a feint of invading Canada, and issued a bombastic proclamation; but after a few weeks of bluster he was hissed out of the army, and was dismissed from the service. The year 1812 closed with little encouragement to the Americans except from their success on the ocean, to be noticed later. Hull had surrendered all Michigan; Van Rensselaer, unable to control his militia, had sacrificed an army at Queenstown;

Smyth had ended his brief military career in a fiasco. The only American success on land this year was the repulse of about seven hundred British at Ogdensburg, New York, by a force under Jacob Brown, a Quaker farmer, who proved himself the most vigorous American commander yet in the field.

VICTORIES ON THE SEA

In striking contrast with our continued failures in the lake region during this eventful year were the unexpected victories on the ocean. Little was expected of our navy, which was a pygmy compared with that of England; but ere the close of the first year of the war the world was astonished at our naval victories. With no attempt to give a naval history of this war, we must notice briefly a few of the notable sea fights of the year 1812.

The most famous of these naval duels was that between the *Constitution*, a 44-gun frigate, and the *Guerrière*, a British frigate of thirty-eight guns. The *Constitution* was commanded by Captain Isaac Hull, a nephew of the unhappy governor of Michigan. Late in July, while cruising off the Atlantic coast, he came upon a British squadron from Halifax. Hull saw that he and his vessel were lost unless he could escape. He fled, and the squadron gave chase, and for three days and nights the exciting race was kept up, partly by kedging, as there was little wind, when the *Constitution* left her pursuers so far behind that they gave up the chase. The race was one of the most remarkable in naval history, and was very complimentary to American seamanship.

The *Constitution* reached Boston in safety, but soon again put to sea. On August 19 she sighted the *Guerrière*, one of

1773 — ISAAC HULL — 1843.

BY GILBERT STUART, 1814.

From the original portrait in the Metropolitan Museum of Art, New York, owned by Dr. Isaac
Hull Platt.

the squadron that had chased her. The meeting was welcomed by both sides. The English ship was inferior to the American as seven to ten, but this counted little to the audacious tar who represented the Mistress of the Seas. A London paper had boasted that no American ship could cope with the *Guerrière,* and her own captain, Dacres, had only a few days before challenged any one of our frigates to battle. Each vessel recognized the other on sight as a mortal foe, and here upon the rolling deep, eight hundred miles from land, they both prepared for an immediate duel to the death. After wearing an hour for position, with an occasional shot, the two ships came within easy range side by side, and each began to pour broadsides into the other. A few minutes after this deadly fire began, the mizzenmast of the *Guerrière* was shot away, and within half an hour the mainmast fell and the vessel, a helpless wreck, struck her colors and surrendered. The *Constitution* was not greatly damaged. Her loss in killed and wounded was fourteen, while the enemy's loss was seventy-nine. Captain Hull set fire to the remnants of the proud English vessel, took his prisoners and hurried back to Boston to receive the plaudits of his countrymen. Even the Federalists joined in the glad shout of victory that spread over the land.[12] Why so much ado about sinking this one ship, when England had a thousand more? The fact is, this victory meant more than appeared on the surface,—it meant the beginning of the end of the impressment of seamen; it meant an awakening in the American sailor, a self-confidence that he had not felt before; it meant a disputing with England the right of way upon

[12] The victory of the *Constitution* occurred but three days after the surrender of Detroit, and the news of both reached the coast at the same time.

the seas where she had reigned, a queen without a rival. "A small affair it might appear among the world's battles," says Henry Adams; "it took but half an hour, but in that one half hour the United States of America rose to the rank of a first-class power." [13]

The defeat of the *Guerrière*, however, was not the first of our naval victories. Six days before this, the American frigate *Essex*, thirty-two guns, Captain David Porter, had captured the British sloop of war *Alert*, twenty guns.

Next in point of time after Hull's victory came the affair of the *Wasp* and the *Frolic*. The former was an American sloop of war of eighteen guns, Captain Jacob Jones. The *Frolic* was a British vessel of almost the same size and equipment. They met five hundred miles off the coast of North Carolina, and one of the bloodiest of naval battles was the result. The sea ran high, and the two ships, riding upon the waves or sunk within their troughs, poured forth their broadsides with deadly ferocity. They drifted so near together that the rammers of the American guns touched the side of the *Frolic*. At length, after Jones had raked the enemy from stem to stern, and less than twenty of the one hundred and ten Englishmen were left alive and uninjured, the Americans, who had lost but ten in killed and wounded, boarded the enemy's deck and hauled down the British flag. The pitching of the vessels in the rolling sea had furnished a fine test of markmanship, and the result was wholly favorable to the Americans. But they were not allowed to enjoy the fruits of victory, for on the same day the two vessels were captured by the British seventy-four, *Poictiers*, and carried to Bermuda.

Exactly one week after this battle a greater one took place

[13] Vol. VI, p. 375.

far out on the Atlantic, between the *United States,* one of
our largest frigates, Captain Stephen Decatur, and the British frigate *Macedonian.* The two ships compared in size
and force in favor of the *United States* about as did the
Constitution and the *Guerrière.* Again the American gun-
nery was greatly superior to the English. The battle continued nearly two hours, when the British vessel, after receiving a hundred shots in her hull, surrendered, her killed
and wounded being nine times greater than on the *United
States.* The *Macedonian* was brought to America, repaired,
and added to our heroic little navy.

One more of these brilliant victories closed the year's
events. The now famous *Constitution,* "Old Ironsides,"
had put to sea again, under Captain Bainbridge, who had
commanded the lost *Philadelphia* in the Mediterranean, and
had lain for a year and a half in a Tripolitan prison. On
December 29, Bainbridge encountered the English 38-gun
frigate *Java* off the coast of Brazil. A desperate battle of
two hours ensued. The *Java* was entirely destroyed, and
her captain, with some sixty of his men, were among the
slain. Thus ended the wonderful six months' record of our
navy. The Americans had won in all these desperate duels
on the sea, and in each case the proportion of British loss
in killed and wounded was far greater than the difference
in the vessels accounted for. Meantime, three hundred British merchant ships had been captured, chiefly by privateers-
men. The British had also captured many of ours, and in
addition to the *Wasp,* as stated above, they had taken two
little brigs, the *Nautilus* and *Vixen.*[14]

[14] On the night of December 8 a naval ball was given to Hull in
Washington in honor of his victory over the *Guerrière.* While the
festivities were at their height a messenger from Decatur entered the

This marvelous showing in our favor created a tremendous sensation in England as well as in America. "It cannot be too deeply felt," said Canning in Parliament, "that the sacred spell of the invincibility of the British navy is broken." But no one expected this to continue, at least no one expected our little navy to triumph in the end over that of England. Congress was so elated with our successes thus far that it voted, early in 1813, to build four new battle ships of the first class, and six frigates and six sloops of war. The honors on the sea for the year 1813 were about even between the two nations.[16] The first sea fight, between Lieutenant James Lawrence of the *Hornet* and Captain Peake of the *Peacock,* both of twenty guns, resulted as usual. They met in West Indian waters, and after a short, fierce battle the British vessel was destroyed, and her brave commander, Captain Peake, died at his post. So destructive had been the American fire that the *Peacock* sank before all of her survivors could be rescued. Nine of her crew and three of the *Hornet's* crew, who had boarded her, went down with the wreck. Congress voted a gold medal to Lawrence, and put him in command of the *Chesapeake,* the famous ship that had been attacked by the *Leopard* six years before.

Now, for a time, our good fortune suffered a reverse. While the *Chesapeake* lay at Boston, she was challenged to a duel by Captain Broke of the British frigate *Shannon,*

ball room with the news that the *United States* had captured the *Macedonian,* and laid the ensign of the latter vessel at the feet of the President's wife. On this the guests broke forth into the wildest enthusiasm. See Schouler, Vol. II, p. 371.

[16] One reason for the change in our fortunes was that the British admiralty issued an order directing captains not to engage with American ships of superior force.

1781—JAMES LAWRENCE—1813.

BY GILBERT STUART.

From the original portrait in the New Jersey Historical Society, Newark, N.J.

lying off the harbor.   Lawrence accepted the challenge.
Gathering his untrained crew, he went out to meet a ship of
the same size as his own, but with a crew that had been
trained for weeks for just such a purpose.   The action was
short and bloody.   The *Chesapeake,* partially disabled at the
beginning, fell afoul of her antagonist, and was raked from
stem to stern.   Her brave young commander received a
mortal wound, and as he was being carried below he cried,
"Don't give up the ship," and this became a rallying cry to
his countrymen.   But Captain Broke and his men had
leaped aboard the *Chesapeake,* and she soon became their
prize.   The killed and wounded on the *Shannon* numbered
eighty-three, and on the *Chesapeake* one hundred and forty-
six.   The prize was taken to Halifax, and Captain Lawrence died on the way.   England rejoiced exceedingly over
this victory, and well she might, for this was her first naval
victory of importance since the beginning of the war.

This disaster was soon followed by another.   The American brig *Argus,* one of our fastest sailers, while cruising
in the English Channel, captured some twenty merchantmen.   One of these was laden with wine, and of this the
sailors drank freely.   Then they set fire to the captured vessel, and the light revealed the *Argus* to the English brig
Pelican. The two came together in a fierce fight.   Many
of the Americans were intoxicated with the captured wine,
and within an hour the *Argus* struck her colors and became
a British prize.   Her brave captain, William Henry Allen,
who had been an officer on the *Chesapeake* when it was
attacked by the *Leopard* in 1807, was mortally wounded.

In September the American brig *Enterprise* captured the
English brig *Boxer,* both of fourteen guns, off the coast of
Maine.   But both commanders were among the slain, and

they were buried at Portland, side by side, with the honors of war.

By the end of the year 1813 the English had captured seven American war vessels mounting 119 guns, while the Americans had captured twenty-six British war vessels mounting 560 guns.[16] What a marvelous showing for our little navy! But its power was now exhausted. On the day of the capture of the *Chesapeake* by the *Shannon*, Decatur, with the *United States*, the *Hornet*, and the captured *Macedonian*, was blockaded in the harbor of New London, Connecticut, and, watched by a squadron of British ships, was compelled to remain there to the end of the war. His ships escaped destruction by the protection of shore batteries. Whenever he planned to escape, the enemy was warned by blue lights on shore. This was supposed to have been the work of anti-war Federalists, and hence they received the opprobrious designation of "Blue-light Federalists." Chesapeake Bay, the Delaware River, and indeed every port and harbor on the entire Atlantic coast, together with the mouth of the Mississippi, were blocked by cordons of British vessels. Admiral Cockburn, who commanded off the southern coast, burned and sacked the towns and committed many unnecessary deeds of cruelty; while Commodore Hardy, who commanded in New England waters, abstained from all such barbarous practices and proved himself a generous foe and a high-minded gentleman.

One of the last of the American vessels to yield was the plucky *Essex*, commanded by Captain Porter. After her victory over the *Alert*, as noted above, she made a wonderful cruise in the Pacific Ocean, capturing many British whalers. In December, 1814, we find the *Essex* blockaded by two

[16] Johnson's "War of 1812," p. 206.

English ships, the *Phœbe* and the *Cherub*, in the harbor at Valparaiso. At length she was attacked by both in disregard of the neutrality of the port, and the battle that ensued was one of the most dreadful in naval history. The odds against Porter were too great, the *Essex* was almost shot to pieces and took fire, after three fourths of her 225 men had been killed and wounded. The battle had been witnessed from shore by thousands of people who had gathered on the heights to view the magnificent spectacle. Among the crew of the captured *Essex* was a boy of thirteen years, whose name was yet to be placed in the first rank of naval heroes. Other naval battles we must leave unmentioned and give a brief notice to the merchant marine.

The victories of our war ships could do little toward destroying the powerful British navy; it was the moral prestige that they gave the United States that made them important. But it was far otherwise with the inroads of our privateers on the commerce of England. The loss inflicted upon British shipping during the two and one half years of war was incalculable. Congress licensed about 250 ships, and these scoured every sea in search of the defenseless merchantmen, and the prizes they took numbered many hundred.[17] Many of the privateers plowed the seas for months in vain; others were extremely fortunate. The *True-blooded Yankee* took a town on the coast of Scotland, burned seven vessels in the harbor, and captured twenty-seven vessels in thirty-seven days. The *Surprise* made twenty prizes in a month. The *Leo* captured an East India-man worth two and a half million dollars, but it was recap-

[17] It has been estimated that sixteen hundred British merchantmen fell victims to the privateers and the war ships. Many of these were recaptured by British vessels before reaching port.

tured.   No English merchantman was safe in the Irish Sea
or the English Channel.   One American captain issued a
burlesque proclamation, declaring the entire coasts of England and Ireland in a state of blockade.   The merchandise
taken reached many millions in value, and represented the
industries of every clime and every seaport on the globe,—
sable furs from the Siberian desert, silks and tea from China
and Japan, ivory from Africa, Turkish carpets, silks, wines,
gold, and diamonds—all kinds of merchandise carried in
English vessels became a prey to these bold, insatiable rovers
of the sea, the American privateers.

There has been much recent criticism of privateering.
The assertion that it is legalized robbery is true; but war
itself is worse than robbery.   Why should property, especially that which has a military value, be held more sacred
than human life?   How could a nation without a navy cope
at all with a great maritime power except through privateering?   Is it less humane to destroy an enemy's property than
to destroy the lives of his men?   Abolish privateering?
Yes, by all means; but abolish war at the same time, and let
the nations settle their disputes by arbitration.   Had not
privateering been permitted in the war we are treating, the
English could have disposed of our little navy and then
harassed our coasts for indefinite years—until we came to
their terms of peace.   It is certain that Great Britain would
not have been ready to come to peace when she did but for
the fearful wounds she was receiving through the privateers.

FURTHER OPERATIONS ON THE LAKES

We left General Dearborn on the southern shore of Lake
Ontario in the vicinity of Sacketts Harbor, where Commodore Chauncey had built a fleet of fourteen vessels.   The

1779 — STEPHEN DECATUR — 1820.

By Thomas Sully, 1814.

From the original portrait in the City Hall, New York.

monotony of the winter was broken by sporadic raids; but in the spring of 1813 Dearborn planned to capture Toronto (then called York), the capital of Upper Canada. For this purpose he sent General Zebulon M. Pike, the explorer. After a rough voyage in Chauncey's fleet, the troops landed near the town, and were met by an equal number of British and Indians led by Sheaffe. After some hours of sharp fighting the Americans captured the town, when suddenly the ground was shaken by a terrific explosion. The magazine containing five hundred barrels of powder had exploded, and the falling débris killed nearly a hundred men and wounded twice as many. Among the mortally wounded was General Pike, who was struck by the fragment of a stone wall while sitting on a stump talking with a captured British sergeant. The British claimed that the explosion was an accident, and the fact that nearly half the killed were their own men, seems to justify the claim. It is impossible to believe that they would have engaged in such wanton destruction of life after having surrendered the town. The British flag was hauled down, and General Pike died with it folded beneath his head.

Soon after this, Dearborn sent General Boyd, who had succeeded Pike, to capture Fort George. Boyd succeeded after several sharp skirmishes, and over six hundred of the enemy were made prisoners.

At the same time Sir George Prevost, governor general of Canada, sailed from Kingston in a fleet of nine vessels bearing a thousand men for an attack on Sacketts Harbor. But Prevost was wanting in military skill, and he soon withdrew his ships and returned to Canada.

General Dearborn was relieved of his command in June, 1813, and General Wilkinson was called from New Orleans to take command. John Armstrong, author of the famous Newburg addresses, had become secretary of war instead of Eustis, and he planned another invasion of Canada, with Montreal as the objective point. In the autumn, Wilkinson moved from Sacketts Harbor down the St. Lawrence with an army of seven thousand men, while an additional force under Wade Hampton was to coöperate in moving on the Canadian city. But these old generals were jealous of each other, and Hampton refused to serve under Wilkinson. The latter moved on, passed Ogdensburg, and when within ninety miles of Montreal met a British army and was defeated in the battle of Chrystler's Field. Hearing now that he would not be supported by Hampton, Wilkinson abandoned the expedition. Meantime the British in the Niagara region had rallied and recaptured Fort George. But the Americans, before leaving, had wantonly burned the village of Newark, and the British in retaliation crossed over and burned half a dozen towns, including Buffalo, then a village of fifteen hundred inhabitants.

We now come to the most famous American victory in the lake region during the war. Lake Erie was held by a small English fleet commanded by Commodore Barclay, who had fought with Nelson at Trafalgar. The Americans determined to dispute the control of its waters, and Oliver Hazard Perry, a valiant young naval officer, sought and obtained permission to undertake the task. The undertaking was prodigious. The timber of the coming fleet was still standing in the woods; the iron works, stores, canvas, and cordage were in New York and Philadelphia, and there was no railroad or canal by which to transport them. So during the winter scores of sleds and wagons struggled through the deep snows of northern Pennsylvania, bearing the necessary equipment; while over fifty ship carpenters at Presque Isle, now Erie, were busy hewing out the timbers. The work was protected by an excellent harbor inclosed by a bar over which the British could not sail. But Barclay would remedy the evil; he would attack the new-born fleet while crossing the bar, and he watched and waited. Perry's work progressed rapidly. He named his flagship *Lawrence,* after the brave commander whose dying words, "Don't give up the ship," now became the motto of the vessel that bore his name. By the end of July the fleet was finished, and fortune favored it from the beginning. The vigilant Barclay lost his vigilance for a day. He accepted an invitation from a rich Canadian to a Sunday dinner, and took his fleet to the northern shore. On that day Perry's fleet crossed the bar. It was a difficult feat. The larger vessels were lightened and borne up by scows, and after a day and a night of severe toil were launched on the bosom of the lake, and there they stood defiantly when Barclay returned next morning. The British commander now seemed to have lost his desire to fight, and he wheeled about and fled westward. It took Perry a month to find him; but he did so at Put-in Bay about sunrise of September 10, and before sunset of that same day Great Britain was without ships or sailors on Lake Erie.

The two fleets were of nearly the same force. Perry had ten vessels with fifty-five guns, and Barclay six vessels with sixty-five guns. Each had about four hundred men. The battle opened at noon, and for some hours there was an incessant roar of artillery. Several of the English vessels directed their fire upon the American flagship, and by two o'clock over two thirds of her hundred and thirty men were killed or wounded. At length the *Lawrence* seemed about to sink, and the undaunted Perry, waving his banner, passed in an open boat in the face of the enemy's fire to his next largest vessel, the *Niagara*. Presently two of the British vessels fouled, and the Americans taking advantage of this, raked their decks with a murderous fire; but only for twenty minutes, when the British fleet raised the white flag and surrendered.

Perry's laconic dispatch to General Harrison, "We have met the enemy and they are ours," soon became as famous as the noble words of Lawrence, which he had made his motto. This brilliant victory transferred the control of the lake wholly to the Americans, rendered the recovery of Michigan comparatively easy, and gave to the young American commander an undying fame.

Before the battle of Lake Erie the land forces of both belligerents had been gathering in northwestern Ohio. The British and Indians were there under Colonel Henry Proctor and Tecumseh, the Americans under General Harrison, of Tippecanoe fame. The fall of Detroit had roused the blood of the young men of the West, and they determined to wipe out the dishonor. Early in the year 1813, General James Winchester was moving through western Ohio with a thousand Kentucky troops, and before the close of January he reached Frenchtown on the river Raisin, eighteen miles from Malden. Here he met Proctor with a large body of British and Indians, and a battle was fought in which the Americans were defeated, and many of them taken prisoners. Then occurred one of those scenes of carnage so common to Indian warfare. Many of the Americans while retreating were ambushed and tomahawked; others were butchered in cold blood after they had surrendered. Next day Proctor started back to Malden with his

1775 — JACOB BROWN — 1828.

BY JOHN WESLEY JARVIS.

From the original portrait in the City Hall, New York.

prisoners, among whom was Winchester, and left thirty wounded Americans at Frenchtown. But ere they had gone far, two hundred Indians turned back and massacred the wounded men and set fire to the buildings. "Remember the river Raisin" became the rallying cry of their surviving comrades in the Northwest. The American loss in this affair was about four hundred killed or wounded, and over five hundred captured.

After this disaster, Harrison with twelve hundred men built Fort Meigs at the rapids of the Maumee. Proctor besieged this fort in vain for some time, and then turned his attention to Fort Stephenson. This fort stood on the site of the present city of Fremont, in northern Ohio, and was held by a hundred and sixty men, commanded by Major George Croghan, a nephew of General George Rogers Clark, whom we have met in the Revolution. Proctor's demand for a surrender of the fort, with the usual threat of Indian massacre, was answered by the brave Croghan, that every man would die at his post rather than surrender the fort. Croghan had one small cannon, a six pounder, which he masked and placed so as to enfilade a ditch up which the British were approaching. On they came with sublime confidence, and leaped over the pickets, shouting, "Show the Yankees no quarter." Next moment the cannon, loaded with a double charge of slugs, was discharged, and this, followed by a rifle volley, mowed down every man in the ditch. Again the plucky Britons filled the ditch, and again the single piece was discharged, with the same result. It was now night, and next morning the British had disappeared.

As the summer passed the two armies lay watching each other, until on September 12 the Americans were electrified with the famous dispatch, "We have met the enemy and they are ours," which meant that Lake Erie had passed into American hands. But this was not all. Harrison's army was about to be more than doubled. Ohio was yet in its infancy, and the older state of Kentucky was the main dependence of the Northwest. And Kentucky did nobly. Governor Shelby, who had fought by the side of Sevier at King's Mountain, marched northward with thirty-five hundred troops, and Colonel Richard M. Johnson came with a thousand cavalry. Harrison now determined to invade Canada. He sent Johnson to Detroit with his mounted thousand, but the enemy had fled; and Michigan, which Hull had surrendered without a blow, was recovered without a blow. The main army was then conveyed in Perry's fleet to Canada and set ashore below Malden. But Proctor, though he had nearly a thousand regulars and more than three thousand Indians, refused to fight, burned his stores, and abandoned the fort. Tecumseh, who commanded the Indians, was chagrined at the apparent cowardice of Proctor, and compared him to a fat dog that had carried its tail erect till it became frightened, when it dropped its tail and ran.

Harrison moved up the river and was joined by Johnson's cavalry. Proctor continued his flight; the Americans pursued. The pursuit was vigorous and comparatively easy, as Proctor neglected to destroy the bridges across the streams. The British army was overtaken at Moravian Town on the Thames River. Here, it is said, Tecumseh made a stand and informed Proctor that the disgraceful flight should be continued no farther; and the result was the battle of the Thames, and the death of one of the greatest of Indian warriors. Harrison had little to do with planning the battle; it was the work of Johnson, whose cavalry, aided slightly by Shelby's riflemen, did all the fighting on the part of the Americans. The American loss of life was slight; the British army, after losing nearly twelve hundred in killed and wounded, became demoralized, and almost all the survivors were made captives, Proctor escaping with a few followers by flight through the swamps and wilderness. The Indian leader Tecumseh was among the slain, and he was said to have met his death at the hand of Richard M. Johnson, a future Vice President of the United States. Among the spoils were six brass cannon captured from Burgoyne at Saratoga thirty-six years before and surrendered by Hull at Detroit.

The campaign ending with the battle of the Thames wholly destroyed the alliance between the British and the Indians, killed the most dangerous Indian enemy since the days of Pontiac, and destroyed all hope of an Indian confederation of tribes. It also resulted in the restoration of Michigan, in the capture of a small British army, cleared the entire Northwest of the enemy, and ended the war in that section. Harrison now stationed a thousand men at Detroit under Lewis Cass, disbanded his Kentuckians and sent them rejoicing homeward, and with the remainder of his troops embarked on Perry's fleet for Buffalo.

Two severe battles in the region of the lakes took place the following summer,—Chippewa and Lundy's Lane. In March, 1814, Wilkinson was relieved from the service, and thus ended a long and exceedingly checkered military career. The command now fell to General Brown; and, aided by a few young and vigorous spirits like himself, the ablest of whom was Winfield Scott, he soon infused new life into the army. And it was quite time for such a change; for Napoleon had abdicated the throne of France and retired to

Elba, thus setting free a large number of British veterans, who "had not slept under roof for seven years," and fourteen thousand of these were now sent to Canada to fight the Americans.

At the beginning of July, 1814, we find Brown in the neighborhood of the great waterfall with some thirty-five hundred effective men and a few Indians, while General Riall, the British commander at Fort George, had a somewhat larger force, partly on garrison duty at the neighboring posts. On hearing of the American advance, Riall hastened forward with two thousand men and took a strong position at Chippewa, just above the falls. Here he was met by General Scott with thirteen hundred men, and after a fierce battle of one hour the British broke and fled.

This battle of Chippewa is noted as the only one during the war in which two armies of regulars, nearly equal in numbers, fought on an open plain with no advantage of position.[18] Whatever advantage there was belonged to the British; they were slightly greater in numbers, they opened fire first, while the Americans were crossing a bridge, and Scott had to form in line while under fire. The result was wonderfully gratifying to American pride. Not only did the Americans win the battle in less than an hour, but their killed and wounded numbered less than half those of the British.[19]

Twenty days after this battle the two armies met again, in a more desperate encounter. Riall had taken his stand at Lundy's Lane, within a mile of the boiling Niagara, on the Canadian side, and in easy hearing of the thunders of

[18] Adams, Vol. VIII, p. 43.
[19] In this battle on the American side was the famous Indian, Red Jacket, whom Halleck has immortalized in a poem.

the mighty cataract. His army was augmented on July 25 by the arrival of his superior, General Gordon Drummond, with a fresh body of troops, many of whom were Wellington's veterans, and the army now exceeded three thousand men. The effective force of the Americans had dwindled to 2644 men. In the evening glow of that broiling summer day the American advance guard of 1300 under Scott met 1800 of the enemy led by Riall, and the battle was immediately opened. Brown heard the firing and reached the field with the rest of the army about dark; the British were reënforced at the same time, and the battle continued. The Americans suffered severely from an English battery on a little hill in the midst of the fighting line. General Brown ordered Colonel James Miller to capture it. "I'll try, sir," was the modest answer, and half an hour later the work was accomplished, every man at the battery having been shot down or having fallen at the point of the bayonet. For five hours in the darkness the battle raged, each army directing its fire by the flash of the enemy's muskets, while the thunder of artillery answered the roar of the falling river in the rear. Three times the British surged up the hill to recapture the stolen battery, but they were always repulsed. Soon after eleven o'clock the firing ceased as if by common consent. At midnight the Americans gathered up their wounded and retired to their camp at Chippewa, leaving the heavy guns to the enemy.

This murderous night battle at Lundy's Lane was an extraordinary one. Brown was wounded, Scott was wounded, and the command devolved on Ripley, one of the brigade commanders. Drummond was wounded, and Riall was wounded and taken prisoner. The total American loss, 853, was about one third of the army. Drummond reported a loss of 878. The American army then proceeded to Fort Erie at the head of the Niagara, and took a strong position. Drummond now committed the most serious blunder of his life. He made a determined night attack on the fort and was repulsed with a loss of over 900 men, while the American loss was but 84. Soon after this the Americans attacked the British in camp, and each side lost several hundred, after which the British withdrew and gave up the siege.

Before these events had fully taken place the British had determined on an invasion of New York from another quarter, and their chances seemed excellent. Early in August eleven hundred more of Wellington's veterans reached Canadian soil, and more were coming. For two reasons the British needed to possess Lake Champlain and northern New York. First, their supplies, cattle and provisions had been drawn from the unpatriotic residents of New York and Vermont, and Congress was about to make a determined effort to stop this traffic. Second, the British had overrun a large part of the coast of Maine, and had required the people to take the oath of allegiance. This territory England determined to hold at the coming of peace, and to do this a solid military basis was necessary.[20] Hence northern New York must be conquered and held.

At Plattsburg, at the head of Lake Champlain, General George Izard held five thousand men, and on the lake Lieutenant Thomas Macdonough commanded a little fleet of five vessels and a few gunboats. But Secretary Armstrong ordered Izard to Sacketts Harbor with three fourths of the army. Izard obeyed and left General Alexander Macomb at Plattsburg with scarcely fifteen hundred effective men, soon to be joined by several thousand militia from Vermont

[20] Adams, Vol. VIII, Chap. IV.

1752—SAGOYEWATHA, RED JACKET—1830.

By Robert W. Weir, 1828.

From the original portrait in the New York Historical Society.

and New York.   While the Americans were in this weakened condition, Sir George Prevost marched from the St. Lawrence Valley at the head of a veteran army of at least twelve thousand men, over the same route taken by Burgoyne thirty-seven years before, and with a larger and better army than that of Burgoyne.   Prevost was supported by a British fleet under Commodore George Downie.   The attack by land and water was to be simultaneous, and it took place a year and a day after the noble victory of Perry on Lake Erie.   The two fleets were nearly equal in force. Downie had little opportunity to show his fighting qualities, as he was killed early in the action.   Macdonough has been pronounced by McMaster the greatest naval commander in America before the Civil War.   He was but thirty years old, but he had seen severe service in the Mediterranean against the piratical Barbary States.   The battle opened fiercely and continued for two hours.   It seemed to be going against the Americans, when Macdonough made a move that won him the victory.   He had taken the forethought to lay a kedge anchor at each bow of his flagship, the *Saratoga,* by the aid of which, if one broadside were disabled, the other could be turned on the enemy.   He now made use of this means and reopened the battle with renewed vigor.   Presently the English flagship, the *Confiance,* struck her colors, and finally the whole fleet surrendered except a few gunboats, which escaped.

On the same day Prevost attacked Macomb with a large portion of his army, but the latter defended his position with success.   The loss on each side was slight, nor were the killed and wounded in the naval fight nearly so great in proportion to the numbers engaged as in the battle of Lake Erie.   Prevost, with no supporting navy, gave up the expedition and returned to his familiar haunts on the St. Lawrence; and the Empire State has ever since been free from invasion by a foreign enemy.

THE WASHINGTON CAMPAIGN

James Madison had been reëlected President over De Witt Clinton, who had been supported by the Federalists and the disaffected Democrats. Madison would have made an excellent President in time of peace; but he was ill fitted to manage a war. His first secretary of war, Eustis, displayed a woeful incapacity in military affairs; and his second, John Armstrong, was but a shade better. The Czar of Russia had offered his services in bringing peace; but while Madison eagerly accepted the proposition, and sent Gallatin and James A. Bayard to join John Q. Adams, minister to Russia, at St. Petersburg, England refused, and the war went on. Nearly a year later England made direct overtures to the United States for peace. The President again accepted, and sent Henry Clay and Jonathan Russell to join the other peace commissioners in Europe; and while the negotiations were in progress, the armies in the field kept on battering one another.

The British government determined to strike the heart of its enemy by attacking our large cities along the coast. The first of these expeditions, under the command of General Robert Ross, who had served under Wellington in Spain, and had stood by the side of Sir John Moore when that hero fell at Corunna, reached the Chesapeake early in August, 1814. The army consisted of thirty-five hundred veterans, soon increased by a thousand marines from the fleet of Cockburn.

For months rumors of the coming of the enemy had been

afloat, but almost nothing had been done for protection. The President had urged Armstrong to prepare for defense; but the latter, with singular dilatoriness, had done nothing. At length Madison appointed General William H. Winder to command the defense. Winder possessed little military ability, but he was willing, and with great effort he collected an army of five hundred regulars and fifteen hundred militia.

Ross landed at Benedict, on the Patuxent River, some forty miles southeast of Washington, and by easy marches moved northward toward Bladensburg. The inhabitants could easily have impeded his march by felling trees or by burning bridges, but nothing of the kind was done. Commodore Barney, who commanded a flotilla on the Chesapeake, burned his vessels, and, with his four hundred marines joined the army of Winder. The two armies met at Bladensburg just after noon on August 24, the American army having been increased by militia till it numbered probably six thousand men. The President and his Cabinet were also on the ground at the opening of the battle. Soon after the fighting began many of the militia found safety in flight, and the British would scarcely have been checked but for the brave stand made by Barney and his marines.   Barney held his ground till he was wounded and captured.

The battle over, the British rested two hours, when they marched upon the capital, then a village of eight thousand people.   The President and Cabinet had returned, and were now fleeing in various directions to escape capture.   Mrs. Madison had carefully secured Stewart's famous picture of Washington and the original draft of the Declaration of Independence before leaving the White House.   The British army encamped at nightfall within a quarter of a mile of the Capitol, while details of troops, led by Ross and the notorious Cockburn, proceeded to burn the public buildings. It is said that Cockburn, followed by a rabble, entered the hall of the House of Representatives, climbed into the speaker's chair, and put the question, "Shall this harbor of Yankee democracy be burned?"   The vote in the affirmative was unanimous, and the torch was applied.   The White House was next set on fire, as was also the Navy Yard (by order of Secretary of the Navy Jones), and the triple conflagration lit up the whole surrounding country.   All the other buildings, except the Patent Office, were given to the flames; after which the invading army hastened away and boarded their ships at Benedict.

This destruction of public buildings that had no relation to the operations of war, with many "public archives, precious to the nation as memorials of its origin   .   .   .   interesting to all nations, as contributions to the general stock of historical instruction and political science," [21] will admit of no defense.   We are glad to note that no reputable Englishman attempts to defend the outrage.   Knight says

[21] See Madison's Proclamation.

there was a general feeling in England that the destruction
of these non-warlike buildings was "an outrage inconsistent
with civilized warfare," and he also points out the fact that
from this time to the end of the war the Americans were
victorious in every contest.[22] The first American victory
after this wanton destruction of the capital was won at
Plattsburg, as we have seen; while the second, almost simultaneous with the Plattsburg victory, was the repulse of
Ross's army before Baltimore.

The capture of Washington had been a task so easy that
the British seemed confident of making a prize of the larger
and richer city of Baltimore. After making a raid up the
Potomac, and plundering Alexandria, they sailed up the
Chesapeake and anchored off the mouth of the Patapsco,
September 11. But the city had not been idle. The fate
of the capital had taught the people a much-needed lesson.
Led by the mayor, they threw up embankments on all sides,
and erected batteries; while the militia poured into the city,
till fourteen thousand were present and ready for duty.
General Ross, who had boasted that he would make Baltimore his winter quarters, and who "didn't care if it rained
militia," landed at the dawn of day—the day after Macdonough had killed Downie and captured his fleet on Lake
Champlain—and began his march toward the city. It was
fourteen miles, and five were traversed without an obstacle,
when Ross met General Stricker with three thousand men
to dispute the right of way. A hot skirmish, known as the
battle of North Point, ensued. The British drove the
Americans back; but it took three hours to do this, and it
cost three hundred men, and among the dead was General

---

[22] "History of England," Vol. VIII, p. 378.

Ross, in whose breast had lodged a musket ball from one of the despised militia.[23]

A large fleet under Admiral Cochrane had meantime blocked up the Patapsco, an arm of the Chesapeake; but it failed to pass the guns of Fort McHenry, and hence was unable to throw shells into the city. All day and far into the night the bombarding continued; but at dawn the American flag was still waving from the walls of the fort. On that night the young American poet, Francis Scott Key, had rowed to the British fleet under a flag of truce to beg the parole of a friend, and the British admiral detained him during the night. Eagerly he watched the fluttering banner above the fort, lit by the powder flashes; and when at dawn he found it still waving, he wrote the beautiful national hymn, "The Star-Spangled Banner." The enemy now abandoned the siege, and the soldiers returned to the fleet, which sailed away to foreign waters to return no more.

WAR IN THE SOUTH

Soon after the battle of the Thames, General Harrison resigned his commission; and another future President, one who was to play a great part in American history, was made major general. No other American commander during the war, except, perhaps, Jacob Brown, can be compared in vigor and energy with Jackson. Born in North Carolina[24] a few days after the death of his father, he grew to

[23] Two weeks before this Sir Peter Parker had left his ship, the *Menelaus*, in the Chesapeake to dislodge two hundred militia at the mouth of the Sassafras River; but the British were repulsed, and Parker and thirteen of his men were killed.

[24] The dispute as to whether Jackson was born in North or South Carolina seems to be settled by Parton, his biographer. According to him, the Jackson family lived in South Carolina very near the boundary to

manhood in poverty and obscurity. At the time of Tarleton's fearful raids through the South we find Jackson, then a boy of thirteen years, among the fighting patriots. He was taken prisoner, and here the spirit of the man appeared in the boy. A British officer ordered Jackson to clean his boots, but Jackson refused, stating he was a prisoner of war and not a servant; whereupon the officer struck him with his sword, inflicting a wound that left a scar which he carried to his grave. When released from prison, he walked forty miles to his home while suffering with smallpox. He lost both his brothers in the war, and his mother died from exposure while ministering to the wants of the patriots. Thus while yet a boy Jackson found himself without parents or immediate friends. On reaching his majority, after having read law for a time, he migrated to the then far West, and made his home in Tennessee. Here he became successively the public prosecutor, a planter, a storekeeper, a judge, and a member of Congress; and he was now commander of the Tennessee militia. He became the first representative of his adopted state in the Lower House of Congress, and served also a short time in the Senate.

Early in the War of 1812 the Creek Indians became hostile; not that they had a grievance against the United States, but through the influence of Tecumseh, who had visited them, and because British agents in Florida had offered them five dollars apiece for scalps of Americans, men, women, or children.[25] In August, 1813, the most dreadful Indian massacre

line between the two colonies. In March, 1767, the elder Jackson died, and his wife, on the day of the funeral, was taken to the home of a relative who lived across the boundary in North Carolina, and here, a few days later, she gave birth to Andrew. Her two other sons, Hugh and Robert, had migrated with them from Ireland two years before.

[25] Johnson's "War of 1812," p. 179.

in American annals took place in southern Alabama. It is known as the massacre of Fort Mims. This so-called fort was a stockade inclosure made for cattle by a farmer named Mims, and to this the settlers came for protection when the Indians became hostile. There were now more than five hundred men, women, and children gathered in the place, when a thousand Creek warriors, led by a half-breed named Wetherford, burst upon them and slew more than four hundred in a few hours. Nearly two hundred of the inmates were volunteers, and so brave was their defense that about half of the Indians were killed.

The country was horrified at the news of the massacre at Fort Mims. Tennessee first came to the rescue; her legislature voted thirty-five hundred men to march into the Indian country under the command of Jackson. With a band of cavalry under General Coffee and a large body of militia, Jackson overran the territory of the Creeks, defeated them with great slaughter at the battles of Talladega and the Horse Shoe, and forced the tribe to sue for peace. It was soon after this that Jackson was appointed major general and given command of the southern military district of the United States; and as the government at Washington had been paralyzed by the invasion of Ross, he was left independent and practically dictator over his district.

In the autumn of 1814 the rumor spread through the country that England was about to send a large fleet to the Gulf of Mexico, with New Orleans as the objective point. The rumor proved true. General Ross of Washington fame was appointed to command the expedition to southern waters; but Ross fell before Baltimore, and General Sir Edward Pakenham, who had won an enviable fame in the Peninsular War, was chosen for the place. Pakenham was

1778 -- SIR EDWARD MICHAEL PAKENHAM, G.C.B. — 1815.
From a painting in possession of Lord Longford, London, England.

a brother-in-law of the Duke of Wellington, and with him sailed Generals Gibbs, Keane, and Lambert,—all famous commanders in their day. The fleet of more than fifty vessels, commanded by Admiral Cochrane, bore at least sixteen thousand veterans and a thousand heavy guns. The avowed object was to "rescue the whole province of Louisiana from the United States;" and so confident were the British of capturing New Orleans that they brought with them a collector of the port and the machinery of city government.

Jackson heard of the approach of the British, and after making an incursion into Spanish Florida he began his long horseback ride through the wilderness to New Orleans, arriving there on the 2d of December. He found the people in a wild state of excitement and without defense; and great was the commotion when the magic news that Jackson had arrived ran through the city. The British fleet arrived on December 10, entered Lake Borgne, and destroyed the American flotilla of six gunboats. The news of this first blow of the campaign struck terror to the city of New Orleans. Jackson put it under martial law and assumed the power of a dictator. He sent to General Coffee, above Baton Rouge, to hasten to the city with his twelve hundred cavalry, and Coffee made the distance of 120 miles in two days. A brigade of Tennessee militia and another from Mississippi also hurried down the river. There was no time to lose, for sixteen hundred men under Colonel Thornton, who had led the English advance at Bladensburg, occupied the Villieré plantation, but six miles below New Orleans, two days before Christmas. Calling together his regulars, his militia and volunteers, and Coffee's mounted riflemen, Jackson threw them between the enemy and the city. The two armies came together late in the evening, and a severe night

battle, similar to that of Lundy's Lane, was the result.
Neither side could claim a victory. The British loss was
the greater; but the Americans had been greatly aided by
the guns of the *Carolina,* a steamer lying near by in the
river. On the next day, December 24, as the two armies
were recovering from the shock of the battle and laying their
plans for another, a different kind of scene was enacted in a
far-away village across the sea. On that day the two warring nations, through their agents, signed a treaty of peace;
but the telegraph was then unknown, and the war in
Louisiana went on.

Withdrawing a mile toward the city, Jackson began to
intrench his army between a cypress swamp and the river.
So great was his vigilance that for four days and nights he
did not sleep, and he took most of his meals while sitting on
his horse.[26] Meanwhile the British army was greatly re-
enforced by the arrival of Pakenham with fresh troops. On
the first day of the new year the armies met for an artillery
duel. The British used hogsheads of sugar as a breastwork,
and the Americans used cotton bales—both of which proved
ineffective. The battle lasted for several hours, and the
Americans were completely successful, disabling and silenc-
ing every English gun. This was the only time during the
war in which a fair, even fight with heavy guns took place,
and the British officers frankly acknowledged that their defeat was due to the superiority of the Americans in handling
artillery.

These battles were but preliminary. Everybody knew
that the decisive battle was yet to come. A week passed,
and Jackson spent the time strengthening his embankment.
Day and night the work was pushed with the utmost vigor,

[26] Parton, Vol. II, p. 117.

and there was scarcely a horse, a mule, or an ox in the city
that was not pressed into the service. The cotton bales had
been discarded and earthworks thrown up.

The fateful 8th of January was now at hand—and the
vessel that bore the tidings of peace was battling with the
wintry tides in mid ocean. The morning was chill and dense
with fog. Long before the dawn the two armies were astir.
Jackson rose at one o'clock and roused his sleeping army,
and by four every man was in his place. The British were

BATTLE OF NEW ORLEANS

also in battle array hours before the dawn. Pakenham had
intended to make the attack while it was yet dark; but his
plans miscarried, and he failed to do so. After detaching
twelve hundred men for the west bank of the river, he
divided his army, about fifty-five hundred men, into three
parts. General Gibbs with twenty-five hundred was to strike
the Americans on the left, farthest from the river and near a
cypress swamp; General Keane with twelve hundred was to
attack the right, along the river bank; while Lambert was
to hold the remainder in the center as a reserve. The main
attack was that of the British right, to be made by Gibbs.

There was some forced merriment along the lines; but the feeling that they were entering a death trap could not be shaken off. Colonel Dale, who commanded Keane's Highlanders, handed his watch and a letter to a friend and said sadly, "Give these to my wife; I shall die at the head of my regiment."

Behind the earthen breastwork crouched the American army, thirty-five hundred strong, with a thousand in reserve. Twelve cannon frowned over the parapet. Soon after daybreak the scarlet lines of the British columns were seen through the fog near the cypress trees. A little later the American cannon opened on the advancing foe, and great lanes were cut through their ranks; but on they marched toward the works until they came within musket range. The musketeers then poured in one murderous volley after another, and the top of the American works for half a mile was an unbroken line of spurting fire. The slaughter of the British was frightful. The killed and wounded fell in heaps. One cannon, loaded to the muzzle with musket balls, mowed down two hundred men at a single discharge. No army, however heroic, could stand before such a storm, and the British columns began to fall back in disorder. At this moment General Pakenham rode from the rear to the head of the retreating column and cried, "For shame, remember that you are British soldiers." Next instant a musket ball shattered his right arm and another killed his horse. He leaped on a second charger and kept on cheering his men, apparently unconscious of his wound. But his time was short. A grapeshot tore open his thigh and killed his second horse, and the two fell together. The wounded general was caught in the arms of friends; but ere they could bear him to the rear, a third shot entered his body, and after gasping for a few minutes his life was gone. Scarcely had Pakenham been borne away when Gibbs received his death wound, and at almost the same moment Keane, who was fighting valiantly on the river bank, was severely wounded; and Lambert became the commander of the army. A very few of the English floundered across the ditch and climbed the American parapet; but none survived except Lieutenant Lavack, who was made a prisoner. Major Wilkinson was one of those who mounted the parapet, but he instantly fell, riddled with bullets. The Americans, struck with admiration of his heroism, leaped forward to save him; but he was dying, and lived only long enough to request that his commander be informed that he died like a soldier and a true Englishman.

Between this main attack made by Gibbs and the river, Keane had made a similar one on the American right and had suffered a similar repulse, but with less loss of life. A simultaneous battle was progressing on the west bank of the Mississippi. The American loss in the main battle east of the river was but eight killed and thirteen wounded,[27] but including the west side the loss was seventy-one. The British left seven hundred men dead upon the field, and twice as many were wounded. The battle continued for two hours; but the chief attack with its fearful slaughter had occupied but twenty-five minutes. The Americans forbore to cheer at their marvelous victory on account of the appalling scene of death and despair that lay before them, and they did all in their power to aid and relieve the

[27] In a letter to a friend in 1839, Jackson stated that in the main battle his loss was six killed and seven wounded. See Parton, Vol. III, p. 633.

wounded.[28]   Lambert decided not to risk a second attack. He withdrew Thornton from the west side and retreated toward his ships, and on the 27th the whole army reëmbarked and sailed away, and were seen no more on the shores of Louisiana.[29]

NATIONAL FINANCES

Aside from the passing of necessary laws for carrying on the government and the war, the chief business of Congress and the administration was to wrestle with the financial problem, and the problem proved an insoluble one at the time.   Albert Gallatin, the secretary of the treasury for thirteen years, was a great financier; and had not Congress persistently disregarded his advice, the story of the War of 1812 would not be so humiliating to the American reader. It was doubtless the incompetency of Congress that brought about the serious condition during the war — a distrust by the people of the credit of the government.   The internal revenue system of old Federalist days had been done away; the embargo and non-importation laws had depleted the Treasury, and Congress, against the advice of Gallatin, refused to recharter the United States Bank at the expiration of the old charter in 1811, thereby cutting off the one sure source of government loans.   The members of Congress seemed to think that the people would readily make loans to

[28] At the close of the battle some five hundred of the British rose unhurt from among the dead and gave themselves up as prisoners. To save their lives, they had dropped down and lain as if dead until the battle was over. Parton, Vol. II, p. 209.

[29] Lambert stopped at Mobile and captured a fort; Cockburn ravaged part of the coast of Georgia late in January; and the war on the ocean continued for some months before the treaty of peace became known.

the government when not even the interest could be paid except through other loans. But the people were slow to risk their money with their government. The first loan of eleven millions, called for in the spring of 1812, was taken but slowly, as previously stated. The next year a loan of sixteen millions was authorized, and Gallatin succeeded in placing it only with great effort, paying six per cent interest for the greater portion of it, and selling the stock at eighty-eight cents on the dollar. Another loan of seven and one half millions was soon afterward placed, the discount being the same. Only a small portion of these loans was taken by New England, which was still under the sway of the Federalists. At the same time many people of that section actually lent money to the enemy by purchasing British bills of credit, and they also sold supplies to the British and Canadians.

Exasperated at this, President Madison, in December, 1813, recommended that Congress pass an effective embargo act, and it was done without delay. Then arose a mighty cry from New England. In Massachusetts many public meetings were held to denounce the law as unjust and oppressive. Madison was not, perhaps, altogether without a vindictive spirit in this matter. It can be believed that one of his objects was to punish New England for its persistent opposition to his policy. This embargo was removed in March, 1814.

At an extra session of Congress in 1813 the Democratic party departed from another of its theories. It laid a direct tax and an internal revenue tax on the people. It imposed a stamp tax, and laid taxes on salt, sugar, carriages, and the like. Most of the people saw the necessity of these measures, and responded cheerfully. The next year Madison reported that they had paid the extra taxes with the "greatest promptness and alacrity."

In January, 1814, a bill was passed to refill the ranks of the armies, offering a bounty of $124, in addition to a tract of land of one hundred and twenty acres, to every one who would enlist for five years, or during the war. Another loan, twenty-five millions, was then authorized (March, 1814); but the people were slow to respond. Months passed; Washington was captured by the enemy; the specie of the country drifted to the New England banks. Public credit fell to the lowest ebb; every bank in the Middle and Southern states suspended specie payments; the state banks floated great quantities of paper, and all sorts of corporations issued so-called ticket money, good only in the locality in which it was issued. The country at large was without a stable and adequate currency, and was on the verge of bankruptcy. The Boston banks would receive the notes of a Baltimore bank only at a discount of thirty per cent, and the treasury notes, issued from time to time, at a discount of twenty-five per cent.[30] It was found that the new loan could be secured only at the ruinous rate of seventy-five cents on the dollar.

At this juncture, Mr. Dallas, who had succeeded Gallatin in the treasury,[31] recommended that a national bank be established. After months of sparring, Congress passed a bank bill; but Madison vetoed it in the belief that it would not furnish the needed relief. Another bank bill was soon introduced; but before it could be passed the news of peace was received, and a further consideration was postponed.

[30] The government issued $40,000,000 in treasury notes during the war.

[31] Mr. Campbell of Tennessee served a short time between the terms of Gallatin and Dallas.

OBSERVATIONS

The agents of the two belligerents had met at Ghent, Belgium, in midsummer, 1814.[32] The instructions from their respective governments were such that it seemed at first impossible to reach an agreement. The English demanded, among other things, that America cede large portions of northern New York and Maine, and set apart a broad tract in the Northwest for the Indians. But when the news of the defeat of Prevost at Plattsburg and of Ross at Baltimore arrived, they abandoned their extravagant demands; while the Americans, on the other hand, yielded on the impressment question. The treaty, as finally arranged, is more remarkable for what it omitted than for what it contained. It was little else than a mutual agreement to stop the war, as both nations were tired of it. The subject of impressment was omitted with the understanding that, as the European wars were apparently over, England would no longer need to follow the practice. There was no cession of territory by either side. The treaty provided for the restoration of boundaries as fixed in 1783, and for peace with the Indians, and left all the old boundary disputes and the fisheries question, as also the British right to navigate the Mississippi, for future negotiation. Both nations agreed to use their best endeavors to promote the entire abolition of the slave trade. The news of peace and of the victory at New Orleans reached the Northern states at about the same time, and the rejoicing was tremendous.

The dying Federalist party had opposed the war to the

[32] The American commissioners were Albert Gallatin, James A. Bayard, Henry Clay, Jonathan Russell, and John Q. Adams. The English commissioners were Lord Gambier, Henry Goldburn, and William Adams.

last, though many of its members had fought bravely in the armies.   The legislature of Massachusetts made a call for a convention of the New England states to meet at Hartford in December, 1814.   Twenty-six delegates assembled, and they sat for three weeks with closed doors.   The fact that the sessions were secret gave ground to the rumor that the assembly was treasonable and sought to destroy the Union. What its discussions were, was never known, except from its report embodying a set of resolutions, afterward made public.

To one who reads this report there can be no doubt that the proceedings of the convention were unpatriotic.   "A severance of the Union by one or more states, against the will of the rest," says the report, "and especially in a time of war, can be justified only by absolute necessity."   Then it proceeds to show that the necessity had come, averring, however, that absolute proof was not yet conclusive that the time for disunion had come.   On state rights we find, "That acts of Congress in violation of the Constitution are absolutely void," and that the "states which have no common umpire must be their own judges and execute their own decisions."   Here was a reproduction of the Kentucky and Virginia resolution in a more virulent form.   The convention made a demand also on the government for a share of the taxes collected within those states, and it proposed certain radical amendments to the Constitution, urging that the New England states "persevere in their efforts to obtain such amendments until the same shall be effected." [33]   The apparent intention was to force these demands upon an un-

[33] Among these proposed amendments are these: That no new states be admitted to the Union except by a two-thirds vote of both houses of Congress; that Congress have no power to lay an embargo

willing administration while it was hampered by a foreign war, or in case of refusal to make such refusal a pretext for dismembering the Union.

The supposed object in calling the Hartford convention was to protest against the refusal of the general government to bear the expenses of the Massachusetts militia, which the governor had recently called out to protect the state. The report complains bitterly of this, but does not state that the sole reason for this refusal was that the governor refused to place his militia under the command of Federal officers. An additional object of the convention was obviously to hamper and cripple the administration to the last degree, at a moment when the country was overrun by a foreign foe, to overthrow the party in power, or to break up the Union. The men of this convention were among the leading Federalists of the country, and with all their good qualities it is evident that their patriotism was shallow. The very fact that the Democrats had adopted the loose construction theories of the old, the real Federal party is conclusive proof that the Hartford convention acted, not on principle, but from partisan hatred. But its work came to naught. The news of peace that soon reached America rendered the whole proceeding ridiculous; and the members that composed the convention, as well as the party they represented, thus brought on themselves an odium from which they never recovered.

The war on the part of Great Britain was a serious and costly blunder. She did not acquire a foot of land, nor es-

for more than sixty days; that a President be ineligible for reëlection, and that a President be not elected from the same state two terms in succession. See State Documents, No. 2, p. 41, edited by H. V. Ames.

tablish a principle, nor win a friend. She might have con-
ciliated America with a few slight concessions, and have
made us an ally against Napoleon. She could have dealt
that monarch a stunning blow by opening her ports to our
commerce, and thus reducing to a nullity all his pretensions
to blockade her coasts. But she suffered the dispute with
us to come to blows, and thereby lost her monopoly on the
sea, never to be regained; sacrificed thousands of lives; and
expended money enough to have raised the pay of her sailors
to such a figure as to prevent desertions, and to render impressment unnecessary. A remarkable feature of the war
is found in the high mortality of British commanders. Seven
sea captains were slain in action, besides Generals Brock,
Ross, Pakenham, and Gibbs, Tecumseh, and Sir Peter
Parker.

On the other hand, the Americans gained greatly by the
war, though this did not appear in the treaty, nor at first
on the surface. The war had been expensive to the United
States also. It had cost thirty thousand lives and a hundred million dollars; the currency had been so debased as
to threaten every business interest in the country; the capital
had been captured and burned; a portion of the people had
been disaffected and had given aid and comfort to the enemy.
But with all this, the war had been a successful one to the
Americans. It had brought commercial independence and a
final separation from European affairs, so necessary to national development. Europe had decided long before that a
republican government could not succeed, and ancient
Greece and Rome were always held up as examples; and
even France, which had become a republic within that generation, had again relapsed into a monarchy. It was believed
that our government would also fail, and great was the con-

tempt across the Atlantic for the United States. But when, without a great leader, we held our own on the land for nearly three years, and more than held our own on the sea against the greatest naval power of the earth, the whole world was astonished. Before this war, the United States was never considered a first-class power; since then it has never been considered anything else. It was then that the nations began to realize that America was a rising giant, and that it demanded their respect; and they have never since withheld it.

In our home relations our success was equally marked. The people for the first time began to feel a national consciousness; they say with clearer vision than before that the nation had a future, a destiny, that no European interference could disturb. French and English factions in American politics forever disappeared. Soon after the close of the war began that wonderful tide of emigration from Europe that has poured an unceasing stream upon our shores from that day to the present. Then, also, began that wonderful era of prosperity which has swept down through the century like a tidal wave, and which has no parallel in the history of civilization.

NOTES AND ANECDOTES

War in the Mediterranean. — During the war the Dey of Algiers had again practiced his depredations on American vessels. In the spring of 1815 Decatur sailed into the Mediterranean with a fleet of ten vessels. Two days later he fell in with the Dey's finest frigate in search of American merchantmen. In half an hour Decatur had captured her, and a few days later another met a similar fate. Decatur then forced the Dey to sign a humiliating treaty, giving up all his prisoners without ransom, and making indemnities for all his extortions. He then sailed to Tunis and Tripoli and exacted similar reparation; and from that time American shipping was safe in the Mediterranean.

Stories of Tecumseh. — Tecumseh was probably the greatest orator ever known among the Indians. His language was remarkable for poetic beauty. When he addressed an audience, his face shone with a passionate emotion that worked like magic on his hearers. He was a man of sensitive dignity, as shown by the following incident: When he and his warriors held the famous conference with Harrison, he looked around, after concluding his address, for a seat; but none had been reserved for him, and he seemed offended. A white man quickly offered him a seat near General Harrison, saying, "Your father wishes you to sit by his side." "The sun is my father," answered Tecumseh; "the earth is my mother, and I will rest on her bosom," and he sat down on the ground.

Tecumseh promised Harrison that in case of war between the whites and the Indians he would not permit his warriors to massacre women and children, and he kept his word. At the siege of Fort Meigs, while the Indians were murdering some prisoners, Tecumseh ran between the Indians and the prisoners, and brandishing his tomahawk dared the former to kill another man. Then turning to General Proctor, who had witnessed the massacre without protest, he exclaimed, "Why do you permit this?" "Your Indians cannot be restrained," answered Proctor. "Begone," cried Tecumseh, "you are unfit to command; go and put on petticoats."

At the opening of the battle of the Thames, Tecumseh turned to his friends and said, "Brother warriors, I shall never come out of this battle alive; my body will remain on the field." He then unbuckled his sword, and, handing it to a chief, said, "When my son becomes a noted warrior, give him this, and go tell my people that Tecumseh died like a warrior and a hero."

Stories of Jackson. — In the early part of the war Jackson raised two thousand troops and was sent down the Mississippi as far as Natchez. But as no enemy appeared, he was ordered, in the spring of 1813, to disband the army. Jackson was very indignant at this order. It was cruel and outrageous, he said, to lead men five hundred miles from home and turn them out without money or food. He chose to disobey the order; he marched the men back to Tennessee, at his own expense. But the government afterward assumed the expense. The general had three good horses; but these he gave to the sick, while he walked with the rest. While tramping along, some one said, "The general is tough," and another added, "As tough as hickory." From this he soon came to be called "Old Hickory," and the name clung to him through life.

Jackson engaged in a disgraceful street fight with the future Senator Benton and his brother, and the latter inflicted a terrible wound in Jackson's arm with a pistol shot. The future President was laid up for many weeks. He was still in bed when the Tennesseeans were arming to avenge Fort Mims. A friend called on Jackson and expressed his deep regret that the commander of the militia was not in condition to lead the army against the Creeks. Jackson's eyes flashed instantly, and he answered, "The h—l he isn't," whereupon he leaped from his bed, and an hour later he was astride his horse at the head of the army. He carried his arm in a sling during the entire campaign. On one occasion when the soldiers mutinied for want of food and started in a body for their homes, Jackson called on them to halt, and they refused. He then rode in front of the column, and with a volley of oaths and the fire flashing from his eyes, drew his musket with his one well arm, and declared he would shoot the first man that took another step. The men sullenly went back to their duty. After the Creeks had been crushed, Jackson set a price on the capture, dead or alive, of the half-breed Wetherford, who had led the Indians in the campaign, as also in the massacre at Fort Mims. One day as Jackson sat in his tent a big Indian chief walked in and said: "I am Wetherford. I have come to ask peace for my people. I am in your power; do as you please with me. I am a soldier. If I had an army, I would still fight; but my warriors hear my voice no longer. Their bones are at Talladega and the Horse Shoe. Do as you will with me. You are a brave man. I ask not for myself, but for my people." Jackson was astonished at this visit. He had intended to put Wetherford to death; but now felt that he could not do so. He gave the chief his liberty on his promise to keep peace in the future — and the promise was kept.

Jackson's wonderful nerve and physical courage were never shown to greater advantage than in his duel with Charles Dickinson in 1806. Dickinson was one of the richest men, and certainly the best marksman, in Tennessee. He and Jackson had long been enemies, and he frequently tried to provoke Jackson to a duel with intent to kill him. At last he succeeded by reflecting on the character of Jackson's wife, and the challenge came. The two parties rode north into Kentucky, and at daybreak, on May 30, the duel was fought. Jackson was an excellent shot; but he could not compare with Dickinson, and every one expected that he would be killed. At the word "fire," Dickinson fired instantly, and a puff of dust was seen at Jackson's breast; but he stood like a statue, with clenched teeth. Dickinson stepped back and cried, "My God, have I missed him?" General Overton, Jackson's second, drew his pistol and ordered Dickinson to stand still. Jackson deliberately fired and shot Dickinson through the body. As they went to the inn it was noticed that Jackson's boots were full of blood. "General, you are hit," cried Overton. "Oh, I believe he has pinked me a little," said Jackson; "but don't mention it over there," pointing to the house where Dickinson lay dying. It was found that Dickinson's aim had been perfect, but that his bullet had only broken a rib and raked the breastbone. Jackson, asked how he could stand motionless with such a wound, said, "I should have hit him if he had shot me through the brain." See Parton, Vol. I, p. 299.

Prohibition of the Slave Trade. — As we shall soon have to deal with the great question of slavery, it is well to notice here the national prohibition of the African slave trade. A part of one of the compromises of the Constitution was that Congress must not interfere with the slave trade before 1808. Long before this time, however, the Southern states put an end to the traffic, each within its own bounds. But in 1804 South Carolina reopened it (after it had been closed in that state for fifteen years), and in the remaining four years imported about forty thousand negroes. In 1807, Congress passed a law to take effect January 1, 1808, prohibiting the trade, under severe penalties. In 1820 an additional act made the traffic piracy punishable by death. But in spite of all vigilance of the government, aided by the British government, there continued a smuggling trade up to the Civil War. In all this period there was but one execution for smuggling negroes, and that after the opening of the Civil War.

CHAPTER XXII

DAWN OF NATIONAL CONSCIOUSNESS

NOTHING is more interesting to the student of American political history than the gradual change wrought in the Democratic party during the first sixteen years of the nineteenth century. The party had been founded on the principles of strict construction of the Constitution; but it did not gain control of the government until the Federalists had committed the country to a policy of broad construction. Had the early theories of Jefferson on construction been strictly carried out, the Union could not have existed a quarter of a century. Jefferson was wise in being able to see the necessity of abandoning his former theories. His party was founded on the theory of strict construction and state rights, and yet no President ever departed farther from this policy than he in the purchase of Louisiana, and in the laying of an unlimited embargo. He believed that the nations could live in harmony without war; his party waged a foreign war eleven years after it came into power. One of the party's theories was that no navy was necessary; it voted in 1813 to build a navy. Another was its opposition to direct taxes and internal revenue; it established both in 1813. At first the party opposed internal improvements at national expense; in 1806 it passed a law to build the Cumberland Road, and internal improvements have flourished from that time to the present. For years the party opposed a national bank; in 1816 it established one. What, then, can we say of a party that abandons the very foundation stones on which it was built? Simply, that it was wise enough to grapple with new problems, to adapt itself to new conditions. What, then, of Thomas Jefferson, who had been forced to discard, one by one, nearly every plank on which he had stood at his first election to the presidency? As noted on a former page, it was not state rights, nor a weak central government, to which Jefferson gave his lifework. These were but means, which he erroneously believed to be necessary means, to a sublimer end. The end was the rule of the democracy, a government by the people. And this he won,—not immediately, not fully during his lifetime; but he started the current, which gathered in force and in later years became irresistible.

RECUPERATING

Marvelously soon after the close of the war the people returned to their respective vocations and set about repairing their broken fortunes. But it was the government, rather than the people, that had suffered. The great question now before Congress was that concerning the adjustment of the finances. The money of the country was in a frightful condition. The sources of issue exceeded four hundred in number. Much of the "wild-cat" money, as it was called, was counterfeit; much came from alleged banks that had no existence.[24] Mr. Dallas of Pennsylvania had proved himself an able financier. He now sought to bring about specie payments as soon as possible, and to do this he again urged upon Congress the advantage of chartering a second United States Bank. The charter of the old bank founded by Hamilton had expired in 1811, and, as we have seen, a re-

[24] McMaster, Vol. V, p. 307.

charter was defeated in Congress. But now a twenty-year charter for a national bank, with $35,000,000 capital, was readily obtained. The government subscribed $7,000,000 of this and the remainder was taken by individuals and corporations. The bank paid the government a bonus of $1,-500,000 for the charter. It had a wonderful effect in restoring confidence, and in a short time the national debt was steadily decreasing, while the people were busy and prosperous and happy.

To the two great industries of the country, agriculture and commerce, a third, manufactures, was now added. The temporary suspension of commerce, through Jefferson's embargo and the war,[35] had forced the people to begin manufacturing on a large scale to supply their own wants. Before the embargo all the cotton and woolen cloth, tools, china, glass, and the like were brought from England; but at the close of the war hundreds of manufactories, encouraged by societies formed for the purpose, by prizes and by special acts of state legislatures, had sprung up, and most of these articles were made at home.

Soon after the coming of peace the country was flooded with all manner of merchandise from England, and the people, seeing their new industries threatened, called upon Congress to protect by tariff laws what the embargo and the war had protected for them before. The response was the tariff of 1816, fathered by William Lowndes of South Carolina. By this tariff duties were raised to an average of about twenty per cent,[36] and this not only greatly increased the revenue, but proved ample for protection; and the busi-

[35] During the war the duties on foreign imports had been doubled.
[36] Tausig's "Tariff History," p. 19.

ness of manufacturing increased and flourished throughout the land.

There was little speculation as to who would succeed Madison to the presidency. It seemed to be generally understood that James Monroe would be chosen, the only objection being that he was a Virginian, and Virginia had furnished all the presidents thus far except Adams. Monroe, however, would have been eclipsed, and would probably have been beaten, by the more brilliant De Witt Clinton of New York, but for the fact that Clinton had bolted the regular party candidate four years before, and had permitted himself to be the candidate of the anti-war Democrats and the Federalists. He never rose again to national favor, and Monroe now had clear sailing. The Federal party was no longer formidable. The war, which the party had so diligently opposed, had ended happily, and this continued opposition, with the odium of the "Blue Lights" and of the Hartford convention, was a burden too heavy to be borne; and after casting 34 electoral votes for Rufus King against Monroe's 183, the party disappeared from national politics. Daniel D. Tompkins, the vigorous war governor of New York, was chosen Vice President.

The time for retiring, after a long and useful public career, now came to James Madison. With his accomplished wife, known as "Dolly" Madison, he retired to his rural home at Montpelier, Virginia, and there he grew old gracefully amid the scenes of his young manhood. He was the last survivor of the illustrious band that had framed the Constitution, dying in 1836, after twenty years in private life. No President in his declining years ever enjoyed a deeper reverence of the whole people than did Madison.

Monroe has been called the last and least of the great Virginians. He was less original than his great predecessors, it is true, nor was he brilliant or dashing in any sense; but none was better fitted for the presidency at this moment than he, for the people were now dreaming of national greatness, and were not in the mood for hero-worship. Monroe had made few enemies. He was so open-hearted, generous, amiable, and industrious that he had won the confidence of all classes. "If his soul were turned inside out," said Jefferson, "not a blot could be found upon it." Soon after the inauguration the new President made a tour of the country, ostensibly "to inspect the national defenses," but in fact to strengthen patriotism, to win over disaffected elements, and to obliterate party lines. And his tour was eminently successful. In New England the remaining Federalists vied with the Democrats in doing honor to this "last of the revolutionary fathers." In every town he was met by the leading men, and was cheered by thousands of school children, and by young men and women of every walk of life. It was said that the farmer left his plow in the furrow, the housewife left her clothes in the tub and her cream in the churn and hastened to the towns to see this real President of the United States. While the presidential party was in New England a Boston newspaper gave rise to the well-known expression, "Era of good feeling," which is still used to characterize the administration of Monroe. From New England the President passed through northern New York, to Sacketts Harbor, Niagara, and thence to Detroit, returning through Ohio, Pennsylvania, and Maryland. This tour, covering three and a half months, was followed by another to the South, and their great usefulness in cementing the Union and awakening a livelier sense of patriotism was denied by no one.

Monroe had chosen a strong Cabinet. John Quincy Adams became secretary of state, William H. Crawford, secretary of the treasury, Crowningshield of Massachusetts, secretary of the navy, while John C. Calhoun took the war department and William Wirt became attorney general. Of these five men, three — Adams, Crawford, and Calhoun — were yet to become important figures on the political stage.

One of the most notable episodes of this quiet administration was that known as the Seminole War, notable mainly because it brought prominently before the public, for the second time, a remarkable character, a future President — Andrew Jackson. The Seminole Indians, a wandering portion of the Creeks, together with some Spaniards and negroes escaped from their masters, kept stirring up trouble with the Americans along the northern border of Florida, which then belonged to Spain, and Jackson with fifteen hundred men was sent against them. He was successful at every turn, and the war was soon over. In this brief campaign Jackson showed that spirit of lawlessness so characteristic of him through life. Monroe was careful not to offend Spain, and through Calhoun, his secretary of war, he instructed Jackson not to lead his army on Spanish soil. But the general thought he knew best, and he led the army across the border without ceremony.[17] He captured St. Marks and Pensacola, both on Spanish territory, and even sent General Gaines against St. Augustine, which was not at all concerned in the war; but Calhoun recalled Gaines,

[17] Jackson always claimed that he had secret orders from the President, through John Rhea, a member of Congress, to conquer Florida. Jackson had said, in a letter to the President, "Let it be signified to me through any channel (say Mr. John Rhea) that the possession of the Floridas would be desirable, . . . and in sixty days it will be accomplished." This authority he and Rhea claimed to have received;

and the town was not taken. Again Jackson exhibited his lawless propensities in dealing with two English captives — Ambrister and Arbuthnot. Ambrister was a young Englishman, who was taken in the act of leading the Indians against the Americans. Arbuthnot was an old Scotch trader suspected of stirring up the Indians. A court-martial sentenced both to death; but it reconsidered the decision in the case of Ambrister and gave him a lighter sentence. But Jackson, believing both men to be guilty, reversed the second decision of the court and ordered both men to be put to death, and it was done. Great was the indignation in England against Jackson when the facts became known. He was denounced as a murderer all over England; but Parliament was more considerate and decided not to allow the matter to make trouble between the two nations, as it was evident that the two men had violated international rights. A British statesman, however, said that if the ministry would but raise a finger, all England would rush to arms at a moment's notice.

But Jackson's trouble was not over. He made enemies in Washington. There were several secret cabinet meetings in which his conduct was discussed. All the cabinet were against him except John Quincy Adams; but none wished to become his open enemy, so the meetings were kept secret. Now Jackson thought that Calhoun was his warmest friend and most faithful defender in the Cabinet; but Calhoun made the remark in one of these meetings that Jackson ought to be court-martialed. This was the costliest

but Monroe always denied having given it. In 1830 the subject came up again, and the aged ex-President, under oath, declared that he had not granted the authority. Whether Jackson and Rhea were right and Monroe had forgotten, was never known. See *Magazine of American History*, October, 1884.

sentence ever uttered by John C. Calhoun, as will be shown in a later chapter. Many of the people denounced Jackson, and he was wroth; but Monroe skillfully soothed his feelings, gave up the Spanish forts, and avoided war with Spain. And yet Jackson's tribulation was not at an end. Congress took up the matter. Jackson had enemies in Congress, and a motion was made in the House to censure him for hanging the two Englishmen, and was debated for three weeks, much to the chagrin of the administration; for Monroe had already settled the matter, and England demanded nothing. The war being over, Jackson came to Washington and remained during this strange debate. At length he was acquitted and came out with flying colors.[38] He then made a tour through the North, and was received with great demonstration everywhere. An immense banquet was given in his honor in New York City. This was on Washington's birthday, 1819, and on that very day, John Quincy Adams, secretary of state, and Don Onis, minister from Spain, signed the treaty conveying Florida from Spain to the United States.[39]

THE MISSOURI COMPROMISE

We must now introduce the reader to a great public question, which first became prominent at this period, and which thereafter, with brief intervals, was the most overshadowing public issue for half a century—the slavery question. It first came up as a sectional question in connection with the admission of Missouri into the Union, and resulted in the Missouri Compromise. The rising West had been rising

[38] In this debate Clay denounced the conduct of Jackson, and thus incurred his everlasting enmity.
[39] See note at end of chapter.

with great rapidity. Streams of emigration from the East had poured into the great valley of the Mississippi, and one new state after another had joined the famous sisterhood. Louisiana had been admitted in 1812, and four years later her northern sister of kindred name, Indiana, became the nineteenth state. Indiana was the first of six states to be admitted in six successive years, the others in order being Mississippi, Illinois, Alabama, Maine, and Missouri. It was the last of these that brought up the momentous issue that was destined to shock the country almost to its destruction, and to be settled at last in blood. The Missouri Compromise was purely a slavery question, and a rapid glance at the existence of slavery in America before this date is here in place.

The enslavement of the African race for commercial purposes had its beginning in southern Europe about half a century before the discovery of America by Columbus. It was transplanted to Central and South America by the Spaniards, and it existed there for a hundred years before being introduced into the English colonies of North America. Soon after the small beginning made in Virginia the institution grew and spread to other colonies as they were founded; and at the opening of the Revolution there were about six hundred thousand slaves in the colonies. The slave-traffic during the colonial period was very lucrative and was carried on chiefly by English traders. At various times the colonies attempted to restrict the evil, but in each case the attempt was crushed by the British Crown, simply because the trade was profitable. As early as 1712 Pennsylvania passed a law to restrict the increase of slaves, but it was annulled by the crown.[40] Virginia made a similar attempt, a

[40] Wilson's "Rise and Fall of the Slave Power," Vol. I, p. 4.

few years later, by laying a tax on imported negroes. South Carolina attempted to restrict the trade in 1761, as did Massachusetts a few years later; but in each case the effort was summarily crushed by the Crown. As late as 1770 King George wrote the governor of Virginia, commanding him on pain of the royal displeasure "to assent to no law by which the importation of slaves should be in any respect prohibited or obstructed." Thus while the mother country prohibited slavery on her home soil, she not only encouraged but enforced it in her colonies.[41] But the colonists were in part to be blamed, for they purchased the slaves; otherwise the traffic would have died out.

Slavery in the colonies was first opposed by the Quakers and Pennsylvania Germans in the latter part of the seventeenth century. John Wesley, the great founder of Methodism, visited the South in later years and pronounced the institution the "sum of all villainies." At the opening of the Revolution all the colonies had slaves; but the Northern states soon began to emancipate, not so much from motives of morality as because the institution was unprofitable. Massachusetts abolished slavery by a decision of the courts; Pennsylvania provided for gradual emancipation in 1780; New Hampshire, Connecticut, and Rhode Island in 1784; New York in 1799; New Jersey in 1804, and so on. There were a few left in New Jersey as late as 1850. Jefferson inserted a clause against the slave trade in the Declaration of Independence, but it was struck out. The Ordinance of 1787 kept slavery out of the Northwest.[42] The law of

[41] Before 1772 slaves were held in England. In that year Chief Justice Mansfield decided, in the famous Somerset case, that it was illegal to hold slaves in England, and that decision, which freed about fourteen thousand blacks, has never since been reversed.

[42] In 1784 Jefferson introduced an ordinance for the government of

1808, prohibiting the slave trade, brought relief to all op-
posers of the institution, for it was generally believed that
the artery of slavery was now severed, and that it would
eventually die out in the South, as it had in the North; and
little was heard on the subject during the next ten years.
But this hope was a delusion. Whitney's cotton gin, a simple machine for separating the seed from the fiber, which enabled one man to do the work of three hundred before its
invention, brought cotton to the front and rendered it
eventually the chief agricultural staple in America. More
slaves were needed to raise cotton in the growing states
along the Lower Mississippi, while some of the Eastern
states had more than they needed, and hence was established
the interstate slave trade. Meantime slavery was fastening
itself upon the South with a firmer grasp, and at the same
time the conviction was slowly taking possession of the
northern heart that the whole system was wrong and should
be checked. On both ethical and economic grounds the
North came to oppose the extension of slavery. The South
was quick to see that the only way in which to prevent future legislation unfriendly to slavery was to increase the
number of slave states, and thus to increase its representation
in the United States Senate.

the Southwest, the territory "ceded already or to be ceded" to the
United States, afterward Kentucky, Tennessee, Mississippi, etc., in
which a clause prohibited slavery in the territory after the year 1800;
but this clause was struck out by a majority of one. Had it been carried and been effective, slavery would have been confined to a few
Atlantic states in the South, and would doubtless have died a natural
death. But a certain member from New Jersey, who would have voted
for it, was absent on the day when the vote was taken. Thus the entire
course of American history was changed by the absence of one man
from Congress on a certain day in 1784. See Greeley's "American
Conflict," Vol. I, pp. 38-40.

A vast region was added to the United States by the Louisiana Purchase, and as the time approached for this to be carved into states, the all-important question arose, Slavery or no slavery in the great West? Missouri was the first of the trans-Mississippi territories to apply for statehood, and on its application the first great battle between the North and the South was fought. The slave-holders had stolen a march by settling in Missouri with their slaves; and when the application for statehood came to the Fifteenth Congress, it provided for slavery in the new state. But it was clearly seen that if Missouri were admitted with slavery, it would be very difficult to keep it out of any part of the Louisiana Purchase. Slavery in Missouri must therefore be opposed, and the man for the occasion was at hand.

There was a young man in the House from New York, named James Talmadge, who now rose and moved to strike out the slavery clause in the Missouri bill, or, more exactly, that there be no further introduction of slavery into Missouri, and that all children born in slavery after the admission of the state should be free at the age of twenty-five years; and his speech in support of the motion was the most eloquent heard on the floor of Congress since the time of Fisher Ames. Talmadge was powerfully aided by John W. Taylor, also of New York, and the two succeeded in defeating the Missouri bill with slavery. But the Senate rejected the House measure, and it was left over till the next Congress. During the interval the subject was discussed on all sides, and the agitation was intense; but the people could do but little, as the next Congress had already been elected.

The Missouri question was not only an ethical and an economic one, it involved also a deep constitutional principle. Had Congress the power to lay restrictions on new states that were not laid on the original thirteen? Would the new states be coequal with the old if admitted under such limitations? The members from the South took the ground that the Constitution gave Congress no such power. They argued also that the treaty ceding Louisiana to the United States contained the express provision that all property rights must be protected by the United States. Those from the North, with some exceptions, contended that as Congress had full control in governing the territories, it had the power to place conditions on their admission as states.

One notable feature of the debate was that no one from either section stood up for slavery as a moral or an economic benefit to the country; all agreed that it was an evil. But the South contended that making a slave state of Missouri would simply scatter and lessen the evil without increasing it.

The Sixteenth Congress, ever memorable for the Missouri Compromise, met in December, 1819, and this great question soon came up for final solution. As Talmadge was not a member of this Congress, Taylor was the champion for free Missouri. The leaders on the other side were Henry Clay, the speaker, John Tyler, a future President, Charles Pinckney, a framer of the Constitution, and William Lowndes. Again the House adhered to its antislavery position, and again the Senate disagreed. In the Senate the debates even surpassed those of the House, the leader for slavery in Missouri being William Pinkney of Maryland, with Rufus King of New York as his leading opponent. The Senate was balanced, half from slave states and half from free states; but there were a few northern senators who, from constitutional grounds, or from a desire to please the South, voted with the southern members. One from Indiana, and both from Illinois, now voted with the South, and the two houses again reached a deadlock.

It happened that at this time Maine, which had belonged to Massachusetts from colonial days, was asking for admission as a separate state; and the Senate, acting on a suggestion made in the House by Mr. Clay, brought in a bill to admit Maine, and to this bill they attached the one to admit Missouri, with slavery. This was passed February 16, 1820, whereupon Senator Thomas of Illinois made a motion to amend the bill by annexing a clause prohibiting slavery in all the remainder of the Louisiana territory north of thirty-six degrees and thirty minutes north latitude, the southern boundary of Missouri. This became the famous compromise line. It was adopted by the Senate, but the House rejected it; and still again each House voted to stand its ground. Then a joint committee was appointed, and this committee agreed to admit Maine and Missouri separately, leaving the Thomas amendment to the Missouri bill. This report was adopted by both houses; and Missouri, with the Thomas compromise line, was admitted as a slave state. President Monroe signed the Maine bill on March 3, and the Missouri bill March 6, 1820.

But this did not end the strife concerning Missouri. The act of March, 1820, was simply an act enabling the territory to form a constitution for statehood. When the people of Missouri adopted a constitution, they inserted a clause making it the duty of the legislature to exclude free negroes and mulattoes from the commonwealth. This brought on another great debate in Congress. The objection to this clause was based on the ground that the Constitution guarantees to the citizens of any state all the privileges and immunities of the citizens of the several states. The two houses again failed to agree, and again the decision was made through a joint committee. Henry Clay was the mover and the chairman of this committee, and from this fact he became known as the author of the Missouri Compromise.[a]

This committee reported a bill to admit Missouri on an equal footing with the original states, on the condition that its constitution should never be construed so as to authorize any law by which a citizen of any other state should be excluded from the privileges which he enjoyed in other parts of the Union; and that the legislature of Missouri should pass a solemn act declaring its consent to this condition. This was accepted by both houses, and became a law on the 28th of February, 1821; Missouri accepted the condition and became a state in the Union.

The Missouri contest had far-reaching results. It has generally been considered a victory for the South, in that Missouri was actually admitted as a slave state. But the compromise on the line of thirty-six thirty probably brought equal or greater advantage to the North. This part of the act was repealed thirty-four years later; but meantime it did great service in keeping slavery out of Iowa and other portions of the Northwest.

But there was a deeper principle involved in this decision. The fact that a compromise line had been agreed on, thus giving Congress power over slavery in the territories, and that Missouri was admitted with a condition which was not imposed on the original states (both in accordance with broad construction), opened the eyes of the South to the

[a] Clay had appointed the House members of the committee that arranged the first compromise of the year before, and his selection of men favorable to the compromise aided also in crediting him with being the author of it.

fact that broad construction had taken deep root in the
Democratic party, and to the further fact that the status of
slavery would, in a great measure, rest henceforth on the
will of Congress. As Professor Burgess has pointed out,[44]
this new revelation to the South brought about within the
next ten years a division in the Democratic party. The portion more favorable to non-interference with slavery, which
became the Democratic party of Jackson, went back, to
some extent, to the early doctrine of Jefferson, and became
strict constructionists, the chief object being to protect
slavery from Congress, which, in the Lower House, must
ever be dominated by the North. The other portion of the
party at length became the Whig party, under the leadership of Clay. These mighty political forces were set in motion by the Missouri Compromise.[45]

MONROE'S SECOND TERM

James Monroe was elected to the presidency a second time

[44] "The Middle Period," p. 104.
[45] The aged ex-President, Thomas Jefferson, was one of the first
to see the deep significance of the Missouri question. Though unfriendly to slavery, he favored its extension into Missouri, as it would
dilute and scatter the evil without increasing the number of slaves.
Jefferson was alarmed at the rise of parties on geographical lines. To
John Adams he wrote concerning the Missouri debate (December 10,
1819): "From the battle of Bunker's Hill to the Treaty of Paris we
never had so ominous a question. . . . I thank God that I shall not
live to witness the issue." Jefferson was greatly alarmed for the
future of the country. After the compromise line had been settled,
he wrote: "The question sleeps for the present, but is not dead," and,
"This momentous question, like a fire bell in the night, awakened me
and filled me with terror. I considered it at once as the knell of the
Union. But he seems later to have regained hope. On December 26,
1820, he wrote to Lafayette, "The boisterous sea of liberty, indeed, is
never without a wave, and that from Missouri is now rolling toward
us; but we shall ride over it as we have over all the others."

by a unanimous vote, save one.* This unanimity indicated, not the overshadowing greatness of the President, nor his inherent power to draw all men unto himself, but rather that party lines had been extinguished, that no other aspirant had secured a following, and that the mediocre President was considered a safe man, and was trusted and loved by all the people.

In December, 1823, President Monroe set his hand to a document that has made his name more famous in foreign lands than that of any other of our early presidents except the name of the Father of his Country. In his annual message to Congress that year he laid down a principle of foreign policy to which the government has adhered with the utmost tenacity from that time to the present, and this policy took the name the world over of the Monroe Doctrine. This "doctrine" grew out of the rebellion against Spain of her possessions in the New World. When, in 1808, Napoleon put his brother on the throne of Spain, Mexico and the Spanish colonies of Central and South America rebelled, and won a temporary freedom; but on the restoration of the old monarchy they returned to their old allegiance. When, however, Spain attempted to reimpose on them her old colonial system, after this taste of liberty, they again rebelled, and declared their independence. After six years of warfare, Spain being too weak to subdue them, the United States acknowledged their independence. In 1823 the king of Spain invoked the aid of other European powers (the same that had formed the "Holy Alliance" a few years before) to aid him in putting down a rebellion at home, and

* An elector from New Hampshire, claiming that Washington should stand alone in being unanimously chosen to the great office, voted for John Q. Adams.

presumably to aid him in subduing his rebellious American colonies. England had built up a flourishing trade with South America, which she wished to maintain, and Mr. Canning, the British premier, now suggested that England and the United States join in aiding these new-born republics to maintain their freedom. But the United States preferred to act alone, and its action consisted in a simple declaration by the President, in part as follows:—

"The occasion has been judged proper for asserting as a principle . . . that the American continents . . . are henceforth not to be considered as subjects for future colonization by any European powers. . . . We should consider any attempt on their part to extend their system to any portion of this hemisphere as dangerous to our peace and safety." The message further states that the United States would not interfere with any existing possessions in America of the countries of Europe, but as to those which had won their independence, "we could not view any interposition for the purpose of oppressing them, or controlling in any other manner their destiny, by any European power, in any other light than as the manifestation of an unfriendly disposition toward the United States."

This is the famous "doctrine," the language of which is said to have been written by Secretary Adams; but, being embodied in the message of Monroe, it took his name, and has thus been known ever since. The first part, as quoted above, was directed chiefly against Russia, as that country had taken possession of Alaska, and was extending its settlements down the Pacific Coast. By this a stand was taken against further colonization in America by European powers. The second part was intended to protect republican government in South America.

The doctrine was not new with Monroe. Its roots may be found in the neutrality proclamation of Washington, in his farewell address, and in Jefferson's warning against "entangling alliances." The attitude of non-interference in European affairs expanded until it resulted in a determination to oppose all European interference in matters wholly American. It was a settled policy of the government for years before being officially proclaimed by Monroe. It was now eminently effective. Russia ceased her encroachments on the Pacific coast, and the European alliance abandoned all intention of aiding Spain against her former colonies. On various occasions since then has this doctrine been called into operation, the most notable being in 1865 against France in Mexico, and in 1895 against England in Venezuela.⁴⁷ The twofold object of the Monroe Doctrine is to guard against that which may be "dangerous to our peace and safety," and to protect republican government in the Americas. The Monroe Doctrine is not a part of international law, nor has it been placed on the statutes of our country; it is simply a policy, a declaration of an attitude taken by the Executive of this government with reference to the relations of the European powers to the republics of this hemisphere. It is a mistake to believe that the doctrine is becoming obsolete; it is more firmly embedded in the American heart at this time than ever before. A still greater mistake is the opinion held by some that the ultimate object of the United States is to absorb the republics south of us into our government. Nothing is farther from the truth. What the future attitude of the United States on this subject may be, we do not pretend to prophesy; but for

---

⁴⁷ For a fuller account of the Monroe Doctrine in operation, see Elson's "Side Lights," Vol. I, Chap. IX.

the present it is safe to say that if any South or Central American state were to seek admission to our Union as a state, or even as a dependent territory, the united voice of our people would be against it.

One of the great subjects that attracted the attention of Congress during the administration of Monroe was that of internal improvements. In the last week of Madison's administration a bill was passed to set apart the bonus received by the government from the bank, and also the proceeds of the shares held by the government, for the purpose of constructing roads and canals. The leading advocate of this bill was John C. Calhoun, and in the light of subsequent events it is interesting to note that at this period no statesman had broader national views than Calhoun. He not only claimed that internal improvements were constitutional under the "general welfare" clause, but that they would go far toward strengthening the government and counteracting all tendencies toward sectionalism and disunion. But there was much opposition to the bill on the old strict construction grounds, and among its opponents was President Madison, who, on the day before retiring from office, vetoed the bill.

Five years later, in 1822, a bill to repair and operate the Cumberland Road, which it will be remembered was authorized in 1806, was passed by Congress and vetoed by President Monroe. Two years later, however, an act for making surveys, plans, and estimates for national routes became a law. This was a second entering wedge, the first being the authorizing of the Cumberland Road nearly twenty years before. After this the government set apart money from time to time for internal improvements; but the coming of the railway rendered the constructing of

1758 — JAMES MONROE — 1831.

By Gilbert Stuart, 1817.

From the original portrait in the possession of Hon. Thomas Jefferson Coolidge, Boston, Mass.

roads and canals less urgent, and national aid in later years was confined chiefly to the improvements of rivers and harbors.

Closely associated with the subject of internal improvements was that of the tariff, which received much attention at this period. Notwithstanding the tariff of 1816, the people suffered a money panic two years later, caused chiefly by the reaction from the disturbed condition during the war, and by the inflation due to the springing up of several hundred local banks. Most of the people, however, believed that a higher rate of protective duties would prove a cure-all for the ills of the country. Led by Henry Clay, who had now become the champion of the "American System" of protection, this party passed a tariff bill in the House in 1820 which was defeated in the Senate by a single vote. But the people continued their clamor for higher protection, and in 1824 the second general tariff of the century was enacted into law. By this tariff the duties on wool, hemp, lead, and many other articles were increased, and an average scale of about thirty-three per cent was reached. This tariff was not a sectional measure.[48] Among its opponents were Daniel Webster, Mr. Cambreling of New York City, and several leading men from the South. The North and the border states, led by Clay, were its chief supporters.

The Seventeenth Congress, expiring in 1823, had done nothing, almost nothing—except to intrigue and plot and counter-plot concerning the presidential succession. Monroe's term was passing into history; somebody must succeed him, and for the first time the whole country was at sea concerning the choice of a candidate. The Federal party had disappeared, and the Democratic party had absorbed

* See Burgess's " Middle Period," p. 115.

the whole people; but this did not bring political harmony. Four candidates early loomed up on the political horizon, each with his personal following, and each claiming to represent the true democracy: Henry Clay, the man of the people, the idol of the House of Representatives; John C. Calhoun, the brilliant young South Carolinian, able, far-sighted, patriotic; John Quincy Adams, son of former President Adams; and William H. Crawford of Georgia, ex-minister to France, now secretary of the treasury, and, as many believed, a designing, intriguing politician. Crawford was Monroe's chief rival for the nomination in 1816, and so sure did he feel that he would succeed Monroe that in 1820 he piloted an act through Congress known as the "Crawford Act," which gave greater power to the president in the appointment of civil service officials. By this act, which stands on our statutes to this day, the tenure of civil service officials was reduced to four years, whereas before this such officials had been appointed without a definite time limit. This gave an immense appointive power into the hands of every incoming President. Eight years were yet to elapse before the national party convention was to come into existence; the congressional caucus still assumed the right to name candidates. But the caucus for this purpose had lost its force with the people. The last of these was held at this period, and it nominated Crawford; but it was attended by less than half the members of Congress.[49] The other candidates were nominated by various state legislatures.

As the canvass progressed, another star was added to the

---

[*] About this time Crawford suffered a severe stroke of paralysis, from which he never fully recovered; but during the campaign his friends kept the fact from the public as best they could.

constellation; and now there were five. As near the close of the War of 1812 a star had risen in the South that soon outshone all the others, so it was now, and it happened to be the same star,—Andrew Jackson. The rude but virile state of Tennessee had, as early as 1822, boldly put forward this grim old hero of New Orleans, who was now nearing the completion of his three-score years; and great numbers of people, weary of the intrigues of the trained politicians, turned instinctively to this "man of the people" and made his cause their own. But the constellation was soon again reduced to four, as Calhoun quietly dropped out and accepted second place on the ticket. The election came; the people spoke through the electoral college, electing Calhoun Vice President, but failing to choose a President; and for the second time in our history, and the last thus far, this momentous duty fell to the House of Representatives. Jackson had received the highest number of electors, ninety-nine; Adams came next with eighty-four, Crawford secured forty-one, and Clay thirty-seven. The Twelfth Amendment provides that the House may vote for the three highest only, and this shut Clay out, as he was fourth in the list. But for this, Clay might easily have become President, had he chosen to vote and to work for himself, for he was speaker of the House and was very popular in that body.[50] The House dallied with the great subject, and before it came to a vote every member turned aside to pay homage to a stranger who appeared upon its floor. He

---

[50] Again, Clay would have been third on the list instead of Crawford, but for a trick played on him in Louisiana. When the legislature of that state chose electors, it did so when two or three of Clay's friends, who held the balance of power, were absent, and thus the state voted for Jackson and Adams instead of Clay.

was an aged, thin-faced, kindly man, whom every American revered as a father,—Lafayette, the friend of liberty.

In the dark days of the Revolution, when in the bloom of his young manhood, this doughty Frenchman had left his youthful wife and his luxurious home to offer his life and his fortune in the holy cause of liberty; and now at the end of half a century he returned to visit the land he had never ceased to love. And never in the history of the United States has any other foreigner received the glad welcome, the universal homage of the people, that he did. Lafayette had greatly changed. His love of liberty was still warm and young; but the blithe step was gone, his hair was silvered, and his brow was furrowing with age. But greater was the change in the land that his eyes now looked upon,—then a few distracted colonies struggling toward the light, now a nation that commanded the world's respect, with its rising cities, its opening industries, its continental domain.

General Lafayette arrived in New York in August, 1824. As he traveled through the country, men and women of every rank hastened to the towns to see this hero of a past generation and to join in the universal shout of welcome. He visited every state in the Union, and spent the winter in Washington. Congress voted him $200,000 and a township of land in Florida, which he was asked to accept, not as a gift, but as a partial recompense for his Revolutionary services; and the gift was acceptable indeed, for he had lost his fortune in the various changes of the French government. In June, 1825, he was in Boston, on the greatest gala day that Boston ever saw, and laid the corner stone of Bunker Hill Monument, on the fiftieth anniversary of the famous battle. After a visit of nearly fourteen months

the nation's guest departed for his native land in the
Brandywine, named for the battle in which he had been
wounded, in southern Pennsylvania.

We return to the presidential election. The eyes of the
nation turned to Henry Clay. His power in the House
was so great that it was generally believed that he held
the election in his hand. Clay was no friend of Jackson,
nor of Crawford; and even he and Adams were not, and
had never been, close political friends. But a choice must
be made, and one of these three must be chosen. At length
Clay announced that he would vote for Adams; his adher-
ents followed his example, and Adams was elected, receiving the votes of thirteen states, while seven states voted
for Jackson and four for Crawford.

Adams made Clay secretary of state, and the Jackson
party raised the cry that there had been a bargain, a corrupt bargain, between Adams and Clay. This cry was kept
up for four years, and it played an important part in the
next presidential election.[51] Clay got into trouble with
John Randolph about the matter. Randolph was a remarkable man in many ways. He had entered Congress in 1799,
when scarcely more than a boy, and had soon attracted attention by his tall, awkward appearance, his ungovernable
temper, his keen wit and biting sarcasm. During his long
career in Congress he made many an enemy quail, when the
object of his sarcasm and pointed out by his long, bony
finger. As a wit he has never been equaled on the floor of

---

[51] Through Adams's Diary we learn that some of Clay's friends did
approach Adams on this subject before the election; but there is not
the slightest proof that Adams made any promises. The cry of corrupt bargain had, in fact, been raised before the election in the House
in the hope of coercing Clay to vote for Jackson. Clay's acceptance of
a place in the Cabinet was a blunder that he should have avoided.

Congress. He usually talked as he chose about any one; and on this occasion he referred to Adams and Clay as "the Puritan and the Blackleg." Clay was angry when he heard this. He had chafed restively under public accusations. Now he could contain himself no longer. He challenged Randolph to a duel. Randolph was not angry with Clay. He had called him a blackleg; but he often used such terms without expecting them to be taken too seriously. But Clay was not to be appeased, and the two men met on the field with loaded pistols. They each fired once without effect. Clay fired again, the bullet passing through his antagonist's coat. Randolph then fired into the air, threw down his pistol, and stepped toward Clay with extended hand. This was too much. Clay's face changed in an instant; he threw his pistol to the ground and ran to meet Randolph, and the latter said with mock seriousness, "Mr. Clay, you owe me a new coat."—"I'm glad the debt is no greater," said Clay; and the two men indulged in a long, fervent handshake.[5]

JOHN QUINCY ADAMS

As a boy of seven years John Quincy Adams had stood with his mother and viewed the famous battle of Bunker Hill from afar; and this may be considered the beginning of the longest public career in American history. Two years later this boy, who never knew a boyhood, was a regular postrider making daily trips from his village to Boston. At the age of eleven he accompanied his father to France and began a course of severe study. At fourteen he was a private secretary to our minister at St. Petersburg. At

[5] For a full account of this, see Benton's "Thirty Years' View," Vol. I, pp. 70-77.

1767 — JOHN QUINCY ADAMS — 1848.
By Edward D. Marchant, 1847.
From the original portrait in the New York Historical Society.

eighteen he had visited every country in Europe; and, returning to his own land, he was graduated at Harvard two years later. No American statesman ever lived a more strenuous life, none had a more varied experience, and none a cleaner record. When elected President in 1825 Adams had been a professor at Harvard, and a practicing lawyer in Boston. He had served in the legislature of Massachusetts and in the United States Senate. He had aided in framing the Treaty of Ghent, had been minister to five European courts, and had completed his eight years as secretary of state. No man in America was by training better fitted for the presidency than Adams; and few were less fitted by natural temperament.

No President ever entered upon the great office with a clearer sense of duty, or with nobler motives than did Adams. But like his father before him he was wanting in tact, in the ability to manage men. He was a man of the sternest puritanic integrity; he subjected himself to severe discipline in his private life and public duties. He judged other men by his own high standard of morality, and saw their faults rather than their virtues.[53] His manner was cold and repelling, and with all his wide acquaintance he had no intimate personal friend, nor did he make any effort to win friends. He enjoyed little popularity among his own class, and still less among the masses of the people. As Ezekiel Webster wrote his brother Daniel, Mr. Adams's support came "from a cold sense of duty, and not from any liking of the man." On the whole, Adams was, with all his defects, one of the most admirable public characters in our history; and his greatest service was rendered in the House

[53] Schouler, Vol. III, p. 400.

of Representatives, where, after his term as President, he spent seventeen years of his old age.

The single presidential term of Adams may be recorded in small space, as both Senate and House were against him, and they refused to pass any administration measure of importance. In his first message the President recommended a system of internal improvements on a far larger scale than had been hitherto undertaken; but Congress opposed such extensive improvements, and Adams was left powerless to carry out his projects.

Early in this administration the Panama Congress, a convention of the American republics to be held at Panama, became the prominent public question. The object was to deliberate on a continental policy concerning commercial intercourse, to restrict the extent of blockades, to establish firmly the Monroe Doctrine, and the like. Clay was its chief promoter in the United States. His object was to organize the Americans against Europe for commercial advantage and self-protection. He won Adams and the Cabinet to favor sending delegates, and Adams announced in his message that this would be done. But the Senate was obstinate, professing to fear "entangling alliances," though its real object was to thwart the administration. At length, however, after long delay, the bill passed. But the victory of the President was a barren one, for the Panama Congress had adjourned before our delegates reached the place.

The only other matter of national importance — except the "Tariff of Abominations," to be noticed later — that belongs to Adams's term of office, was that concerning the Indians of Georgia. When Georgia ceded her western lands to the United States in 1802, the latter engaged to remove the Indians from the bounds of the state when it could be done peaceably. Various treaties and purchases were made subsequent to this, but in 1824 the Indians declared they would sell no more land. The white people of Georgia became enraged at this and demanded that the government carry out its contract. A treaty was made at Indian Springs, in 1825, ceding the Indian lands; but the tribes refused to accept it, and put to death the chiefs who signed it. President Adams then notified Governor Troup of Georgia that he was expected to discontinue his survey of the Indian lands until the United States government had completed its negotiations with the Indians.[64] Whereupon the governor became frantic, and blustered and fumed against the United States to his heart's content. President Adams was not appalled by the irate governor; he sent General Gaines to Georgia with instructions to prevent the survey of the lands, by force, if necessary. The next year, 1826, another agreement with the Indians was made by the United States government. By this agreement a large portion of the Indian lands were secured to Georgia. But the Georgians were not content with the incompleteness of the work, and the governor was again defiant, and even prepared to resist the power of the United States.

President Adams, while careful to uphold the dignity and authority of the government, was unwilling to allow the matter to come to blows without being sure of the support of the country. He therefore laid the subject before Congress; but Congress refused to give the matter serious attention. This encouraged the Georgians in their attitude toward the Creeks, and they also laid claim to jurisdiction over the lands occupied by the Cherokees within the state. In 1827 the legislature passed a law in accordance with this

[64] See Ames's State Documents, No. 3, pp. 25-36.

claim, though the lands had been solemnly guaranteed to the Indians in a treaty in 1785; but Governor Troup declared this treaty not binding on the state, on the ground that Georgia and the United States were equal and independent powers! The Indians appealed to President Adams for protection in their rights; but he, about to retire from office, chose not to embarrass his successor by committing the government to any policy in the matter.

By anticipation it may here be stated that the trouble with the Cherokees continued under Adams's successor. Georgia claimed jurisdiction over their lands; they resisted and appealed to the President, who refused to aid them. The matter came before the United States Supreme Court, and was decided, in 1832, against the Georgians.[55] But President Jackson sympathized with the state and refused to enforce the decision of the court. At length, a few years later, some sort of agreement having been reached, the Cherokees, who had made commendable progress in agriculture and education, were removed to the Indian Territory, beyond the Mississippi, where they still remain. The action of Georgia throughout was little short of nullification.[56]

As this presidential term drew to a close the country prepared itself for a fierce contest. Adams was a candidate for reëlection, with Andrew Jackson as his opponent. Unlike Adams, Jackson was popular; he could win friends and he could win crowds. He had risen from the lower walks of life, and the people regarded him as one of themselves. Adams was looked upon as an aristocrat, and, moreover, he refused to turn a hand to secure his own election. Many of the public servants who held their offices at his discre-

[55] Worcester *vs.* Georgia.
[56] See Ames's State Documents, No. III, p. 36 *sq.*

1773—JOHN RANDOLPH OF ROANOKE—1833.

By WILLIAM HENRY BROWN, 1830.

From the original silhouette in the Historical Society of Pennsylvania.

tion, including some of his own Cabinet, were openly working for Jackson, but he refused to notice the fact. Even those who worked for his election received no word of gratitude or encouragement from him. He took the high ground that the influence of the office should not be used to further an election. One would think that such fidelity to duty would have been rewarded; but it was not. Jackson was elected by a large majority of the popular vote, as well as of the electoral college.[57]

MEANS OF TRAVEL AND INVENTION

Nothing impresses the student of the history of this period more than the progress made in the invention of machinery and in the means of travel. We have noticed the great flow of humanity across the Alleghanies to the valleys of the Ohio and Mississippi, and the consequent admission in rapid succession of five new states of the West and South. This movement of the population from the seaboard to the interior of the continent awakened an intense desire for better modes of travel. The first important advance in this line came through the general use of the steamboat. By the time of Monroe's second election the western rivers, as well as those of the East, were covered with steam craft. These were not to be compared with the river steamer of the present day. It required thrice as many hours to run a hundred miles upstream as to return with the current, but the improvement over the flatboat of earlier days was very marked. So it was also along the seacoast. All the leading ports were now connected by lines of steam

[57] All the states except two, South Carolina and Delaware, now chose electors by a popular vote; these two still retained the old system of choosing by the legislature.

vessels, and a journey from one coast city to another became
a pleasure trip, and consumed far less time than in the old
days of the stagecoach.

But this was not enough for the rising West. The mountain walls that nature had thrown between the Eastern
states and the valley of the great river must be overcome,
if in the power of man to accomplish it. The great cones-
toga wagon still lumbered across the mountains and the valleys, from Philadelphia to Pittsburg. But relief was soon
to come, and it came in two forms, — the railroad and the
canal.

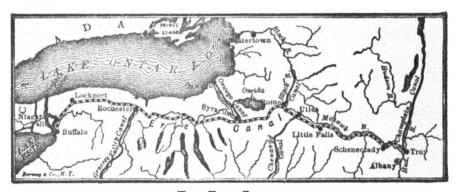

THE ERIE CANAL

The first great canal to be completed in America was the
Erie Canal from Albany to Buffalo, 363 miles, — often
called Clinton's Big Ditch, as Governor De Witt Clinton
was its chief projector. In October, 1825, after eight years'
toil of thousands of men with pick and spade and wheel-
barrow, the great work was finished, and Governor Clinton
led a tandem fleet from Buffalo to Albany amid the acclama-
tions of the multitudes that gathered along the banks. The
motley fleet bore a bear, two eagles, two Indian boys, and
other things typical of the land before the coming of the

white man,[58] and its coming was announced by a continuous line of cannon placed along the route. From Albany Clinton proceeded down the Hudson, and, pouring two kegs of Lake Erie's water into the sea, pronounced the communication between "our Mediterranean seas and the Atlantic Ocean accomplished."

The Erie Canal proved a wonderful boon to New York. The cost of transporting merchandise from Albany to Buffalo had been over $100 a ton; now it fell to one tenth of the former price, and this opened a vast market to the merchants and manufacturers of New York City, which soon became the chief metropolis in America. Farmers hastened from all sides to purchase farms along the canal, and the price of land rose rapidly. But not only was New York benefited by the canal. The farmers of Ohio, Indiana, and Illinois could now purchase their axes, plows, and other utensils for a fraction of what they had formerly paid for them, and indeed the business of the entire country was affected by this great improvement.[59]

One of its effects was to cause a rage for canals to spread over the country. Philadelphia saw its western trade threatened with ruin. This led the people of Pennsylvania to decide on digging a canal between their two chief cities, and the work was soon begun.[60] The great Ohio Canal joining Lake Erie with the Ohio River, from Cleveland to Portsmouth, was begun in 1825. The Chesapeake and Ohio Canal extended from Pittsburg to Washington. Many other canals of smaller pretensions were built, and many

[58] McMaster, Vol. V, p. 132.

[59] It is interesting to note that in 1903 the people of New York voted to expend $101,000,000 for the improvement of the Erie Canal.

[60] This was never completed; or rather, when it was completed, it was part railroad.

were begun and never finished, for another and far superior mode of inland transportation was now attracting the attention of the people.

The vast network of railroads that now covers the United States had its beginning at the time we are treating. John Stevens, an inventive genius of the highest order, who had done almost, if not fully, as much as Robert Fulton for the steamboat, was now the chief advocate of steam railways. A road was soon built from Philadelphia to the Susquehanna, but the cars first used were drawn by horses. The action of Pennsylvania in projecting canals and railways alarmed the people of Baltimore lest Philadelphia steal its western trade, and they decided to build a railroad to some point on the Ohio River. Work on it was begun in July, 1828, and this was the origin of the Baltimore and Ohio Railroad. The first steam locomotive was brought from England in 1829, where experiments in steam railways had been in progress for over ten years, but it proved a failure. In 1831, however, a locomotive was successfully used in South Carolina, and within a few years others were in operation in various parts of the country. But for years after this beginning many of the cars, even on the steam roads, were still drawn by horse power. The roads were owned by the state and the cars and engines by individuals or corporations. Any one owning a car or an engine had the use of the road. The engines were rude machines compared with those of our own times, but they went faster than the horses, and this caused much confusion. Eventually the railroads passed into the hands of private corporations, and horses were everywhere supplanted by the steam engine.

Some of the greatest inventions of our modern civilization belong to this period. The rapid progress in steam navigation by land and water brought about a wonderful stimulus in manufacturing and created a great demand for labor-saving machinery. Hence came the sewing-machine, the threshing-machine, the mower and reaper, and a few years later the telegraph and many other inventions of great usefulness. The first flannel made by machinery was produced in Massachusetts in 1824; the first illuminating gas was made from coal in New York in 1827. Thus one invention followed another, and they played a great part in laying the foundations of our present industrial prosperity.

The newspapers, numbering two hundred at the beginning of the century, seventeen of which were dailies, had now greatly increased in number; but their subscription rates were still high, as printing was a cumbersome business, the modern steam press being yet a thing of the future. The majority of the people did not take a newspaper. The postmaster was often the only one in a town who took a paper, and on its arrival the villagers would gather about him to hear him read the news.

NOTES

Boundaries. — Two important boundary lines were agreed on while Monroe was President. The boundary between the United States and British America west of the Great Lakes was fixed in 1818. From the Lake of the Woods the forty-ninth parallel was made the boundary westward to the summit of the Rocky Mountains. West of this lay the Oregon country extending to the Pacific and claimed by both the United States and England, and it was decided that both occupy it jointly for ten years; but twenty-eight years elapsed before the ownership was settled.

In 1819 the United States purchased East and West Florida from Spain for $5,000,000. Before this the United States had claimed that Texas was a part of the Louisiana purchase; but this claim was now given up and the boundary decided on was as follows: The Sabine

River from the Gulf to 32° and thence northward to the Red River, up
the Red River to the one hundredth meridian, north to the Arkansas
River, up this river to the crest of the Rocky Mountains, north to 42°,
and west on this parallel to the Pacific. Thus the United States did not
reach the Pacific at any point. The Pacific slope north of 42° belonged to
the Oregon country, and south of 42° were the possessions of Mexico,
known as the California country. The United States did not take
possession of Florida until 1821, when Andrew Jackson became the
first governor.

Migration to the West. — A wonderful movement of the population to the West began soon after the war with England had closed.
Every road leading westward from the East was covered with lines of
moving wagons, plodding their weary way over hills and mountains,
streams and valleys. At Haverhill, Massachusetts, 450 emigrants
passed through the town in thirteen days. At Easton, Pennsylvania,
511 wagons, bearing over 3000 persons, passed in one month. These
were moving to the great valley of the Ohio River, and in the South
a similar movement to the new states of Alabama and Mississippi was
going on.

A farmer wishing to better his worldly condition would sell all his
goods that he could not take with him, and provide himself with a
strong, light wagon, covered with canvas. In this he would pack his
goods, leaving only room enough for himself and his family. Thus
equipped they would bid adieu to old neighbors, friends, and kindred,
often to meet them no more in this life, and start out upon the long and
toilsome journey of hundreds of miles through the wilderness. Sometimes whole communities went together and settled in the same neighborhood in the West; but more frequently they moved by isolated families.
Arriving in the western wilderness, the pioneer would purchase a
quarter section of land of the government, of some land company, or
of some settler who had preceded him and failed, paying two or three
dollars an acre, on the installment plan. If the land were wholly un-
improved, the family would live in the moving wagon until a cabin
could be built. The cabin was made of logs, notched at the ends so
as to fit at the corners, and laid one above another until the house was
about ten feet high. There was but one room, one door, and one window. The door was made of rough boards swung on leather hinges,
and opposite the door was left an open space on the ground for a
fireplace, the chimney being built outside of flat sticks like laths, and
plastered with mortar. The floor was made of planks hewn out with
the ax, and the roof of lighter planks resting on rafters made of sap-

1767 — ANDREW JACKSON — 1845.

BY RALPH E. W. EARL, 1819.

From the original portrait in possession of Colonel Andrew Jackson, Cincinnati, O.

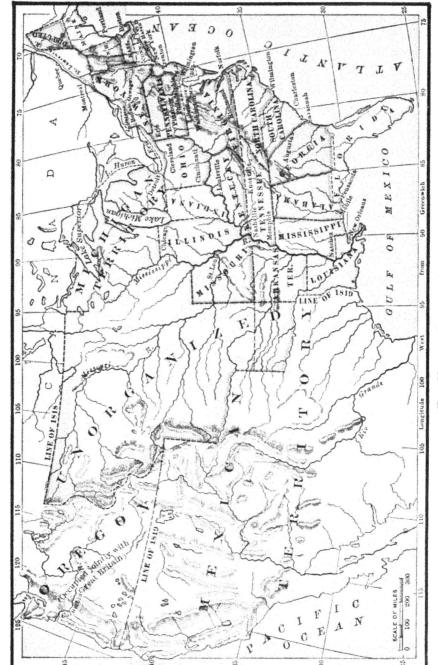

THE UNITED STATES, 1830

lings. In such a home many a good family lived for ten or twenty years, the ancestors of many of the leading men of the nation to-day. The cabin built, the pioneer would begin battling with the forest, clearing a few acres each year, carrying his grain perhaps twenty miles on horseback to the nearest mill. Soon his land would become more productive; and at length, if thrifty and industrious, he would build a good house and abandon the cabin. Other movers would settle near, then a town would be founded, and another, and another, and eventually a railroad would be built through the new settlement. The community is transformed in twenty-five years; the markets are near, the comforts of life have multiplied, the farm of the first settler is now worth thousands of dollars, and he has added other hundreds of acres to it. His children settle on the farm or enter the business or the professional world, and the "old settler" spends his declining years amid peace and plenty; and he gathers his grandchildren about him and tells of the days of long ago, of the long journey in the moving wagon, and of the time when the forest frowned on every side and the wolves howled about his lonely cabin in the wilderness.

CHAPTER XXIII

THE REIGN OF JACKSON

AMERICAN LIFE IN 1830

THE census of 1830 footed up nearly thirty million people, scattered over about half the present limits of the United States. West of the Mississippi River was a vast unbroken wilderness, save for Missouri and some parts of Louisiana and Arkansas. Texas and California still belonged to Mexico, and the ownership of Oregon was unsettled. Little else than a wilderness were Michigan, Illinois, and large tracts of other fast-growing states east of the Mississippi. The great cities of the West are all of recent growth. Cincinnati was then a considerable town and was called the "Queen City of the West;" but Chicago was a rude wooden village, and the buffalo still roamed over the sites of Omaha, Denver, and San Francisco.

Changes were rapidly going on in the East. Virginia was no longer the first state in population, nor even second. New York was now first, Pennsylvania still held second rank, while Virginia was relegated to the third place. The three leading cities each boasted a millionaire of untold wealth — Girard of Philadelphia, Astor, the New York merchant-prince, and Lawrence, the founder of the Boston cotton mills.[61] The telegraph was unknown at this day, and our present vast network of railroads was just making

[61] Schouler, Vol. IV, p. 6.

a beginning. The old stagecoach days were not yet over, and their relics are still to be found in various parts of the United States. Any one who travels through the country will find here and there a house very different from the ordinary farmhouse. These are usually large stone buildings, two stories high, with spacious rooms and halls, situated in old towns or on the main roads, twenty miles or more apart, and are always old. They are relics of the stagecoach period, and were called inns or taverns. In some neighborhoods the aged people still remember and eagerly tell of the good old days when travelers from all parts of the country would lodge there; or when political meetings were held at the inn, and the people would come together to discuss public questions and sing their political songs over the social glass; or when the young people from far and near would assemble and spend the night in carousal and merrymaking.

The American of that day was known abroad as the Yankee. Every country has its typical citizen, and the typical American, whose likeness has been preserved to us in the well-known picture of "Uncle Sam," was tall, lean, wiry, and awkward. He had a roving, keen, inquisitive eye, and no stranger could escape him without gratifying his appetite for news. He was the keenest bargain driver in the world. To foreigners he was courteous, but he would flare up in an instant, if any one spoke against his country.

There were few rich men and almost no poverty. The chief subjects that engaged attention were religion, politics, and moneymaking.[62] The great majority of the people were religious, though the intolerant spirit of colonial days had passed away. Nearly every man was interested in politics.

Schouler, Vol. III, p. 4.

He took pride in the fact that he was part of the state, and had a voice in shaping the laws. But the most conspicuous characteristic of the Americans was the widespread desire to become rich. In wealth there is power, and here were no social castes to keep a man down, however humble his birth; and the American sought wealth, not only for the distinction and comfort that it brings, but also that he might give his children advantages that he did not have in his youth.

Democracy reigned supreme by 1830. "The principle of the sovereignty of the people," says De Tocqueville, "has acquired in the United States all the practical development that the imagination can conceive. The people are the cause and the aim of all things; everything comes from them and everything is absorbed by them."[63] The Declaration of Independence had set forth the dogma that the rights of man are inherent and the gift of nature; but half a century passed before that principle became triumphant. It reached high-water mark in American history at the time of Jackson's presidency. The principles of Federalism were wisely retained in the general government, but the current of democracy, set in motion by Jefferson in the closing decade of the eighteenth century, had swollen into a tidal wave, and Federalism existed now only at the will of the democracy. Nothing illustrates this triumph of the people more than the rapid spread of the suffrage and of religious liberty. When the Constitution went into operation a property qualification or a religious test was required in nearly every state, and probably not more than one hundred and fifty thousand of the five million people could vote.[64] The

---

[63] "Democracy in America," Chap. IV.

[64] Thorpe's "Constitutional History of the American People," Vol. I, p. 97.

1782—JOHN CALDWELL CALHOUN—1850.

BY WILLIAM JAMES HUBARD, 1832.

From the original portrait in the Corcoran Art Gallery, Washington, D.C.

new states forming constitutions, with rare exceptions, recognized manhood suffrage without the religious or property test. The old states brought about the same results by amending their constitutions, and by 1830 the suffrage of the adult white male population was almost universal.

THE PEOPLE'S PRESIDENT

Andrew Jackson, "the people's man," was now President. He was the first of our Presidents, but not the last, to rise from the ranks of the common people; all his predecessors were from the so-called higher class of society. Until long past middle age, Jackson had shown no inclination toward a political career. If he had any ambition beyond the quiet life of a planter, it was a military ambition. Twice he resigned from the United States Senate before finishing his term. He made little impression in Congress, and seemed to dislike public life. Thirty years after his first service in the House, he was recalled by Gallatin as a tall, lank, uncouth frontiersman, with long hair gathered in a queue and tied at the back with an eelskin. After resigning from the Senate in 1797, he lived an obscure life till the battle of New Orleans, when he suddenly sprung into a world-wide fame. As above stated, he did not like public life, and there is reason to believe that his candidacy for the presidency annoyed rather than pleased him [65] until it reached a certain point, until he believed himself to have been defeated by a corrupt bargain between Adams and Clay. Then the contest assumed a different form, a victory to be won, and his

---

[65] "Do they think," said Jackson, in 1821, "that I am such a darned fool as to think myself fit for the presidency? No, sir; I know what I am good for. I can command a body of men in a rough way, but I am not fit to be President." Parton's "Life of Jackson," Vol. II, p. 354.

old warrior spirit arose, and he left no stone unturned until he was seated in the presidential chair.

The outgoing President refused to attend the inaugural ceremonies, as his father had done twenty-eight years before. He felt that he had good grounds for taking such an attitude. The facts in brief are these: During the campaign in the preceding summer, Jackson's wife was shamefully attacked, and the poor woman, who was doubtless innocent, died a few weeks before the inauguration. Jackson believed that her death was partially due to these attacks, and he felt very bitter against every editor who had published them. The administration organ at Washington had copied them, and Jackson, believing that Adams had something to do with their publication, and also remembering the "corrupt bargain," refused to call on Adams, according to custom, when he reached the Capital City some days before the inauguration; and hence Adams refused to attend the ceremonies. He remained in the city for a week, then quietly left for New England.

The inauguration of the new President was a grand affair; the day was fine, and the crowd was vast. The people had flocked from every point of the compass to see the people's man made President. Jackson, despite his want of early training, was capable of assuming the manners of the most highly cultured. He was not in the least overawed by the presence of the great, nor did he affect to show contempt for the refinements of social life. His address to the great audience that now stood before him revealed no tendency to cringe, nor was it marred with a taint of bravado. "His manner was faultless," writes an eyewitness who was not his political friend,[66] "not strained, but

* Thompson's "Recollections of Sixteen Presidents," p. 146.

natural. There was no exhibition of pride or ostentation — no straining after effect or false show." The ceremonies over, a great public reception with refreshments was held at the White House, and the rabble had full sway. They trampled the fine carpets with their muddy boots, stood on chairs and upholstered furniture, and among other things smashed an immense, costly chandelier. "Let the boys have a good time once in four years," said Jackson, — and nothing he ever said gives a deeper insight into the cause of his popularity.

Jackson chose as his secretary of state the rising, smooth-tongued Dutch politician of New York, Martin Van Buren, who a few months before had been elected governor of his state. Samuel D. Ingham was made secretary of the treasury, and John H. Eaton secretary of war. The Cabinet was now increased to six members, the postmaster-general being admitted to it, and the first incumbent of the new office was William T. Barry of Kentucky.

During the early months of 1829 an affair at Washington, known as the Eaton Scandal, created much public excitement. This matter would not merit the notice of serious history but for the permanent effect it had upon the administration. Many years before this time, a William O'Neal had kept a tavern at Washington, and his house became the lodging place of many of the government officials. Among the boarders was Senator John H. Eaton from Tennessee. O'Neal had a daughter, a witty young beauty, known over the city as Peggy O'Neal. She was quite free with the inmates of her father's house, and especially with Mr. Eaton, — until the gossips were set going and her name became tainted. At length Peggy O'Neal married a Mr. Timberlake of the navy, but he died by suicide in the Mediterranean; and in January, 1829, Mr. Eaton, who was still in the Senate, married the widow. Mrs. Eaton now set out to gratify the ambition of her life, — to become a leader in Washington society. But her former history was exhumed, and most of the society ladies of the city refused to recognize her. This was the state of affairs when Jackson arrived in the city. Eaton had been one of his chief campaign managers, and the O'Neals had a warm place in Jackson's heart, as he also had been their guest while serving in the Senate a few years before.

Remembering the slanders against his own wife, now deceased, believing Mrs. Eaton to be innocent, and believing also that the gossip about her was inspired by Henry Clay with the object of ruining her husband, Jackson determined to espouse the cause of the Eatons. He appointed Mr. Eaton to his Cabinet, and did everything in his power to clear the name of his wife, and to give her a standing in society. He wrote scores of letters, he called Cabinet meetings, he attended stately dinners — all for Mrs. Eaton. But the women who held the key to the inner sacred circle declined to open the door to Mrs. Eaton. General Jackson now practically informed the members of his Cabinet that their political fortunes depended on the recognition by their wives of Mrs. Eaton; but these men were powerless; their wives simply refused, and that was the "end of it." Even the President's niece, the mistress of the White House, made a stand. "Anything else, Uncle, I will do for you, but I cannot call on Mrs. Eaton." "Then go back to Tennessee, my dear," said the President, and she went back to Tennessee." Thus the hero of New Orleans, the old iron

---

*" Six months later, however, this niece, Mrs. Andrew Jackson Donelson, was reinstated in the White House.

warrior who had never known defeat in battle, was completely defeated by the women. The Cabinet was now inharmonious in the extreme, and after hanging together till the spring of 1831, it broke to pieces and a new Cabinet was formed.[88]

Aside from disrupting the Cabinet, the Eaton Scandal had another and still more marked effect on American history. It built the fortunes of the secretary of state. Martin Van Buren was at this time a widower and without daughters, and he could well afford to give his energies to the cause that was so dear to his chief. He called on Mrs. Eaton; he arranged balls and dinners for her; he spoke of her virtue in every social circle; he sought out the British and Russian ministers, both bachelors, and secured their aid in pushing Mrs. Eaton to the front. And he succeeded, not in having her recognized in Washington society, but in intrenching himself in the heart of General Jackson. Never from this moment was there a break between the two, though as unlike they were as winter and balmy spring. It was soon after this time that Jackson decided to name Van Buren as his choice for the presidential succession, and his decision was final, for his party was all powerful, and he swayed the party as Jefferson had done thirty years before.[89]

The chief members of the new Cabinet were Edward

[88] Mr. Eaton was sent as minister to Spain. He died in 1856; but his famous wife lived to be very old, dying long after the Civil War.

[89] In a letter dated December 31, 1829, to Judge Overton of Tennessee, Jackson adroitly names Van Buren for the succession. This letter was to be used in case of Jackson's death, and his health was then frail. But he grew stronger, and the letter remained a secret for nearly thirty years. See Parton, Vol. III, p. 294. But Parton wrongly gives the date as December, 1830. See Von Holst, Vol. VI, p. 163.

Livingston, secretary of state, Lewis Cass, secretary of war, and Roger B. Taney, attorney-general.   Here may be mentioned also Jackson's "Kitchen Cabinet," composed of a few of his intimate friends, private advisers, but not members of the real Cabinet.   These men were said to meet the President in a private room, which they reached by means of the back door, hence the name.   Chief among them were Francis P. Blair, editor of the *Globe*, founded in opposition to the *Telegraph*, which was under the influence of Calhoun; William B. Lewis, who had managed Jackson's first campaign and was a master politician; and, above all, Amos Kendall of Kentucky, afterward postmaster-general. Kendall was a strange character.   Silent, wiry, seedy, and slovenly in appearance, he glided in and out of the President's private room more like a spirit than a man.   But withal he was frugal and honest, and was possessed of remarkable political sagacity.   He devoted all his powers to upholding the name and fame of the President, and was content to remain almost unknown himself.   It is believed that Jackson owed more to Amos Kendall than to any other man for the successes of his administration.

THE CIVIL SERVICE

For three things the "reign" of Jackson will ever be remembered in our history: The radical changes made in the civil service; nullification in South Carolina; and Jackson's crushing the life out of the United States Bank.

Andrew Jackson was a man of intense patriotism, and he did much for which the country should hold him in greatful remembrance.   But for one thing he deserves no credit, and that was his debauching the civil service, his introducing, or permitting to be introduced, the spoils system into national politics. Before the advent of Jackson civil service officials usually held office for life or good behavior. The Crawford Act of 1820, limiting an appointee to a four years' tenure, had not been enforced. During the forty years preceding Jackson's term but few public officials had been dismissed; but Jackson ignored all precedent and removed clerks, postmasters, and customhouse officials by scores and hundreds, for purely political reasons. This "spoils system" had been in practice in New York and Pennsylvania state politics. It was the spirit of triumphant democracy that brought it into national politics. Jackson could have crushed, or at least deferred it, but did not do so.[10] The system, the motto of which was "To the victors belong the spoils," took a powerful hold on the country and was followed by Jackson's successors for many years; each became a victim to the system whether he would or not; and it is only in recent years that the movement known as Civil Service Reform has in part brought us back to the old practice of the early Presidents.[11]

JACKSON AND CALHOUN

Now in addition to the line by which we have traced the career of Jackson to this point, let us follow another, almost

[10] See Sumner's "Jackson," p. 147; Von Holst, Vol. II, p. 14.

[11] Would that all our Presidents had the conception of the great office held by Washington! Here is an extract from a letter he wrote to a friend concerning another friend who had applied for an office: "He is welcome to my house and to my heart; but with all his good qualities, he is not a man of business. His opponent, with all his politics hostile to me, is a man of business. My private feelings have nothing to do in the case. I am not George Washington, but President of the United States. As George Washington, I would do this man any kindness in my power — as President of the United States, I can do nothing."

parallel with this one for a long distance, when they diverge never to meet again.   In this second line we trace the life of another of the most striking figures in American history. Von Holst, the German historian, pronounces the life of Calhoun more tragical than any tragedy ever conceived by the imagination of man.

The points of resemblance in the lives of Jackson and Calhoun are very remarkable.   They were both of Scotch-Irish descent, born in the Carolinas, of revolutionary Whig parentage, and each was left fatherless at an early age. They were both tall and spare in frame, of pure morals and undaunted courage, and each was a born leader and commander of men.   They both entered Congress at the early age of thirty years and were leaders in the same great political party.   In 1824 they were both candidates for the presidency, one withdrawing and accepting second place, the other being defeated; they were elected four years later, President and Vice President on the same ticket.[13]

But these two lines are not wholly parallel; there is here and there a notable divergence.   Jackson was entirely without a higher education; Calhoun was a graduate of Yale. Jackson disliked the tedious work of lawmaking; he was sent to Congress three times, and resigned each time without finishing his term; but he was a superb commander on the battlefield.   Calhoun, on the other hand, never took the field, but he was a leader in Congress from the time he entered it in 1811 to the end of his long political career of thirty-nine years, with the exception of the few years when he was not a member.

For many years Jackson and Calhoun were fast friends.

[13] This parallel is adapted from Greeley, "American Conflict," Vol. I, p. 88.

1791 — ROBERT YOUNG HAYNE — 1839.

By Samuel Finley Breese Morse, 1820.

From the original portrait in possession of Mrs. William Alston Hayne, San Francisco, Cal.

Calhoun aided Jackson to the presidency in 1828. Jackson gave as a toast at banquet, "John C. Calhoun, an honest man, the noblest work of God." The great ambition of Calhoun's life was to become President of the United States. It was almost a passion with him, and entered into all his political acts. But Jackson had gained such a powerful hold upon the Democratic party that no one could be elected without his support, and any one he might name was likely to become his successor; yet it was believed from one end of the land to the other that Calhoun would be the fortunate one upon whose shoulders the mantle of Old Hickory would fall.

But an evil day came. Calhoun's hopes were blasted forever, and he became a changed man, so changed that the Calhoun of later years could scarcely be recognized to be the same man as the brilliant young patriotic leader of his earlier years. It happened on this wise: It will be remembered that Jackson in the Seminole War of 1818 caused trouble by trespassing on Spanish soil. Calhoun was at that time secretary of war in the Monroe Cabinet. The subject was discussed in secret cabinet meetings, and in one of these meetings Calhoun suggested that Jackson be subjected to a court of inquiry with a view to his punishment. At the same time Jackson believed that Calhoun was his warmest friend and most faithful defender in the Cabinet. It was soon after this that Jackson had toasted Calhoun as an honest man, the noblest work of God. Their friendship thus continued for many years longer when, in 1830, Jackson heard of the attitude Calhoun had taken in the Monroe Cabinet. Jackson was dazed at the information. He at once wrote Calhoun asking if it could be true. In vain did Calhoun assert that he had never questioned Jackson's

patriotism or honesty; in vain did he explain that whatever
he may have said in Monroe's Cabinet was in accordance
with official duty, and never intended to mar their personal
friendship. But Jackson was unable to distinguish between
personal and political friendship. He denounced Calhoun
most bitterly, and gave him to understand that their friendship was forever at an end. And so it was; they were never
after reconciled.[13]

A breach between two political leaders is not an unusual
occurrence, and may often be passed over as of little importance. Sometimes, however, such a quarrel may change
the entire working machinery of the government. This
quarrel and permanent breach between Jackson and Calhoun became a momentous turning point in the life of the
latter. Calhoun's great ambition to become President was
now blasted. He was a disappointed man, and the effect of
his disappointment can be traced through his entire subsequent course. He was a national man, with broad national
views, and one of the most brilliant and attractive men in
the nation till this time. After this change came over him
he was a sectional man and gave his great talents to the interests of slavery as long as he lived.[14] Slavery during its
career in America had many champions of admirable talents,
but no other compares at all in ability with Calhoun.
The one weapon which he constantly used in dealing his
powerful blows was state rights, or, more properly, state

[13] This incident was not the origin or the sole cause of the rupture
between Jackson and Calhoun. They had been growing apart for some
years.

[14] I would not be understood to mean that the quarrel with Jackson
was the sole cause of Calhoun's change of heart; but without this quarrel he might have become President, and remained broad and national
in his sympathies.

sovereignty. And this brings us to the notable outbreak of the time, a product of this doctrine, —

NULLIFICATION IN SOUTH CAROLINA

The grievance that caused the outbreak in this little state by the sea had been brewing for ten years, and especially for six years — since the defeat of Jackson for the presidency by John Quincy Adams. It had its origin, not in the quarrel between the President and the "great nullifier," nor even in the tariff, as is generally supposed, but in a growing discontent of the people, a feeling that the interests of the North and the South were not identical, and that the government was falling into the hands of the North.[76] This feeling was intensified by the tariff of 1828, and a few years later it broke into open defiance. During the ten or fifteen years preceding this the North and the South had changed places on the subject of the tariff. At the close of the recent war with England the South was more favorable than the North to a protective tariff. One cause of this was, it is asserted, that the South at first expected to work its own cotton; but this it could not do. Slave labor had not the intelligence to manufacture; white labor could not flourish by the side of slave labor, and the cotton mills were built in New England and Liverpool. Since, therefore, the South could only raise cotton for sale, it came to prefer a low tariff so that it might purchase manufactured articles more cheaply, and through fear that a high tariff would disturb the cotton market in England. New England, on the other hand, was at first so wedded to commerce as its chief industry that it favored free trade or a low tariff. But as its manufactories grew and clamored for more protection, and

[76] See Harvard Historical Studies, No. III, p. 5.

as it was further discovered that protection did not seriously injure commerce, that section came to favor a high protective tariff. Thus in the years following 1816 the two sections veered around and exchanged places on this great national question.[76]

The duties of 1816 were raised in 1824, and these again in 1828. This last measure was called the "Tariff of Abominations." It was supported by the free traders and made as obnoxious as possible by them in the hope that the country would become surfeited with protection; but New England swallowed it. This tariff gave occasion for the pent-up feelings in South Carolina to find an opening; but before continuing the subject, let us turn aside to notice an episode, indirectly connected with it, which brought on the most famous debate that ever took place in the United States Senate.

It was in January, 1830, that Senator Foote of Connecticut introduced a resolution to limit the sale of public lands, or rather to inquire into the expediency of doing so, and from this arose the great debate which took a wider range, lasted over two months, and covered nearly every great question that had agitated the government since its foundation. At length, however, the debate narrowed down to the great rising issue between the North and the South, with slavery as its background, and threats of nullification and

[76] It must be stated, however, that South Carolina was an exception in the South from the beginning. In this state high protection was never popular. In 1789 Senator Pierce Butler from that state "flamed like a meteor" against the proposed tariff, and charged Congress with "a design of oppressing South Carolina." In 1816, when Calhoun supported the protective tariff, he did so against the wishes of his constituents and was censured for it. He afterward came to agree with his constituents.

disunion as its immediate exponents — and it culminated in the famous oratorical contest between Robert Y. Hayne and Daniel Webster.

Senator Hayne was a man of finished education and of refined and fascinating manners; he was as pure as a child in morals, as charming and unassuming in his ways;[77] he had a soft, winning voice, was an able lawyer, and was possessed of much oratorical ability. And yet Hayne would scarcely be known to our national history but for the fact that he drew from the greatest of American orators the greatest oration of his life. The speech of Hayne was one of the notable speeches of the period. It covered two days, and was made to a crowded chamber. In it Hayne advocated with much power the right of a state to render null and void an unconstitutional law of Congress. The Southerners gathered around him at the close to show their delight at having a champion, as they believed, who was more than a match for Webster.

On the next day, with but one night for preparation, Webster rose to reply. He took the floor like a gladiator entering the arena; his appearance, always impressive, was especially so that day. He was at the prime of life, forty-eight years of age; and his raven black hair, high forehead, shaggy brow, broad shoulders, and deep, melodious voice made an impression on the audience never to be forgotten. Webster's argument was that the Constitution is supreme, the Union indissoluble, and that no state has the right to resist or to nullify a national law. His well-known closing peroration, ending with the words, "Liberty and Union, now and forever, one and inseparable," is one of the most eloquent passages in the English language.

[77] Sargent's "Public Men and Events," Vol. I, p. 171.

This great oration awakened the people to the fact that a new prophet had arisen among them—and so he was, a prophet of nationality. The old Federalist party had originally stood on the ground of extreme nationalism; but that party had ceased to be, and the Democratic party had now been in control for thirty years. This party was equally patriotic with its predecessor, but less pronounced on nationalism, and had some great upheaval occurred within these thirty years, who can tell what might have become of the Union? But now at this new menace to the integrity of the Union the new champion of the old doctrine of nationality arose in the person of Webster.

But Federalism had not been dead, nor even sleeping, nor had it hovered as a disembodied spirit during those thirty years. Not only had its best principles been in a great measure adopted by the democracy; but a bridge of living Federalism had spanned this chasm of thirty years, from Hamilton to Webster, in the person of the great interpreter of the Constitution, John Marshall. It was Marshall above all men who gave to the Constitution the meaning that it has to-day.[78] And now as the great jurist was grown old and ready to close his earthly labors, it was Webster who took up the cry of nationality and sounded it forth with a trumpet sound; and it took hold on the national mind, and increased more and more for thirty years, when it was strong enough to put down the mighty rebellion against the Union in the sixties.

. But Webster was not the only one, not even the chief one,

[78] Marshall, in his great constitutional decisions, did an incalculable service to the country during this formative period; first, in strengthening the national government; second, in sustaining the power and dignity of the Federal courts; and third, in restricting the power of the states.

ie fact th
o he was
y had or
m; but t
ty had so
vas equa
ced on a
ed with
become a
integra
ne of s

ping, no
se thirty
at meas-
Feder-
Hamil-
of the
ove all
it has
d and
took
impel
eased
ough
the

one,
able
en-
and
of

1755 — JOHN MARSHALL — 1835.

BY CHESTER HARDING, 1828.

From the original portrait in the Athenæum, Boston, Mass.

to whom the nation owes its preservation in the thirties. This honor must be awarded the Democratic President. Webster was only a voice, and the case required action. Webster's doctrine was too new to take immediate hold upon a people who had so long been schooled in the doctrine of state sovereignty. The condition required action; it required one with power, and Jackson had the power. Had he the inclination, the will to do it? That was the great question in the spring of 1830.

The muttered rumblings of nullification were increasing in South Carolina. There was much dissatisfaction with the tariff of 1828 in other states, and some were belligerent in their utterances,[19] but none except South Carolina was so audacious as to defy the government. But what would Jackson do? He was a southern man. Would he decide against his own section and espouse the cause of the Union, the doctrine of this rising sun of Massachusetts? In a unique way it was decided to discover the views of the President on this great subject. A banquet was to be held in Washington on the birthday of Thomas Jefferson, the great apostle of democracy, April 13, and Jackson was invited to be present and to give a toast on a subject of his own choosing. He readily saw that the general object was not so much to honor Jefferson as to foster nullification and disunion and to make Jefferson the "pedestal of this colossal heresy," and the immediate object to discover his own views on the subject. Jackson attended. Many toasts were given, all bearing on state rights, and savoring of nullification.[20] Jackson was then called on for a volunteer toast. He arose

[19] See the case of Georgia, Ames's State Documents, No. IV, pp. 14-16.
[20] Benton.

amid profound silence, for his views on the exciting subject were unknown. He announced his subject: "The Federal Union: It must and shall be Preserved;" and he denounced as treason all movements toward nullification and disunion. His speech fell like a bomb in the ranks of the South Carolinians; they saw that they could get no sympathy from Jackson, that he was for the Union at all hazards. This occurred two and a half months after the great debate between Webster and Hayne, and a month before the final break between Jackson and Calhoun.

Notwithstanding the ominous warnings, the South Carolinians rushed on where angels might have feared to tread. Their state was in great turmoil; but it was in Washington that the seeds of disunion were nourished into growth under the leadership of Hayne. But Hayne was not the real leader; those who looked deeper than the surface could see the master hand of Calhoun beneath it all. Again in 1832 some tariff duties were raised, and South Carolina grew desperate. In November, 1832, the crisis came. A convention with the governor of the state as chairman, met at Columbia, and solemnly decided the tariff of 1828 and that of 1832 null and void in that state after the first of the following February, authorized the calling out of the militia, forbade any appeal to the Supreme Court, and declared that if the government attempted to use force, the state would set up a government of its own. This was the famous ordinance of nullification. It was a bold and daring step for the little state to make, especially with such a man as Jackson to deal with at Washington. A few weeks after this the President came out with his famous December proclamation to the people of South Carolina, in which he showed them the folly of their action, appealed to them to pause in their

The Rats leaving a Falling House.

RESIGNATION OF JACKSON'S CABINET, 1831.

From a lithograph in possession of Chief Justice Mitchell, Philadelphia, Pa.

madness, and warned them that if they went on, the soil of their beloved state would be drenched in blood; for the general government could not and would not yield to their demands.[21]

The government, however, did yield to a compromise, the author of which was Henry Clay. By this compromise the duties above twenty per cent were to be reduced gradually for ten years, when the uniform duty should be twenty per cent. It was agreed to by Calhoun, but was signed with reluctance by the President, as it was a partial yielding to the hotspurs of South Carolina. At the same time, however, he had put through Congress the so-called Force Bill, which enabled him to send troops to South Carolina to enforce the collection of the revenue. This he did under General Scott; but no blood was shed and all was soon peaceful. South Carolina had made one serious miscalculation from the first. She expected other cotton states to follow her example; but instead of doing so, nearly all of them condemned her action. This fact doubtless explains her willingness to yield to compromise.

THE RE-ELECTION AND THE BANK

When Jackson first became President he had no thought of a second term, but at the urgent request of his friends, he decided to stand for reëlection, and Van Buren, whom the Senate had rejected as minister to England, was elected Vice President. From Jackson's private correspondence we learn that he would have preferred to spend the remainder of his days at the Hermitage, near the grave of his de-

[21] To this the legislature of South Carolina made a rather defiant answer, and solemnly declared that any state had the right to secede from the Union. Ames's State Documents, No. IV, p. 43.

parted wife, and that with all his successes and with all his friends and admirers, he was a "sad and lonely old man." His chief object in consenting to serve a second term, if elected, was to carry out his designs against the United States Bank. His leading opponent was Henry Clay, whose party used the name National Republican.

There was another party also in the field in this election of 1832—the Anti-Masonic party. It arose in the following way: A man named William Morgan of New York published a book disclosing the secrets of Freemasonry and in so doing awakened the implacable hostility of the Masons. One day he was abducted at Canandaigua, carried away in a closed carriage to Fort Niagara, and was never afterward seen or heard of by his friends. It was believed that he was sunk into the depths of Lake Ontario, and the deed was ascribed to the Masons. A violent wave of indignation against the Masonic fraternity spread through New York and adjoining states. Anti-Masonic societies were formed on all sides and they resolved themselves into a political party and entered the arena of national politics for the election of 1832. This party nominated William Wirt, twelve years attorney-general of the United States, for President, and carried one state, Vermont, in the election. The party soon dissolved, and it would scarcely be remembered but for the fact that it introduced into national politics three statesmen destined to great renown in the coming generation,—William H. Seward, Thurlow Weed, and Thaddeus Stevens,—and the more important fact that it instituted the national nominating convention, an example soon followed and still followed by all other parties.

But the real contest in 1832 was between Jackson and

1782 — THOMAS HART BENTON — 1858.

From an enlargement of an original Brady negative in the possession of Frederick H. Meserve,
New York.

Clay; and there was but one prominent issue—the United States Bank.[82] Jackson was hostile to the bank and sought to destroy it. Clay was its friend, and he made a bold move, which proved to be a blunder. He had put through Congress, in the midst of the campaign, a bill to recharter the bank. The old bank charter had four years yet to run, and there was no need of such haste; and Clay's sole object was to force the issue by forcing the President to sign or to veto the bill, and it was sent to him on the 4th of July.

The country waited in deep anxiety for the action of the President. The test was a severe one. Jackson was known to be altogether hostile to the bank; he had thundered against it in his first annual message in 1829, and again in 1830. He had said again and again that Nicholas Biddle, the bank president, and the directors were using their influence and the bank's money to corrupt the people and carry the elections, and that no such corporation should exist in a free government. Could he sign the bill in the face of all that? But could he veto it and risk awakening the wrath of the people within four months of the election? The money of the country was still good, and there were yet no signs of corruption. What could Jackson do? Whatever Jackson may have been, he was no coward. He waited six days and then vetoed the bank bill. As the news of this spread, the majority of the people were struck with consternation, for most of them had come to believe that the bank was necessary to the prosperity of the country.

The issue of the campaign was now settled—it was the bank and nothing but the bank. The great trio in the Senate, Clay, Webster, and Calhoun, combined against Jackson, and the bank officials, led by "Nick" Biddle, were active

[82] For an account of the bank see *supra*, p. 62.

in assisting them. Their claim was that the financial equilibrium was so disturbed by the veto that widespread ruin must result. On the other hand, Jackson railed against the bank; his followers took up the cry, and ere long the whole Democratic press was accusing the bank of corruption, and they kept it up until the masses of the people believed that there was truth in the accusation—and so there was.

For some time before the election the popular tide set toward Jackson, and Clay received but forty-nine electoral votes out of two hundred and seventy-five.

This appeal to the people sustained Jackson on the question before the country; but the old bank had four years yet to live; and the next year Jackson made the boldest stroke ever made by a President of the United States. He removed the government deposits from the bank, on his own authority. He had determined to destroy the institution, and fearing that by his death or through some great change in Congress, the bill to recharter it might yet become a law, he decided to ruin the bank by withholding the government moneys on which its life depended. Calling his Cabinet together, he made known his purpose. But the entire Cabinet, except Mr. Taney, the attorney-general, disapproved. It was believed that such an act would ruin the business of the country by ruining this great fiscal corporation, which had practical control of the finances of the nation, and hundreds of smaller banks dependent on it. But Jackson believed the bank to be corrupt and even insolvent, and he was determined on his course; nothing could stay his hand. By the charter no one but the secretary of the treasury had power to remove the public money from the bank. Jackson ordered his secretary of the treasury, Mr. Duane, to do this; but Duane refused and was immediately dismissed from the

Cabinet. Taney was then transferred to the treasury, and he immediately proceeded to obey his chief.

Little can we realize at this day the excitement into which the people were thrown by this action of the President. Public meetings were held in every part of the country to protest against it. Thousands who had voted for Jackson the year before now believed he had gone entirely too far. Petitions came from all sides praying that he replace the bank funds.[83] Jackson, when approached on the subject, would become furious; he would walk the floor like a caged lion. "Go to the monster, Nick Biddle," he would say, "he has millions; it's all a job of the politicians; I will not yield a hair's breadth." [84] And he did not yield.

But the trouble did not stop here. In a few months the business of the country was greatly disturbed. Banks closed their doors and manufactories were shut down. Distress meetings were held in every center of trade, and they poured their memorials into Congress by the hundreds. Congress met in December, and the Senate debated the subject for weeks amid the wildest excitement. The leader against Jackson was Clay; but Clay had been so recently defeated by Jackson that personal grievance was thought to have something to do with his opposition. Clay's right-hand man was Calhoun; but his recent quarrel with the President weakened him also with the people.

[83] The government deposits in the bank, amounting to near $10,000,000 at this time, were removed gradually in the course of business. The accumulating surplus was placed in "pet banks" to the amount of $11,000,000, when Congress passed a law loaning the unused surplus to the various states. But after three quarterly payments, aggregating some $28,000,000, had been so distributed, a financial crash, to be noticed later, put a stop to them.

[84] Schouler, Vol. IV, p. 161.

Jackson was not without friends in the Senate, the ablest and most devoted of whom was Thomas H. Benton, thirty years a senator from Missouri. Benton was a national character, known as "Old Bullion," from his hard money proclivities. Many years before, he and Jackson had been enemies and had fought an impromptu duel,[85] but all this was changed, and with unwearied effort and much ability he now defended Jackson against the combination in the Senate. He claimed that the sudden distress of the country had been caused by the willful designs of the bank directors with a view of overthrowing Jackson's popularity and forcing him to replace the deposits. The bank refused its accustomed loans to business men, and had forced smaller banks to the wall by demanding immediate payment in coin of all debts due it. Benton also showed that the old bank in 1811, in order to force the government to grant a recharter, had brought on the country a temporary distress of the same kind and in the same way. He drew from this a strong argument against the existence in a free country of a corporation so powerful as to be able to do this. His points were well taken, and in the end had great effect on the people.

The fury of the Senate against the President did not abate; but that body was powerless. It was under the magic spell of Clay, and would have impeached Jackson beyond a doubt, but the Constitution gives all power of impeachment to the House, and the House was Democratic by a majority of fifty. The Senate, however, rejected Taney as secretary of the treasury, and adopted strong resolutions of censure against the President; who in turn sent a long written protest, which the Senate refused to receive. Ben-

[85] See note on p. 59.

1777 — ROGER BROOKE TANEY — 1864.

By George Peter Alexander Healy.

From the original portrait in the Robing Room of the Supreme Court of the United States, Washington, D.C.

ton then gave notice that he would move to expunge the resolutions of censure from the Senate journal, and that he would succeed in this or keep up the subject to the end of his official life.   He did succeed about three years later, after the Senate had changed political complexion.

FOREIGN RELATIONS AND INDIAN WARS

So great were the domestic achievements of the Jacksonian epoch that little notice, usually, is given to foreign affairs; yet these were important, and in every dispute with a foreign power, as well as in his contests at home, the old warrior President was successful in the end.   First came a wrangle with France.   The United States held a claim of $5,000,000 against that country for spoliations of American shipping after 1803.   In a treaty of 1831 Louis Philippe, the newly crowned King of France, acknowledged the claim. But three years passed and the money was not forthcoming, whereupon Jackson came forth in a vigorous message in which was couched a menace.   This offended the French Chambers, and they refused to pay the claim unless the President would modify his message.   This attitude brought from Jackson a second message, threefold more offensive than the first.   In this message he threatened reprisals on French commerce.   Congress then took up the matter; but the French government soon ended the trouble by paying the claim.   The administration demanded and received payment also of long-standing claims against Spain, Denmark, and the Sicilies.   These things touched the popular heart and strengthened the administration.   But still more were the people pleased with the opening of the West India trade.   Great Britain had closed the ports of the West Indies to American ships some years before.   The Adams administration had sought with unwearied effort to have this trade reopened, but in vain.   Jackson renewed the negotiation through his secretary of state, Van Buren, and by making some concessions to British commerce, won a complete victory.

Our relations with Mexico were strained during the whole of this administration, and so continued for more than ten years longer.   Mexico emancipated her slaves in 1827, but her northern province, Texas, refused to do so, and soon afterward revolted under the leadership of Sam Houston. Jackson sent an army under General Gaines to the gulf coast "to keep Texan Indians off our soil," but in fact to connive with Houston.   Gaines's troops deserted freely and joined Houston, and received no rebuke from the government. Jackson even demanded damages of Mexico and threatened reprisals, when the damage claims should have come from the other side.   Nothing was plainer than that, contrary to his usual honesty, Jackson was unfair in his dealings with Mexico.

Two Indian wars marked the administration of Jackson. The first occurred in the Northwest and is known as the Black Hawk War.   Black Hawk, a former pupil of Tecumseh, who had, like that great chief, espoused the cause of the British in the War of 1812, was now chief of the Sac and Fox tribes.   His war with the whites in 1832 arose from the usual cause of Indian wars—land cessions.   General Gaines, and later General Atkinson, were sent against him. Black Hawk was defeated and at length taken captive.   He was then taken east that he might see the greatness of the United States. He called on the President at Washington and visited most of the great cities of the East.   He was highly honored in this tour, thousands of people swarming to the

1767 — MUKATAHMISHOKAHKAIK (THE BLACK HAWK) — 1838.

BY GEORGE CATLIN, 1832.

From the original portrait in the United States National Museum, Smithsonian Institution, Washington, D.C.

towns to see this monarch of the forest. While bearing himself with the dignity of a ruler, Black Hawk was deeply impressed with the white man's government, and returning to his western home, was faithful to his promise to keep the peace in future.

Far more formidable was the war with the Indians of the South, beginning in 1835, and known as the Second Seminole War, the first being that of 1818 with Jackson as the chief figure. The various southern tribes had been slow to remove to the lands allotted to them west of the Mississippi, and in 1834 the President sent General Wiley Thomson to Florida to urge their departure. But the Indians, led by the strong chieftain, Osceola, rose in rebellion. In December, 1835, Major Dade and a hundred soldiers whom he led were ambushed and massacred in a Florida swamp; and on the same day Osceola, with his own hand, assassinated and scalped General Thomson, while the latter was sitting at the table dining with friends. These acts stirred the government to vigorous action. General Scott was sent to take command, and he soon subdued the Creeks, and removed thousands of them to their new home. But the Seminoles were still hostile, and they extended their forays into Alabama and Georgia, attacking mail carriers, stagecoaches, and even towns, from which the people fled for their lives. General Jessup commanded in Florida. He made a treaty with the Indians, but Osceola trampled it under foot and refused to be held by the most sacred promises. Hundreds of the troops perished in the swamps of fevers and of the bites of venomous serpents. At length Osceola came to General Jessup under a flag of truce, and was detained, sent to Charleston, and confined in Fort Moultrie. Jessup was severely censured for violating the sanctity of a flag of truce; but he explained that as this was the only way in which he could stop the career of this treacherous chief who violated every obligation, he felt justified in doing as he did. Osceola died of fever at Fort Moultrie in 1839. But the war went on, continuing in all about seven years, and costing the United States $30,000,000.

CHARACTER OF JACKSON

The student of history must search long to find a parallel to this remarkable man, who has been pronounced "the incarnate multitude," and whose will dominated the government of the United States for eight years. The period was noted for its great men, and yet Jackson stood alone as the transcendent figure of the times. Such leaders as Clay, Webster, and Calhoun were powerless while Jackson occupied the political stage. His popularity in his party was unbounded. The people came to believe that he could do no wrong, and that he stood like an angel with a flaming sword, guarding their interests against the designs of the politicians. It is difficult to rate Jackson as a statesman. He had little training in statecraft, but he was gifted with an intuition that proved remarkable for its accuracy. His insight into human nature was almost unerring.[86]

The most conspicuous element in Jackson's character was his will. This was as inflexible as steel. He usually reached his conclusion on a great subject without apparently considering the matter, and then, deciding on his course with equal suddenness, he bent every energy to attain his object

[86] He could be imposed on, however, by artful politicians. But with the exception of Swartwout, who stole a million dollars as collector of the port of New York, and a few others, his appointments were generally commendable.

1804—OSCEOLA (THE BLACK DRINK)—1838.

BY GEORGE CATLIN, 1838.

From the original portrait in the United States National Museum, Smithsonian Institution, Washington, D.C.

and trample every foe and every obstacle that came in his way. No expostulations of friends or threats of enemies could change his marvelous will. He had a Cabinet, it is true, but no real advisers. He called his Cabinet together, not to seek advice, but to inform them of his intentions, and to bid them what to do. Some of them had ten times his experience as statesmen, but they sat in his presence as children with their schoolmaster, and none that crossed his will or refused to humor his foibles or to bend to his purpose could remain long in his favor.[57] Jackson held his party in a grasp of iron, and his discipline was that of a general commanding an army. He was not a partisan in the ordinary sense; he was simply master. Every contest with him was a battle, and every battle brought him victory. It is a remarkable fact that, except in the case of the Eatons, Jackson gained every important object on which he set his heart during his entire administration. His few apparent defeats were more than victories in the end. He nominated Van Buren minister to England. The Senate rejected his nominee, and Jackson made him Vice President and then President of the United States. He then named former Speaker Stevenson for the place. The Senate again refused its consent, and Jackson left the office vacant for two years, and again sent the same name to the Senate, and it was confirmed. His appointment of Taney to the treasury was also rejected, and he made Taney Chief Justice of the Supreme Court. The Senate at last seemed to gain a crowning victory over the President—by passing its resolutions of censure. This annoyed him exceedingly; but his friends, after laboring for three years, succeeded in expunging the hated censure—and Jackson was ahead again. Both Clay

[57] Schouler, Vol. IV, p. 266.

and Webster were so wearied at their successive defeats at the hands of this untutored President, that they determined to abandon public life,[*] and would doubtless have done so but for the retirement of their unconquerable enemy.

Andrew Jackson had faults—glaring faults. One was his lawlessness. He was a law unto himself, and was impatient of the restraints of civil law. This was shown in his Seminole campaign, as we have noticed. When President he refused to be bound by the Supreme Court, on the ground that he would sustain the Constitution as he understood it, and not as it was interpreted by others. For example, when Georgia had trouble with the Creeks, she condemned a half-breed named Tassells to be hanged. Tassells appealed to the Supreme Court, and the decision was reversed, and the state was cited on a writ of error. But Georgia was defiant, and refused to be bound by this decision. It was now Jackson's plain duty to enforce the decision of the Supreme Court, but he refused to do so. "John Marshall has made his decision," he is reported to have said, "now let him enforce it"—and Tassells was hanged. Very similar was his action in the case of Georgia and the Cherokees, as noted on a preceding page.

Jackson was a man of quarrels. He couldn't be happy without one. He loved his friends and hated his enemies. He was not able to distinguish between a personal and a political enemy, nor was he broad enough to give an opponent credit for honestly differing from him in opinion; but he never grew weary of showering favors on his devoted followers.

Now a hurried glance at the other side of his nature. It has been truly said that Andrew Jackson, with his vast

[*] Sargent, p. 344.

power, could have done his country irreparable harm, had he been a bad man; but this he was not. He was a true child of nature, born with an unhappy temper, of which he never had the good fortune to become master; while the half-civilized society of the frontier had set its mark indelibly upon his life. But his heart was right. No trace in him of selfish ambition of the Aaron Burr type; no enemy, even, could accuse him of dishonesty, or couple his name with political corruption. His devotion to his country was equal to that of Washington. His unjust dealing with Mexico arose from his too great love of country—his longing to see Texas a part of the Union. When he disobeyed orders while a commander in the field, it was because he thought he knew best. When he quarreled with enemies, he doubtless thought he was right and they were wrong, and compromise was a meaningless word with Jackson.

The story of Jackson's home life is scarcely credible to the reader who knows him only in the hurricane of battle, and in the caldron of political strife. In the domestic circle Jackson was the gentlest and most lovable of men. His servants, white and black, revered him as a father. His devotion to his wife while she lived, and to her memory after she was gone, was rarely beautiful. For years after her death he would place her picture in front of him on the table before retiring at night, and alternately look at it and read from the prayer book that she had given him, and late in life he fulfilled his promise to her that he would become a member of the Church. In morals he was as chaste as a child, and one of his striking characteristics was his courtesy and chivalry to women. In appearance he was tall and thin, with an erect military bearing, his iron-gray hair thrown back in ridges from his forehead, while in his eye was a "dangerous fixedness," and down his cheeks deep furrows ran. The prevailing expression of his face showed energy and will power. He would be singled out, even among extraordinary men, says an English writer, as a man of superior cast.

The political influence of Jackson upon the country, especially upon the northern Democrats, was very great. At the time of his power the murmurs of sectionalism and disunion were distinctly heard from the South; but Jackson, while a strong friend of state rights, was an unrelenting foe to sectionalism and disunion. He was national in the broadest and best sense, and this spirit he infused into the multitude. Above all men of his times Jackson was the idol, the oracle, the teacher of the great unformed democracy, the untutored masses, many of whom had but recently received the franchise. What they needed above all things was a lesson in nationality—and they received it from Jackson. Through him vast numbers of men came to love the nation above the state, and it was largely through the memory and influence of Jackson that the northern Democrats came forward in 1861 to aid in saving the Union, which he, through their fathers, had taught them to love.[59]

While we cannot sympathize with the spoils system of Jackson, nor with his harsh treatment of the Seminoles, nor his double dealing with Mexico, nor his belligerent propensities in general, it cannot be denied that he was a true patriot and an honest man. In ability he was almost a Cæsar; and while it is perhaps well that the American people are inclined to place few Cæsars in the presidential chair, may it be hoped that whenever they do they will

[59] This thought is brought out by A. D. Morse, in an able article in the *Political Science Quarterly*, Vol. I, p. 154 *sq.*

choose as honest and unselfish a one as was Andrew Jackson.

MARTIN VAN BUREN

The administration of Van Buren properly belongs to the Jackson epoch; but the term "reign" can be used no longer, as the new President lacked the dictatorial power and the popularity of his predecessor. It was the intense desire of the outgoing President that his favorite from New York become his successor. His wishes were respected by the party, and Van Buren became President—but not without a contest. A new political party had been born. Henry Clay, who had served with the Democrats for twenty years, but who was now at variance with them at all points, determined after his defeat by Jackson in 1832 to break away entirely from the old party. And while casting about for a party name the old Revolutionary name Whig was decided on, and was first used in 1834. The Whig party absorbed the National Republican party, the name by which the opposition had been known for some years past. As the old Whig party in England and the colonies had opposed the high prerogative of the King, the new party now opposed the encroaching power of the Executive. The Whigs did not expect to win in 1836, nor was their party sufficiently united to concentrate on one man. Their aim was to throw the election into the House. Their votes in the electoral college were scattered among four men, William H. Harrison of Ohio, Judge White of Tennessee, Daniel Webster of Massachusetts, and William P. Mangum of North Carolina. Their combined vote, however, reached but 124, while Van Buren received 167. The electoral college made no selection for Vice President, and Richard M. Johnson of Kentucky was chosen by the Senate.

As it was at the inauguration of 1797, so it was now—
the eyes of the multitude were turned toward the setting
rather than the rising sun.   The quick-moving, smooth-
shaven little man who read his inaugural on that bleak
March day in 1837, and promised to tread "in the footsteps
of his illustrious predecessor," won little applause from the
vast crowd compared with that given the aged specter by
his side.   Now for the last time this old warrior, who had
been dictator of American policy for eight years, leaning
heavily upon his staff under his burden of three-score and
ten and the ravages of long disease, came forth and received
the homage of the masses.   A few days later he departed for
his southern home, and the troubles of the new President
began.

Martin Van Buren, the son of an innkeeper and small
farmer of New York, had been initiated into politics by
Aaron Burr, and he was a prominent lawyer before the War
of 1812.   He was a man of greater individuality and ability
than is generally put to his credit by historians.   In 1821
he entered the United States Senate and was the leader in
that body during the administration of Adams.   On the
death of De Witt Clinton in 1828 Van Buren was easily the
foremost man in the Empire State.   Resigning the governorship of that state to take the chief place in the Cabinet of
Jackson, he was by no means a figurehead even there; for it
was largely due to his skill that Jackson made the two brilliant strokes in his foreign policy—opening of the West
India trade and settling the French spoliation claims.   But
with all this, Van Buren could not have become President
without the aid of his powerful friend; and while he inherited the office without the popularity of Jackson, he also
inherited the evils of Jackson's administration.

1782 — MARTIN VAN BUREN — 1862.

BY HENRY INMAN, 1828.

From the original portrait in Metropolitan Museum of Art, New York.

Van Buren has been pronounced the cleverest political manager in American history, and no other man has held so many high national offices. He was small in stature, had a round, red face and quick, searching eyes.[90] He was subtle, courteous, and smooth in conversation. His enemies charged him with being noncommittal on all subjects. At a great tariff meeting in Albany he was invited to make a speech; he did so, and at its close not a man, woman, or child in the audience could tell whether he was for or against a high tariff.[91] For two things the administration of Van Buren is prominent in history: First, the panic of 1837; and second, the establishing of the independent treasury.

THE PANIC AND THE INDEPENDENT TREASURY

This panic was probably the most disastrous that the American people have yet experienced. Every bank in the country suspended specie payments, thousands of leading merchants and manufacturers were forced to the wall, and the business of the country was utterly demoralized. As to the cause of the panic, there are various versions. The Whigs were prompt to put all the blame on the Democrats. It is not unusual in American politics for the party out of power to arraign the party in power, guilty or not guilty, for every disturbance in financial and business circles. Few

[90] Schouler.

[91] One day Van Buren handed an official paper that he had written to a clerk to be criticised, and the latter declared that he couldn't tell what it was about. "Very well," answered Van Buren, "it will answer, then." A member of Congress, it was said, made a bet with another that if Van Buren were asked if the sun rose in the east or west, he would not give a direct answer. The question was asked, and his answer was, "My friend, east and west are altogether relative terms." The reputation of being a wily politician rather than a statesman was very annoying to Van Buren all through his public career.

statesmen have risen above this practice, especially when their own advancement depended on it—and in that degree a statesman becomes a demagogue.

This panic, like most of its kind, was the resultant of various causes, some of which elude the pen of the wisest political economist. A few of the causes, however, are not far to seek. Jackson's specie circular, by which payments for public lands were to be made in coin, when the people had but little coin, hastened the crisis. Another cause was the act of Congress distributing the surplus of the treasury to the various states. This made the states reckless in spending money, and when the payments were withheld, the states found themselves with many expensive projects in hand which they could not carry out. But the chief cause of the panic was the wild spirit of speculation that had seized the people. The national debt was paid, banks everywhere flooded the country with paper money far beyond their ability to redeem in coin; and moreover, English capital poured into the country at this time and played its part in throwing the people off their guard.[92] The wildest schemes of speculation were set on foot. Prices rose and work was plentiful at high wages. Great manufactories were begun and never carried out. Scores of towns were laid out in the West, many of which are not built up to this day. The sale of public lands, which had often fallen below $2,000,000 a year, ran up to $24,000,000 in 1835. Banks sprung up on all sides, and they inflated the country with worthless paper

[92] Von Holst shows that English capital, which was at high tide at this time, also flooded other countries and produced a similar effect. This is conclusive proof that the panic in the United States was not wholly caused by the administration. The President's annual message of 1839 says that $200,000,000 of foreign capital were then afloat in the United States. See "Jackson's Administration," p. 173.

money. Railroads, canals, and all manner of internal improvements were projected. Men were intoxicated with their dreams of growing rich in a night; and the crash came, as it always will under such conditions.

The panic reached its height soon after Van Buren became President, and he was besieged from every part of the country by delegations representing mass meetings, which had condemned the government for bringing about the hard times. The people raged and clamored, and begged the President to bring back good times, of which they seemed to think he had robbed them.

Van Buren's bearing was courteous and firm. His position was very difficult, but he faced the storm with great courage and for once evinced statesmanship of a high order. He assured the people that the object of government was not to manage the private affairs of the people, and that frugality and industry with careful management of business would alone bring prosperity. The President, however, yielded to popular clamor in so far as to call a special session of Congress to meet in September, 1837; and in his message to Congress at this session, a very able state paper, he urged with much force the one and only great measure of his administration—the establishing of the Independent Treasury, which, from its many subordinate branches in the various cities, has come to be known as the "Subtreasury." This is simply a special place or places for the funds of the government. Thus the government becomes the custodian of its own surplus and is divorced from all dependence on the banks. The measure, as urged by the President, was ably discussed during this extra session, and again at the regular session. It was bitterly opposed by the Whigs and by many Democrats. It passed the Senate in June, 1838,

but was defeated in the House.   The administration, however, did not give the matter up, and in 1840 the bill for an
independent treasury passed both houses, was signed by
the President on the 4th of July, and became a law.   A
year later the Whigs had control of the government, and
they repealed the act.   But the Democrats still clung to their
favorite measure, and in 1846 the law was reënacted.   From
that time to the present, this law has been in force, and as all
parties now favor it, it seems to be a fixture in our government.

THE HARRISON CAMPAIGN

The most remarkable presidential contest in our history
was that of 1840.   In spite of anything that the Democrats
could do, they steadily lost ground during the administration of Van Buren.   This was largely because of the reiterated cry of the Whigs that the party in power had brought
about the great industrial depression known as the Panic of
1837.   Every sign seemed now to point to a Whig victory
in 1840.   That party held its convention at Harrisburg in
a newly erected Lutheran church, almost a year before the
election.   Three prominent candidates were before the convention—Henry Clay, William Henry Harrison, and Winfield Scott—all born in Virginia, but now of different states.

Scott was widely known for his deeds at Queenstown
Heights, at Chippewa and Lundy's Lane; but the greatest
work of his life—his march upon Mexico—was still in the
future, and he was not seriously considered by the convention.   The real contest lay between Clay and Harrison.
Against Clay many forces were at work.   He had been in
the forefront of public life for thirty years, and his out-
spoken manner had made him enemies; his views on the

tariff were not popular in the South, and moreover he was a Freemason. This was his weakest point, for the Anti-Masonic party had dissolved, most of its members had joined the Whigs, and they would not have given Clay a hearty support. Harrison, on the other hand, had been out of public life for many years. His views on the great questions of the day were scarcely known, and this, according to our anomalous American politics, was considered a point in his favor as a vote getter. But Harrison had a record. He was the son of a "signer;" he was the hero of Tippecanoe; he had done valiant service in the Northwest during the war with England. He had also served in both houses of Congress, and had been sent by John Quincy Adams as minister to Colombia, South America. After a brief service he was recalled from this mission by Jackson, when he settled down to the quiet life of a farmer at North Bend, an Ohio village near Cincinnati.

The majority of the delegates to this convention preferred Clay; but the leaders, led by that master political manager of New York, Thurlow Weed, and the rising young editor of the same state, Horace Greeley, determined to secure the nomination of Harrison if possible. They succeeded by skillfully manipulating the committees. Clay was disappointed. True, he had written his friends to withdraw his name, if in their eyes it seemed the right thing to do; he had also about this time given rise to the oft-quoted statement, "I would rather be right than be President." Nevertheless he was disappointed at the outcome, and so were his friends. One of these whose heart was set on Clay burst into tears, it was said, when his favorite was set aside. This was John Tyler of Virginia.

Harrison's friends now determined to conciliate the Clay

people by offering to place one of their number second on the ticket.   When looking about for a suitable choice—behold John Tyler in tears! and he was straightway nominated for the vice presidency.**   But Tyler was not a cipher.   He had attracted attention in Congress away back in the days of the Missouri Compromise.   He had been governor of Virginia and a United States senator.   For many years he had been a Democrat, but revolting against the iron rule of Jackson, he became an ardent supporter of Clay.   His selection was a concession to southern Democrats who had broken with Jackson.

The Democrats met in Baltimore and renominated Van Buren.   They put forth a platform of principles, pronouncing against a United States Bank, internal improvements at national expense, a high tariff, and the like.   The Whigs had no platform, and they made no avowal of principles; their sole cry during the campaign was, in substance, Down with the administration.

The wild enthusiasm of the Whigs increased in volume during the summer and autumn.   Harrison was known by his popular military name of Tippecanoe, and the shouts for "Tippecanoe and Tyler too" were long and lusty.   A Baltimore paper having suggested that Harrison was more in his element in his log cabin with his barrel of hard cider than he would be in the White House, the Whigs took up the cry of "Log Cabin and Hard Cider," and made these the emblems of the campaign.   Horace Greeley started a newspaper in New York which he called *The Log Cabin*, and it bounded into great popularity.**   The Whig mass meetings were

** This nomination, it should be stated, was declined by two or three others among Clay's friends before it was offered to Tyler.

** The *Log Cabin* was merged into the *Tribune* in September, 1841.

vast beyond any before known in the country. Men would come for many miles in farm wagons, bringing their families, and remaining whole days and nights at these great meetings. At first the people were counted at these gatherings, but as the crowds grew larger counting became impossible, and they were measured by the acre by surveyors brought for the purpose. The most notable feature of the campaign were the songs,[95] written for the occasion, and learned and sung by the shouting multitudes. As Clay remarked, the country was "like an ocean convulsed by a terrible storm."

The Democrats affected to treat the Whig enthusiasm with contempt, but in reality they were angry, and very much alarmed.[96] They too held meetings, but these fell far short of those of the Whigs in numbers and enthusiasm. They attempted to reason and argue; but the people preferred to sing and shout. And the result was a crushing defeat for Van Buren. He received but sixty electoral votes to 234 for Harrison.

[95] For samples, see Greeley's *Log Cabin* or Elson's "Side Lights," II, p. 234.
[96] Stanwood's "History of Presidential Elections," p. 136.

NOTES

Minor Events. — Imprisonment for debt by the United States courts was abolished in 1833, chiefly through the efforts of Richard M. Johnson, the slayer of Tecumseh. The states soon followed the example of the general government, and the barbarous practice became a thing of the past. — The death of some of the most prominent men occurred within this period. Ex-President Monroe died on July 4, 1831, in the city of New York. The last signer of the Declaration of Independence, Charles Carroll of Carrollton, died in 1832 at the great age of ninety-two years; and James Madison, the last of the framers of the Constitution, died in 1836. John Marshall, America's greatest jurist, and Lafayette, the most highly honored in America of all foreigners, both passed away in 1835. In January, 1835, President Jackson narrowly escaped assassination. While attending the funeral of a member of Congress, a man from the crowd in the rotunda of the Capitol snapped two pistols at his breast. Both missed fire, and the President rushed upon the man with his cane. The man was arrested and was found to be a demented Englishman named Lawrence. He was sent to an insane asylum. The President's escape was very narrow, as both pistols were afterward fired at the first trial.

The Caroline Affair. — In 1837 a portion of the people of Canada, led by William Lyon MacKenzie and Louis J. Papinau, rose in rebellion against British rule in the province with the view of setting up a republic. After a few sharp skirmishes the insurrection was put down, and many of the insurgents took refuge on Navy Island, in the Niagara River. The *Caroline*, a little steamer owned by a citizen of the United States, was employed in carrying supplies to the island, and the British determined to destroy her. On the night of December 29, 1837, a flotilla of five boats set out for this purpose, but not finding her here, they searched until they found her moored at Grand Island, which is part of the territory of New York. The British boarded the vessel, overpowered the crew, killing one man, set the boat on fire, and sent her burning over the falls. The American government then made a demand on the British government for reparation; but the matter was left unsettled for several years, and was at length dropped by the United States.

Meantime, one Alexander McLeod, a worthless resident of Ontario, made the boast that he was the party that destroyed the *Caroline*, and had himself killed one of the Yankees. One day while in Buffalo he repeated his boast, and was instantly arrested and clapped into prison. The British government now made a demand that he be released, and the President would gladly have released McLeod, but he was in the hands of New York State, and she refused to give him up. Great Britain began to mobilize armies and prepare for war. New York, meantime, having no foreign relations, calmly held the prisoner and had him tried before a court at Lockport for murder and arson. It all turned out to be ludicrous in the extreme. It was proved that the blustering braggart, McLeod, had not been present at the destroying of the *Caroline*. His boast was an idle and a false one. He was acquitted, and all signs of war disappeared. Nothing in our history shows more clearly how a trifling matter may disturb the peace of two great nations, and how the defect in our dual system of government, state

1773—WILLIAM HENRY HARRISON—1841.

From the original portrait in possession of Mrs. Russell B. Harrison, Omaha, Neb.

and national, may prove disastrous to the peace of the country. For a fuller account of the *Caroline* affair, see Elson's "Side Lights," Series I, Chap. XL.

CHAPTER XXIV

RISE OF THE SLAVERY QUESTION

TWENTY years had passed since the adoption of that famous compact known as the Missouri Compromise. That measure was expected to give peace to the land, and so it did for about ten years. Nevertheless the debates on it left a sting, a wound that could not altogether heal; and they also awakened here and there a moral consciousness that eluded the grasp of the lawmaker, that could not die; it could only slumber.

During this period there were a few, a rare few, who, like the ancient prophets of Israel, ceased not to cry out day and night against the evil of the land. First among these was Benjamin Lundy. A saddler by trade, he worked for many years at Wheeling, Virginia, until his interest in the black man became so overmastering that he determined to give his life to the cause of emancipation. Abandoning his occupation, leaving his wife and his children behind, he traveled over the country making speeches and organizing societies. He traveled in nearly all the states of the Union, in Canada, Mexico, and the West Indies, in the interest of the cause he had espoused. In 1821 he established *The Genius of Universal Emancipation*. In one of his tours to New England, Lundy met at a boarding house a young man of ardent spirit, who became a convert and co-worker with him in the cause—William Lloyd Garrison. Together the two men went to Baltimore and became joint editors of an antislavery journal. But they soon parted. Garrison now became the leading Abolitionist in the country, and after serving a time in prison for his violent utterances, went to Boston." Here in 1831 he founded *The Liberator*, and in it he denounced all slaveholders with unsparing severity. He demanded the unconditional emancipation of all slaves, and pronounced the Constitution, for permitting slavery, " A covenant with death, an agreement with hell." Another noted agitator was the Rev. E. P. Lovejoy of St. Louis, who, after publishing an antislavery paper for several years, was murdered in November, 1837, by a proslavery mob at Alton, Illinois. Antislavery societies were formed in various states; but they were composed chiefly of the poorer classes, and had little effect on public opinion. And besides, the violence of such men as Garrison produced among the lovers of peace, even in the North, a proslavery reaction. This was intensified by a slave insurrection in Virginia, led by Nat Turner, a negro, in which sixty-one whites, mostly women and children, were killed. This incident sent a shiver of horror throughout the South. It showed what might occur, if great numbers of the bondsmen should rise against their masters. At this moment slaveholding Virginia, through her legislature, seriously considered the subject of emancipation in that state. And here the institution was denounced as it had seldom been denounced at the North. " Tax our lands," said one speaker, " vilify our country, carry the sword of extermination through our defenseless villages, but spare us, I im-

---

" Burgess says if a name, a date, and a place must be given the new movement, the name is Garrison, the date is 1831, and the place is Boston. " Middle Period," p. 246.

plore you—spare us the curse of slavery, that bitterest drop from the chalice of the destroying angel."

There was a rising sentiment against slavery in the North, but it was not yet strong nor widespread. Two or three incidents will readily show that the sympathies of the people were generally with the slaveholder, whose desire was to keep the black man in ignorance, that he might not become dangerous. In 1831 it was proposed to found a school for colored children in New Haven, Connecticut, but a town meeting declared against it as " destructive of the best interests of the city." Two years later Prudence Crandall, a school-teacher of the same state, was cast into prison for admitting colored girls into her school, and the school was broken up by a mob. A similar occurrence took place at Canaan, New Hampshire, in 1835, and in New York the endeavors to suppress the Abolitionists caused serious riots.

The cloud that presaged the coming storm seemed as yet no larger than a man's hand, but its increase, though slow, was steady and irresistible. The antislavery societies numbered three hundred and fifty in 1835. Such men as Dr. Channing, the famous Boston divine, and Wendell Phillips began to defend the Abolitionists, and these were afterward joined by Emerson, John G. Whittier, Theodore Parker, and Henry Ward Beecher. And further, there was a little political party founded in the North, known as the Liberty party. In 1840 it cast but seven thousand votes, but in 1844 the number had increased to sixty-two thousand; still small, it is true, but the increase showed the direction of the political wind. The South now became thoroughly alarmed. Before this most of the southern leaders had frankly confessed that slavery was an evil, and had deplored its existence; but this growing abolition feeling crystallized the South against abolition. The antislavery societies in that section soon dwindled away, and at length the whole South, led by Calhoun, took the ground that slavery is a good—a positive good.[**]

But this new attitude of the South was not caused wholly by the opposition of the Abolitionists. It accepted Calhoun's views partially from economic grounds. The southern people had come to believe that slavery was indispensable to their social and economic welfare, and, believing this, they could not do otherwise than defend it. This new position taken by the South, that slavery is a positive good, together with the fear of insurrection, led that section, including non-slaveholders, to unify in the defense of slavery.

Not long could this great question be kept from the halls of Congress, and in two ways it came to be forced upon the government—through petitions to Congress and the use of the mails for distributing Abolition literature. For many years an occasional petition had come in, chiefly from Quakers, for the abolition of slavery in the District of Columbia. About the time Garrison began his agitation these petitions began to come rapidly. For some years after this the custom of both Senate and House was to receive all such petitions and refer them to a committee, in which they were quietly strangled. This refusal of Congress to consider the petitions did not discourage or quiet the Abolitionists. The petitions increased in numbers, and at length the southern members became irritated at this continuous goading. In 1834 sharp debates began to be heard in the House on the subject, and in March, 1836, a resolution was

[**] This new doctrine was first set forth by Calhoun in the Senate in 1836.

adopted to lay all such petitions on the table, and that no further notice be taken of them. This action only stirred up the Abolitionists to greater efforts, and, during the two years following the adoption of this rule the number of petitions increased tenfold. In January, 1840, the House went still further. It adopted a standing rule that no petitions or memorials concerning the abolition of slavery or the slave trade in any part of the country " shall be received by this House, or entertained in any way whatever." This was known as the " gag rule."

The Senate had arrived at a practice similar to that of the House, and the condition in both was brought about by the radical men of the South. These men felt that they had won a victory; but quite the opposite was true. The Constitution guarantees the right of petitioning the government, and refusing to receive a petition implied a denial of the right to make it. This attitude of Congress drew the attention of the whole country; it led the people to identify the denial of the constitutional right with the interests of slavery; it awakened sympathy with the Abolitionists and made many converts to their cause.

Most of the petitions that came to the House fell into the hands of the venerable John Quincy Adams, who now became the champion of the right of petition. With infinite moral courage he bore every insult, and waged unceasing war on the gag rule in the House, and after continuing his efforts for nearly ten years he won the victory of his life by securing its repeal. When the vote was counted, and Adams saw that he had won, he sank back into his chair and exclaimed, "Blessed be the name of God."

The southern resistance to the use of the mails for the distribution of Abolition literature in the South furnished

1790 — JOHN TYLER — 1862.

BY GEORGE PETER ALEXANDER HEALY, 1842.

From the original portrait in the Corcoran Gallery of Art, Washington, D C.

another cause for national commotion. In July, 1835, a mob of respectable citizens broke into the post office at Charleston, South Carolina, seized a bag of Abolition pamphlets and burned it in the street. The matter was soon brought before the postmaster-general, Amos Kendall, but his decision was undecisive,[*] and in December President Jackson in his message recommended that Congress pass a law refusing the use of the mails to "incendiary publications intended to instigate the slaves to insurrection." This would probably have been done but for the fact that Calhoun took the extreme state rights ground that each state should decide the matter within its own bounds. Thus the South lost the aid of the government in its first battle with the Abolitionists.

These early contests concerning the right of petition and the use of the mails had a profound effect on the future of the country. They directed the eyes of the people to the Abolitionist party, raised it to national importance, and vastly increased its power. They awakened the South to a sense of the fact that an ever increasing party in the North existed for the purpose of attacking slavery at every point, and from this time forth the North and the South drifted steadily apart.

HARRISON'S BRIEF TENURE

The joy of the Whigs at their great victory over the

[*] Mr. Kendall wrote the postmaster at New York City, who had asked his opinion after excluding Abolition matter from the mails, "The postmaster-general has no legal authority to exclude from the mails any species of newspapers." And he adds, "If I were situated as you are, I would do as you have done." To the postmaster at Charleston he wrote, "We owe an obligation to the laws, but a higher one to the communities in which we live."

Democrats was little short of delirium. The winter following the election was one long jollification, and little did they
dream of the disasters that were before them. General
Harrison reached Washington, after a week's toilsome journey, on the sixty-eighth anniversary of his birth. Inauguration day was dreary and cold; a chilling northeast
wind blew all day, yet the new President rode on horseback
in a procession for two hours without overcoat or gloves.
He then stood for another hour in the open air to read his
inaugural address. It was believed that the President in
exposing himself thus without an overcoat, sought to dispel
the floating rumor that he was in poor health. He recovered, however, from this exposure, and the administration
started out on a promising voyage, with Daniel Webster at
the helm as secretary of state.

The President, used to the easy life of his rural home,
now entertained visitors till long after midnight every
night.[100] In the morning he rose at a very early hour and,
against the advice of his friends, he took long walks in the
chilly air. Moreover, the office seekers clamored by the
hundreds for positions; and the President was a man of
such kindliness of heart that it pained him deeply that he
could not gratify them all. His health bore this strain but
three weeks, when he fell ill; and half an hour after midnight
on the 4th of April, an exact month after the day of his inauguration, President Harrison was dead.

The nation was shocked at the sudden death of the President. He was not a great statesman, as compared with
some of his contemporaries, nor a party leader in any sense;
but he was a sincere, honest man, and he had won the esteem
of all parties. Sadly and slowly moved the funeral pageant

[100] Sargent, Vol. II, p. 114.

through the city to the beat of the muffled drums and the mournful wail of the trumpet. The casket in which the dead President lay was enwrapped with the American flag, and the funeral car with nodding plumes was drawn by six white horses, and followed by a vast multitude of sorrowing friends. The body was laid to rest in the congressional burying ground, but in the summer it was taken to the West and was placed in its last resting place at the little town where the President had lived, on the bank of the river Ohio.

TYLER AND THE WHIGS

The Whigs were dismayed at the death of their President. Fifty years had passed since the inauguration of Washington, and no President had before died in office, and the Whigs had not taken such a possibility into account. Tyler at once became President, it is true, but the Whigs were not sure of Tyler. He had been placed on the ticket with Harrison to console the Clay men and to win, if possible, a floating vote from the South. He had been a Democrat until within recent years, and his views on the great issues between the two parties were not known. He had been simply known as "Tyler too," and now for the first time people began to inquire who he really was. One thing, however, was known of Tyler. He was a southern man to the core; he believed in state rights in the narrow sense and not in the broad Jeffersonian sense; he alone of all the senators cast his solitary vote against forcing South Carolina at the time of her nullification.

Congress had been called, by the late President, to meet in May for the purpose of dealing with the finances. In the campaign of the preceding year it was generally under-

stood, though little had been said on the subject, that if the
Whigs elected a President and gained control of Congress,
they would establish a national bank similar to one that
Jackson had killed, and to do this was the chief object in
convening Congress in extra session. Accordingly Mr. Clay
proceeded, soon after Congress met, to frame a bank bill.
But rumors were soon going around that Tyler was not in
favor of a national bank and also that a rupture between him
and Clay was imminent. These rumors proved to be well
founded. Tyler, it seems, had determined to rid himself of
the influence of the great Whig leader. The bill creating a
"Fiscal Bank" was passed by both houses, and was sent to
the President early in August. He returned it in a few days
with his veto. The Whigs were highly indignant and
chagrined at this action of the President, whom they had
elevated to power. But the Democrats were elated with the
veto, and in the evening of the day of its reception many of
the Democratic senators and representatives, headed by a
future President, James Buchanan, marched to the White
House to offer him their congratulations.

The Whigs were discouraged, but a gleam of hope returned to them when the President caused the word to go
out, through his Cabinet, that he would sign a second bank
bill, if purged of the features to which he had objected in the
first. A second bill, creating a "Fiscal Corporation," was
therefore passed, and was sent to Mr. Tyler in September.
Whig hopes now trembled in the balance, for they dis-
trusted their President despite his promise. Five days of
suspense passed, when the bill was returned to the House
with a veto.

The Whigs now burst forth in an uncontrollable storm of
wrath. The entire Cabinet, except Webster, resigned. Clay

1782 — DANIEL WEBSTER — 1852.

BY JOSEPH AMES, 1852.

From the original portrait in possession of Mrs. Charles H. Joy, Boston, Mass.

denounced Tyler and his "corporal's guard" of advisers in unsparing terms, while the friends of Tyler pronounced Clay the self-appointed dictator of the Whig party. Tyler claimed to have vetoed the bill on the pure ground of conscience and his ideas of the public good. This may have been true, but he was utterly in the wrong, nevertheless. That the chartering of the bank would have been a serious blunder few will now venture to doubt, but there was no excuse for Tyler. If he were not a Whig at heart, he should have come out in his true colors before the election. He permitted himself to be elevated to the great office and then he turned against the party that had elected him.[101]

The breach between President Tyler and the Whigs was now irreconcilable. The leaders of the party met in solemn conclave and deliberately read the President out of the party, putting forth at the same time a manifesto to the Whigs of the country. In this they set forth the hopes of the party and disclaimed all responsibility for the acts of the administration. In consideration of the fact that three and a half years of this presidential term yet remained, and of the vast patronage at the disposal of the President, this action of the party was a bold stroke, and admirable for its courage. There was now presented a spectacle, unknown before—a President without a party—and such a creature is almost as helpless in shaping legislation as the commonest laborer in the street.

[101] The opinion of some that the action of President Cleveland in 1896 in opposing his party on the silver question was similar to that of Tyler is entirely erroneous. Free silver was not a tenet of the party when he was elected, and when it became such he had as much right to his convictions on the subject as any other man in the country. Had he been elected on a free silver platform and then turned against it, his case would be parallel to that of Tyler.

The President had evidently hoped to win the Whig party from Clay and to become its head, but that matchless leader held the party in a grasp that could not be broken. Tyler then attempted to form a new party of the milder Whigs and Democrats. Not succeeding in this, he used his utmost efforts to win the Democratic party and to become its standard bearer. He called Democrats into his Cabinet and filled many of the best offices with them. But the Democrats, while they accepted these favors and rejoiced that Tyler had foiled the bank measure, at heart despised the man. They refused to make a man the leader of their party who had been unfaithful to his own; and Tyler was left without a party to the end of his term.

When the Cabinet resigned, Webster, as stated above, remained, his avowed object being to conclude a treaty with England which was then pending. This treaty, fixing the eastern boundary of Maine, was arranged with Lord Ashburton, and is known as the Webster-Ashburton Treaty. Webster, however, continued in the Cabinet for nearly a year after this treaty was concluded, and he was severely criticised by his fellow Whigs. The fact is, Webster and Clay had not been on the most friendly terms for some years, and had Tyler succeeded in forming a new party, Webster would no doubt have gone with him. But the President, failing in this, at length came to desire the retirement of the great New Englander from his Cabinet; not on personal grounds, but because he had now set his heart on a great project, and Webster was not the man to carry it out. His project was the annexation of Texas.

THE STORY OF TEXAS

As stated on a preceding page, when Mexico emancipated

her slaves, in 1827, Texas refused to do so, and there was strife from this time forth between the mother country and her northern province. In 1836 Texas declared its independence, and it was afterward recognized by the United States and by several European powers as a separate nation. This same year, 1836, witnessed the massacre of the Alamo, in which the famous Davy Crockett was killed, and the battle of San Jacinto, in which Santa Anna was routed by General Sam Houston, former governor of Tennessee. Texas desired, however, not to lead a separate existence, but to join the Union as a state. Of the sixty men who signed the declaration of independence, fifty-three had been born in the United States, and this fact explains why Texas soon afterward knocked at the door of the Union for admission. But Texas lay in the slave belt and, if admitted, would become a slave state; and on this ground its admission was sure to awaken strong opposition at the North. President Jackson, with all his courage, hesitated to risk a party rupture by coming out openly for annexation, though he greatly favored it. The matter then rested till the time of Tyler, who, having now alienated his party, had nothing to lose, and he boldly decided on annexation as the great measure of his administration. His hope was to win back the South for the coming presidential election.

But he must get rid of Webster, and this he did by simply freezing him out of the Cabinet. Webster was made to see that his counsels were not wanted, and that he was in uncongenial company, and in May, 1843, he resigned from the Cabinet. Mr. Upshur of Virginia became secretary of state. Upshur was a man of much ability and was fully in sympathy with the interests of the slave power. He would no doubt further the President's project with the utmost vigor;

but suddenly the whole project was thrown out of balance for a time by a calamity such as no human eyes could foresee.

One bright day in February, 1844, a gay company of about a hundred persons made an excursion down the Potomac River in a war vessel. This distinguished company included the President, his Cabinet, and many members of Congress with their families, and also the former queen of the White House, the aged Mrs. Madison. One object of the excursion was to witness the working of the great gun, the Peacemaker, which threw a 225-pound ball. Several times the gun was fired without incident, but on the return, as they neared the city, a heavy charge was put into it for a final salute, and it exploded with a terrific noise. When the smoke cleared away a dozen persons lay dead or dying on the deck. Among the dead were Mr. Upshur, secretary of state; Mr. Gilmer, secretary of the navy; and Mr. Gardner, whose daughter was soon to become the wife of President Tyler. Senator Benton and others were knocked senseless, while the President had a narrow escape, he having been playfully called below by Miss Gardner a moment before the explosion took place.

The President now chose John C. Calhoun secretary of state. The great South Carolinian was not desirous of the honor, but, seeing that he could do a real service for the South, he accepted. With remarkable energy he took hold of the business, and a secret treaty of annexation was arranged with the Texan government. This treaty, sent to the Senate by President Tyler on April 22, 1844, met with fatal opposition. Instead of receiving the two-thirds vote necessary to ratify, the treaty was rejected by a two-thirds

1795—JAMES KNOX POLK—1849.

BY GEORGE PETER ALEXANDER HEALY, 1846.

From the original portrait in the Corcoran Art Gallery, Washington, D.C.

vote.[102] This was a shock to the administration. The Texan question was thus left over, and it became the most vital question in the

The Whigs were united in 1844. Clay was all in all to the Whig conscience in this campaign. The vagaries of Tyler had cemented the party and it suffered with remorse that the noble "Harry of the West," the "Mill Boy of the Slashes," had not been chosen four years before. The Whig convention now nominated him by acclamation and without a dissenting voice, while Theodore Frelinghuysen was placed second on the ticket.

The Democratic convention met a few weeks later in the same city, Baltimore, and attracted far greater interest because of the uncertainty of the outcome. Van Buren was supposed to be the coming man. More than half the delegates had been instructed for him; but there were forces working against him. The chief of these was his attitude on the Texan question. His enemies, by a decoy letter, had obtained from Van Buren a statement that he was opposed to immediate annexation, and this greatly injured him in the South. Other candidates were, James Buchanan of Pennsylvania, who, however, withdrew his name; Calhoun, who followed the example of Buchanan; Lewis Cass of Michigan; and Richard M. Johnson of Kentucky.

The two-thirds rule was adopted, and the balloting began. Van Buren led with a good majority over all others, but fell a little below the required two-thirds. Again on the second

[102] Some voted against the treaty because they did not approve of the method of annexing Texas. They thought it should be done by a vote of both houses.

and third ballots, and so on till seven ballots had been taken, Van Buren kept the lead; but he lost a little each time, and it became evident that his nomination was impossible.   There was a man from Tennessee who had been timidly mentioned for the second place—James K. Polk,—but on the eighth ballot he received a few votes for first place.   And then, by one of those strange stampedes that sometimes take possession of such a body, the convention nominated Polk on the ninth ballot by a unanimous vote.   The news was flashed to Washington by telegraph.   This was the first practical use of that marvelous invention by which time and space are reduced to nothing in the transmission of news, by which a man can converse with his brother man with a thousand leagues of rolling sea between them.

Polk was the first "dark horse" candidate, that is, an unexpected candidate, one not put forward by any party before his nomination.[103]   Polk had been governor of Tennessee, and had served fourteen years in Congress, being four years Speaker of the House; but he was not a well-known statesman nor a national party leader, and the question arose on all sides, "Polk,—who is Polk?"   The convention, after nominating George M. Dallas of Pennsylvania for the vice presidency, adopted a strong platform, pronouncing for the immediate occupation of Oregon and the annexation of Texas.

A third convention was held in the same city during this same week.   President Tyler had attempted to win the Whig party from Clay, but had failed.   He then made efforts to divide the party and failed again.   After this he cast every Whig from his Cabinet and courted the Democrats, equally

[103] Other "dark horse" candidates were Pierce, Hayes, Garfield, and Bryan.

without success. But even now he did not despair. He set out to create a Tyler party, and to build it up he used the government patronage for all it was worth; yet with all this immense power his converts were few. Nevertheless he sent a band of his office-holders to hold a so-called national convention at Baltimore. They nominated him without division, and "Tyler and Texas" became their party slogan. The Tyler party presented a sorry spectacle indeed, but the oversanguine Tyler still had hopes. He seemed to think that the misguided people would yet see their folly and flock to his standard—but they failed to do so. At last the President awakened to the fact, which everybody else knew long before, that he had no following, and he withdrew from the field in August.

There was one man in America who was alarmed at the work of the Democratic convention at Baltimore, and that was Henry Clay. Clay had counted on Van Buren as his antagonist, and as he and Van Buren stood together in opposing the immediate annexation of Texas, that all-absorbing question would have been thrown out of the canvass. But Polk with his vigorous Texas-Oregon platform was stunning to Clay, who well knew that the prospect of acquiring Texas would please the South and that the Oregon plank would please the North, while his own platform dealt with such tame subjects as a protective tariff and the distribution of the land sales. The campaign, as it progressed, waxed hot. The Whigs at first felt confident; but as the summer passed they realized that the fight would be a close one. Clay and Polk were as unlike as two men could be. Clay was the brilliant leader who for many years had been the idol of a great party; Polk was plodding, sturdy, and straightforward. The Whigs ridiculed the idea that their fine thoroughbred could be beaten in the race by the un-known pack horse. But in the fact that Polk was an un-known quantity lay his greatest strength.

In the South the Democrats laid great stress on the ac-quisition of Texas; in the North it was Oregon, and the boundary must be 54° 40' north latitude; and "Fifty-four Forty or fight" became a campaign cry. But the Democrats needed Pennsylvania, and Pennsylvania cared less for Texas or Oregon than for a protective tariff. The Democrats there-fore preached protection throughout the state. Mr. Polk wrote a letter to a Mr. Kane of Philadelphia in which he pronounced himself in favor of moderate protection. This was taken up by the Democratic orators and they brazenly pronounced Polk "a better tariff man than Clay;" they even circulated the statement that Clay had become a free-trader and that the only salvation for the iron industry lay in the election of Polk—and by this means they secured the vote of Pennsylvania. Clay felt himself on the defensive. He wrote letters and letters, defining his position. These did little good or harm until his "Alabama letter," written to a friend in that state, came out in July. In this letter Clay dealt with the Texas question, stating that he had no personal objec-tion to annexation, that if it could be accomplished without dishonor, without war, on just and fair terms, *he would be glad to see it.* This sentiment was directly opposite to that expressed in his well-known "Raleigh letter," and to the equally well-known position of the Whig party on this great subject. It was intended to do good at the South, but in this it failed, and it did immeasurable harm at the North. Clay's friends were thunderstruck; they were chilled to the bone when this letter was published over the land. The Demo-crats rung every change on the phrase, "He would be glad

1777 — HENRY CLAY — 1852.

By Oliver Frazer, 1851.

From the original portrait in possession of Mrs. James B. Clay, Lexington, Ky.

to see it," repeating it over and over from every platform to show that Mr. Clay stood on no real principle, but would hedge on any issue to win the election. In vain did the Whig orators and editors attempt to explain; in vain did Clay write additional letters declaring that he still stood by his Raleigh letter. It was too late; the mischief was done; Clay had signed his political death warrant in writing his Alabama letter, and from this moment the cause of the Whigs slowly declined.

There was a little party at the North known as the Free Soil or Liberty party, and James G. Birney was its candidate. It held the balance of power in a few Northern states, notably New York and Michigan. This party had no hope of success, and many of its members were inclined to vote for Clay, as the less of the two evils. But when his Alabama letter came out they turned fiercely against Clay and supported Birney, who drew enough votes from the Whigs to throw New York and Michigan to Polk and give him the election. The election was held on different days in different states, and the excitement became intense as the long-drawn-out returns came in. At last New York cast her vote for Polk, owing to the fact that many former Whigs voted for Birney, and decided the contest; but Massachusetts, faithful old Whig state as she was, cast her vote for Clay after it was known that he was defeated.[104]

This was the third time that the great Kentucky chieftain made a fruitless race to win the glittering prize of his life's ambition; and it was the last. He had passed the meridian of life, the youthful luster of his eye was fading,

[104] When Congress met a few weeks later it passed a law fixing a uniform day for the presidential election in all the states, and it has continued in force from that time.

and never again could he hope to make so strong a race as he had now made, for the time was near when the destinies of the nation must pass into younger hands.

NOTES

Morse and the Telegraph. — Samuel F. B. Morse had labored for years on the telegraph, and had almost reduced himself to penury. In 1842 he was granted the privilege of setting up his telegraph in the lower rooms of the Capitol. The experiment was successful, and the members of Congress could hardly believe their senses as Morse enabled them to converse with one another from the different rooms. And yet when he asked an appropriation of $30,000 to establish an experimental line from Washington to Baltimore, there was much opposition. Many were the shafts of ridicule thrust at the new invention. One member moved that half the appropriation be used to experiment in mesmerism; another, that an appropriation be made to construct a railroad to the moon. One prominent member pronounced all "magnetic telegraphs miserable chimeras, fit for nothing." Another lost his seat in the House at the next election because he voted for the appropriation. While the debate was in progress, Morse stood leaning against the railing in the House in great agitation. A friend went to console him, and Morse, placing his hand to his head said, "I have an awful headache. . . . I have spent seven years in perfecting this invention, and all that I had. . . . If the bill fails, I am ruined. . . . I have not money enough to pay my board bill." He was greatly relieved soon after by the passing of the bill. His fortune was made, and the name of Morse must forever be inseparable from the telegraph. See Sargent's "Public Men and Events," Vol. II, p. 193.

The Creole Affair. — The *Creole* was a slave ship. While on a voyage from Norfolk to New Orleans in November, 1841, with 135 slaves, a portion of them rose in mutiny, killed the masters of the vessel, and steered to a British port in the West Indies. Here, according to the laws of England, they were free. The slaveholders in Congress determined that a demand be made on England that the slaves be given up, and many from the North agreed with them. At this point a young representative from Ohio, Joshua R. Giddings, rose and made a strong speech in favor of the slaves, claiming that they had a right to use any means in their power to gain their freedom, and that, being on the high seas, their masters had no longer the right to hold them in bondage. Giddings was at once censured by a vote of the House, whereupon he resigned his seat, bade his friends adieu, and repaired to his home in Ohio. His constituents held an election and reëlected him by three thousand majority. He returned to Congress, and from that time to the Civil War he was a leading opponent of the slave power.

The Dorr Rebellion. — Rhode Island, after the Declaration of Independence, retained its charter government, and many of the people were dissatisfied at the limited suffrage. In 1842 a portion of the citizens rose in an effort to secure a new constitution, and they were led by Thomas W. Dorr, a young lawyer. A new government was set up, but the insurgents were dispersed by national aid, and Dorr was taken captive. He was tried for treason, and sentenced to prison for life, but was afterward pardoned. Dorr's principles prevailed in the end, and were embodied in the new constitution.

CHAPTER XXV

THE MEXICAN WAR AND THE COMPROMISE OF 1850

THE lonely administration of Tyler came to an end unwept and unsung. The few friends who had fawned upon him because favor followed fawning, now melted away rapidly since his power to bestow offices on them was drawing to an end, and the last weeks of his term were spent in solitude. Tyler was a man of sanguine spirit and abounding faith in himself, and not until near the close of his official life did he see that he had failed to impress himself upon the country and that the Tyler party could be expressed by zero. He returned to his home in Virginia and soon disappeared from public notice; but sixteen years later, at the outbreak of the Civil War, he reappeared at Washington as president of the "Peace Congress." This came to nothing, and Tyler cast his lot with the South and became a member of the Confederate Congress; but he died the next year. Of the fact that it is perilous for an American public man to betray the party that gives him his power, John Tyler is a conspicuous example—and no one envies him his memory.

James K. Polk, born in North Carolina, was the son of a sturdy farmer and the eldest of ten children. Polk was a serious man, able, industrious, and religious. His defects lay in his narrow partisanship and his tendency for political intrigue. He could see no good in the creed of the Whig party and nothing but good in the creed of his own, nor was he scrupulous as to his methods in winning an election. His Cabinet was a strong one and included at least four men well known to fame. James Buchanan, the bachelor statesman of Pennsylvania, became secretary of state; William L. Marcy of the "Hunker" [106] faction in New York and author of the well-known phrase in our political parlance, "To the victors belong the spoils," secretary of war; Robert J. Walker of Mississippi, who was to find his political grave in "bleeding" Kansas in the following decade, secretary of the treasury; and George Bancroft, America's leading historian, secretary of the navy.[106]

The chief issue of the campaign of the preceding summer had already been settled. Arrangements had been made in the last days of Tyler's administration by which Texas in the following months became a member of the Union. The new state was annexed by a joint resolution of Congress. This raised a cry of "unconstitutional" among northern Whigs, and from the Massachusetts legislature. Little heed was paid to this protest, and a half century later, when Hawaii was annexed by a similar joint resolution, little opposition to the method was awakened. A vast and fertile domain is Texas, an empire in extent, with unbounded resources for agriculture and grazing. Every American rejoices that this broad, fair land is part of our glorious Union,

[106] The Democrats of New York were at this time divided into two factions, the "Hunker," or conservatives, or old-time Democrats, and the "Barnburners," the progressive, antislavery Democrats. The latter, it was said, were ready to destroy the Union in order to get rid of the evils such as slavery, and they were compared to the Dutchman who burned his barn to get rid of the rats — hence the name. The origin of the word "Hunker" is unknown.

[106] After a short service Bancroft resigned and became minister to England. Another literary appointment of Polk was Nathaniel Hawthorne as collector of the port at Salem, Massachusetts.

but no one takes pride in the political intrigues by which it was secured.[107]

But there was an abundance of business left for the Polk administration. "There are four great measures," said the new President with great decision, " which are to be the measures of my administration;" and these were a reduction of the tariff, the reëstablishment of the independent treasury, the settlement of the Oregon boundary, and the acquisition of California. The first of these, the reënactment of the independent treasury bill, was accomplished in 1846, as stated on a preceding page. The second, the reduction of the tariff, dates from the same year. In spite of the plaintive protests from Pennsylvania, the state that had given its vote to Polk because he was " a better tariff man than Clay," the " Walker Tariff of 1846 " was enacted. By it many of the higher duties of the " Whig Tariff of 1842 " were lowered. This tariff was in force for eleven years, and it became popular with all classes. Again the tariff question ceased to be a party measure, and, owing to a surplus in the treasury, the duties of the Walker Tariff were reduced still further in 1857, with the consent of all parties; and there was no further tariff legislation till the opening of the Civil War.

OREGON AND CALIFORNIA

The remote unpeopled region in the Northwest known as Oregon lay between 42° and 54° 40′ north latitude, and extended from the crest of the Rocky Mountains to the waves of the Pacific. The ten-year joint occupation between the

[107] The term "reannexation" was constantly used, because, it was claimed, Texas had been a part of the Louisiana Purchase, but had been ceded back to Spain in part payment for Florida.

1791 — SAMUEL FINLEY BREESE MORSE — 1872.

From an original photograph by Sarony, New York

United States and England had been extended indefinitely, either country to give a year's notice to have it discontinued. This notice was given by the United States in 1846. For some years before this it was seen that Oregon was about to become the home of civilized man. In 1835 Marcus Whitman, with a few companions, crossed the mountains and entered the Columbia Valley as a missionary to the Indians. A few settlers arrived in the following years. In 1842 Whitman came east on business connected with his mission work, and on returning he was accompanied by a train of moving wagons leaving Missouri for the Columbia Valley. It was a long and weary journey, but others soon followed, and within three years some ten thousand Americans had settled in the Oregon country.

The whole of Oregon was claimed by each country. The American claim was based on the discovery of the Columbia River by Captain Grey in 1792, on the explorations of Lewis and Clark, and on the actual settlements.[108] President Polk had said in his inaugural address that our right to all of Oregon was indisputable, and this he reiterated in his first message to Congress. But England had no thought of giving up her seacoast on the Pacific. Yet neither country wished to go to war, and it was decided to compromise, to split the Oregon country in the middle, each to take half. A few Democratic hotspurs in Congress still shouted for 54° 40′, but while this was a good campaign cry, it could not be adhered to. England at last offered to extend the boundary line of 49° to the Pacific, retaining for herself the whole of Vancouver Island. President Polk could not accept this without abandoning his former position, and that of the plat-

[108] The English claim was based on the discoveries of Mackenzie and on the occupation of the country by the Hudson Bay Company.

form on which he was elected. But he could not do other-wise without risking a war far greater than that now brew-ing on the South, and, to let himself down as gracefully as possible, he shifted the responsibility to the Senate by asking the advice of that body. The Senate advised that the British offer be accepted, and 49° was made the boundary between the United States and British Columbia. Our portion of Oregon, some three hundred thousand square miles, in-cludes the entire Columbia Valley, and is of far greater value than that retained by the British. The people of the North were especially pleased with this new acquisition, for it balanced the recent extension of slave territory through the admission of Texas.

This brings us to the last of the four great measures—the acquisition of California. Why should the American Presi-dent put this in his programme? California belonged to another nation, a sister republic. It was the boundless region in the Southwest out of which four or five states and territories have since been carved. Mexico had refused to sell it. By what means, then, could the acquisition be made? By simply conjuring up a quarrel with Mexico, "conquer-ing" the uninhabited territory, and then holding it by "right" of conquest. And a good *casus belli* was at hand. Texas claimed all the territory between the Nueces River and the Rio Grande, which was also claimed by Mexico. But Congress had ignored the claim of Mexico, and had passed an act extending the revenue laws to the disputed ter-ritory. Mexico could not give this up without fighting. Here, then, was cause enough for war.

And yet Polk did not want war. His honest desire was to avoid it. He professed to believe that Mexico would not fight on account of Texas, though all diplomatic relations had ceased at the time of annexation; or even on account of the disputed boundary line, and he congratulated Congress and the country on having acquired the new territory without bloodshed. He apparently expected to acquire California by negotiation or purchase, and he sent John Slidell to the Mexican capital with full power to settle all differences and to offer a good round sum for California; but Slidell was not received by the Mexicans. In his anxiety to avoid war the President made a serious blunder at the beginning. He restored Santa Anna, who was living in exile at Havana, to his Mexican home. Santa Anna was one of the noted characters of his time, imperious, deceitful, revengeful, yet not without bravery and military skill. He was a typical revolutionist of the Latin American states. As early as 1833 he became President of Mexico, and at various times thereafter; but usually after a brief service the people rose against him and sent him for a time into exile. His most recent banishment took place in 1845. President Polk now sent a war vessel to convey Santa Anna back to Mexico, in the hope, first, that he would overthrow the new President, Paredes, which he did; and second, that he would treat with the United States for peace out of gratitude for the favor—which he did not.[100] Polk mistook his man. Santa Anna was not a man of gratitude. On reaching Mexico, he discovered that he could best restore his popularity by making war against the United States, and he instantly set about doing so.

[100] It is believed that Santa Anna promised that if, on being restored, he again got control of Mexico, he would cede California to the United States for a sum of money, but his word was worthless.

ZACHARY TAYLOR IN MEXICO

President Polk, with all his avowals that there would be no war, had taken the precaution to send General Zachary Taylor to the disputed territory with an " Army of Occupation," and a fleet to the Gulf of Mexico. The ownership of this territory should have been settled by treaty, if possible, and its occupation in this high-handed way pointed clearly to the fact that, if California could not be had for gold, the feeble sister republic must be goaded into war. But Mexico had also invited hostilities by placing an army at Matamoras. The Army of Occupation moved on to the mouth of the Rio Grande, and the Mexican general, Arista, crossed the river to meet it. The two armies came together on two successive days, and the so-called battles of Palo Alto and Resaca de la Palma were fought. The Mexicans were worsted, but a few Americans were killed, and this was enough. President Polk at once sent a message to Congress declaring that "American blood had been spilt on American soil," that Mexico had struck the first blow,[110] and that a state of war existed, "notwithstanding all our efforts to avoid it!"

But war, righteous or unrighteous, will always stir the people to action. Congress voted supplies and called for fifty thousand volunteers. Many of the northern Whigs opposed the war, but few of them were willing to go on record as voting against its prosecution.[111] The people quickly responded, and the war was vigorously prosecuted. Taylor's little army was augmented, and he crossed the Rio

[110] This referred to the capture of a few American scouts before the battles above mentioned had taken place.

[111] "The Biglow Papers," written by James Russell Lowell, humorously set forth the opposition of the Whigs.

Grande, occupied Matamoras and relieved Fort Brown. During the summer he advanced up the river, taking one point after another, and in September captured Monterey after a bloody siege. Polk had assured his friends that the war would not continue longer than three months, but even with the capture of Monterey, the chief stronghold in northern Mexico, the Mexicans refused to give up, and Taylor was instructed to press the war to a finish.

There was one man in Washington all this time who was very impatient and restless. General Winfield Scott was the commander-in-chief of the armies, next to the President, and he felt that he ought to be sent to the front to take general command of the war. But the administration held him back for no given reason. The true reason, however, is not far to seek. The President, as above stated, was a narrow partisan. Scott was a leading Whig and had been an aspirant to the presidency. If now he were sent to the front, he might win such laurels as would make him a dangerous candidate for President. Hence he was kept at home. But another horn to the dilemma appeared. Taylor was also a Whig, or was supposed to be, though he had never voted, and his victories in Mexico were now giving him a name among the greatest heroes of the age. He even began to be mentioned as the coming Whig candidate. Something must be done to head off Taylor, and at length the authorities decided to send Scott to share the laurels—not that they loved him more, but Taylor less. Scott was now ordered to proceed to Vera Cruz by sea, to capture that port, and to march overland to the Mexican capital. Taylor was not only to have a rival in the field; he was ordered to send a large portion of his army to Scott. This he did like a true soldier, though it was a bitter medicine to take. Taylor was thus left in the midst of a hostile people with but a fraction of his former army; but strange to say, his greatest victory was yet before him.

Santa Anna had landed at Vera Cruz from Cuba but a short time before the siege and fall of Monterey. Hearing, late in the autumn, of Taylor's weakened condition, he gathered an army of twenty thousand men and marched against him. Taylor was joined by General Wool, who had recently led an army into Mexico, and his force was thereby raised to five thousand men. He took a position in a mountain defile near the fine estate of Buena Vista and awaited his foe. On the 22d of February, 1847, the enemy had almost surrounded the Americans, and the Mexican general sent word to Taylor that if he wished to save his little army from being cut to pieces and captured, he could do so by surrendering at discretion. "General Taylor never surrenders," was the laconic answer, and the battle of Buena Vista was fought. It began on the morning of the 23d and raged all day. Toward evening Taylor saw the Mexicans waver, and his order, "Give 'em a little more grape, Captain Bragg," was vigorously obeyed, and by nightfall the Mexicans were fleeing in confusion. The Mexican loss, including prisoners, reached nearly two thousand, while the American loss was about seven hundred and fifty. Among the slain was a son of Henry Clay. This battle closed the career of Zachary Taylor in the Mexican War; but his fame was now secure. He returned to his native land some months later to receive the highest honors that can be awarded an American citizen. General Scott was now to take the helm and to win even greater achievements than Taylor had done, though not an equal reward. But before recounting the deeds of Scott, let us take a brief note of

THE CONQUEST OF CALIFORNIA

The Mexican War was waged by the United States, not on account of a boundary dispute, as the world was made to believe, but because Ahab coveted Naboth's vineyard, because the slaveholder cast his eyes over the vast fertile Southwest and desired it for his own. More tempting by far than Oregon was this beautiful land of perpetual summer, where "the flowers ever blossom, and the beams ever shine." It was this garden of the West that must now be secured as the chief prize of a victorious war. General Stephen W. Kearny was sent with a competent force at the opening of hostilities to secure this golden fleece. He entered New Mexico, and, capturing the ancient town of Sante Fé without firing a gun, raised the American flag and took possession of the province in the name of the United States. Kearny was then ordered to proceed to California and to take possession of the country, as he had done in the case of New Mexico. Arriving at Los Angeles late in December, he met the explorer, John C. Frémont, who, with Commodore Stockton,[112] had already taken possession of California. Frémont, for whom there was much notoriety yet in store, had attracted attention by his daring exploits in this far western country, and by his romantic marriage with Jessie Benton, daughter of the famous Missouri senator. The Mexican general, De Castro, had moved against the settlers of the Sacramento Valley, who then rallied to the camp of Frémont. In several skirmishes Frémont beat De Castro, at length capturing Sanoma Pass and nine cannon. The Mexicans were driven out of the country and the American settlers chose Frémont governor

[112] Stockton had succeeded Commodore Sloat, who had captured the Mexican towns on the California coast.

of the province—all this before it was known that war existed between the United States and Mexico.[118]

Thus the immense region from the Cordilleras to the sea, on which the President had looked with covetous eyes, fell into his hands like mellow fruit, and almost without bloodshed.

THE GREAT MARCH ON MEXICO

From this moment to the end of the war the chief military glory centers about one man—General Winfield Scott. It had been confidently believed at Washington that Mexico would yield after our first hostile demonstrations, but the Mexicans were defending their country with desperate valor; and now it was seen that nothing short of striking the heart of their republic and humbling them to the dust could subdue them. Accordingly General Scott was borne by sea with twelve thousand men to Vera Cruz, where he entered upon one of the most successful military campaigns of modern history. Arriving on March 9 at the entrance of the harbor, the Americans beheld the old town nestled quietly between the mountains and the sea, and presenting anything but the aspect of war. On a little island at the entrance of the harbor stood the ancient castle of Ulloa, while in the background rose in lonely majesty the lofty peak of Orizaba, its snow-covered summit buried in the skies.

Scott landed his army without incident or opposition. The town and castle were garrisoned by some five thousand Mexicans under Juan Morales. The demand of Scott that

[118] H. H. Bancroft, Vol. XVII, p. 208. Frémont and Kearny had a quarrel over the governorship, and Frémont was court-martialed and dismissed from the service, was but pardoned by the President.

1784 — ZACHARY TAYLOR — 1850.

By John Vanderlyn, 1850.

From the original portrait in the City Hall, New York.

the town surrender was declined, and he opened a tremendous cannonade on the city and its defenses. Hundreds of shells fell and exploded in the streets and on the housetops, causing great destruction of life and property. For five days and nights the continuous roar of artillery resounded from the besieging army, from the fleet of Commodore Conner in the harbor, and from the answering guns of the besieged city. Scott is said to have thrown half a million pounds of metal. Many Mexicans and a few Americans were killed. On the 29th of March the Mexicans surrendered the city and the garrison marched out with honors of war.

Scott now prepared for his great overland march to the interior of Mexico. Sending his advance column under Generals Twiggs and Patterson by way of the road that winds among the mountains of Jalapa, Scott joined them by the middle of April, and here amid the rugged steeps that frowned from every side, he was obliged to fight a desperate battle. Santa Anna, after his disastrous encounter with Taylor at Buena Vista, had collected an army of about ten thousand men, and he met the advancing Americans in a mountain pass near the village of Plan del Rio and under the shadow of a lofty hill called Cerro Gordo. The Mexican commander had chosen his position with admirable skill. The tops of the surrounding hills, save one, were planted with cannon, while the main army occupied a level place between a dashing mountain stream and a rocky wall a thousand feet high.   But Santa Anna left one lofty eminence unoccupied, believing, as he said, a goat could not approach him from that point.   Scott detected the omission, and while he engaged the enemy in front he sent a detachment to scale the unoccupied height and to command the Jalapa road above the Mexican army.   This was done by Twiggs with no less energy and success than the Heights of Abraham at Quebec had been scaled by Wolfe nearly a hundred years before.   Santa Anna saw his mistake when too late to correct it; yet the Mexicans fought bravely, and yielded only when all hope of success had vanished.   A thousand of them were killed or wounded and three thousand were taken prisoners.   Santa Anna started to flee in his carriage, but it was overturned, and he escaped astride a mule, leaving with his carriage a large quantity of gold, his private papers, and his wooden leg.[114]   The American loss slightly exceeded four hundred.

The American army swept on like a tidal wave, capturing everything before it.   Jalapa, Perota with its impressive castle, and Puebla fell successively into the hands of the Americans.   In mid-summer they reached the summit of the Cordilleras, eight thousand feet above the sea, and here they opened their eyes upon one of the sublimest scenes in the world—the panorama of the Mexican Valley, hemmed in by mountain walls with here and there a snow-capped peak gleaming in the sun; the long slopes covered with the luxuriance of a tropical summer; the sleeping valley with its glittering, sunlit lakes, and the ancient city of the Montezumas nestled in the midst.

The 20th of August, 1847, was a great day in the Mexican War.   Scott had advanced slowly from Puebla toward

[114] He had lost a leg in battle in 1837.

the capital city. His four divisions were commanded respectively by Generals Worth, Twiggs, Pillow, and Quitman; and Franklin Pierce, who was soon to outdo his military chief in a presidential race, arrived early in August with twenty-five hundred fresh troops. The army now numbered eleven thousand, and Scott pressed on toward the doomed city as relentlessly determined on its fall as was the inexorable Cortez who had marched over the same route for the same purpose more than three hundred years before. The ever sanguine, irrepressible Santa Anna had gathered another army, much larger than before.[115] On this fateful 20th of August Generals Twiggs and Pillow with forty-five hundred men made a wild, tumultuous dash at daybreak upon the strong Mexican camp at Contreras, held by General Valencia with seven thousand men. In less than half an hour the place was carried and three thousand Mexicans with most of their artillery were captured. A few hours later the strongly garrisoned village of San Antonio was taken. The Mexicans now rallied in great numbers at the village of Cherubusco with its great stone citadel, a fortified convent. This was within four miles of the city gates. After a fierce bombardment of some hours the outer field works were carried. But the convent—from its loopholes bristled many cannon, and numberless sharpshooters plied their deadly work from its walls. War knows no religion, and the American guns were trained on the sacred edifice. After a short, terrific bombardment, the white flag was seen waving above the somber walls of the convent. The Americans had lost a thousand men on this day, and the Mexicans four times that number in addition to the prisoners taken in the morning.

[115] Scott estimated the number at 27,000. See " Memoirs," II, p. 487.

The way was now open for the invading army to march upon the city of Mexico.

President Polk had sent the chief clerk of the state department, Nicholas B. Trist, to arrange for peace, and two weeks were spent in negotiation. This came to naught, and hostilities were resumed. On September 8 General Worth made an assault on the near-by village of Molino del Rey to destroy a cannon foundry; but from a stone castle on the hill of Chapultepec near the town Worth was assaulted with great vigor, and the proportion of American loss was greater than in any other engagement during the war. Some days later the castle of Chapultepec was taken by storm, and on the 14th of September General Scott marched at the head of his victorious army into the city of Mexico.[116] A few hours later the stars and stripes were waving from the walls of the ancient palace of the Montezumas. The war was over; and it is notable from the fact that the Americans won every battle. The Mexicans had fought nobly, but they were wanting in scientific training, and moreover many of them were half-breeds—a cross between the Spaniards and the ancient Aztecs—and were no match for the more virile Anglo-Saxon; and now at the close of a brief war of a year and a half, not only their proud city, but their whole land lay prostrate at the feet of the conquerors from the North.

RESULTS OF THE WAR

A view of Congress during the progress of the war reveals a state of agitation unequaled since the debates on the Missouri Compromise in 1820. The chief result of the war, as

[116] Santa Anna had fled in the preceding night with a large part of his army, after setting free and arming about two thousand criminals from the prisons. These men attacked the invading army from the housetops, but were soon put to rout.

1782 — LEWIS CASS — 1866.

From an enlargement of an original Brady negative, in the War Department, Washington, D.C.

every one foresaw, would be the addition to our national domain of the immense region in the Southwest; and the question rose spontaneously in every mind, Will it be free soil,
or slave soil? Aside from the moral aspects of the question,
the South had the right of priority of claim, for it was the
South that had brought about the war, and its chief object
was to extend slave territory. In another sense the North
had the first right, for this land had already been dedicated
to freedom by Mexico. The Louisiana Purchase was wedge-
shaped, the larger end lying north of 36° 30′. The South
had used up its smaller end beginning with the admission of
Louisiana in 1812, and ending with the admission of Arkansas in 1836. There remained to the South Florida and the
Indian Territory, and now came Texas; but these were no
match for the vast territory in the Northwest to be carved
into free states. Almost from the beginning of the government the states had been admitted in pairs, one in the North
and one in the South, so as to preserve equal power in the
Senate between the free and the slave states. The South
now began to view with alarm the exhaustion of its territory,
while that of the North seemed inexhaustible. Hence came
the Mexican War.

But the South had not clear sailing; there were breakers
ahead. A great majority of the people of the North opposed
the further extension of slave territory, and this feeling
found expression in the national legislature. The storm
broke forth when, in August, 1846, a young Democrat in the
House, from Pennsylvania, having been chosen for the purpose, made the motion that slavery be forever excluded from
the territory about to be acquired from Mexico. His motion, known as the Wilmot Proviso, was an amendment to a
bill for the appropriation of $2,000,000 for settling the dif-

ficulties with Mexico. The whole South flared up in a moment in fierce opposition. The proviso did not become a law, but the principle it involved became the apple of discord between the two sections for years, and even threatened the foundations of the Union.

The treaty of peace, signed at Guadalupe Hidalgo, conveyed to the United States the territory which has since become the states of California, Nevada, and Utah, part of Colorado and the largest parts of the territories of New Mexico and Arizona.[117] Mexico gave up the territory with reluctance but she was prostrate and powerless. She feebly requested, however, that slavery be not established in the ceded territory; but Mr. Trist, who acted for the United States, refused even to mention the subject to his government.

No true American is proud of the Mexican War. · The ceded territory is vastly better off, it is true, in industrial development and in civil and religious liberty, than it could have been had it remained a part of Mexico; but the means by which it was acquired were out of harmony with the general policy of the United States in its dealings with foreign nations, and we rejoice that this innovation did not intrench itself in the national mind and become the settled policy of our country. One honorable thing, however, we did in the matter. We paid Mexico $15,000,000 for the land ceded, and this of our own free will, for Mexico was powerless and could not have resisted had our government chosen to pay nothing. This great acquisition of territory, if Texas be

[117] Five years later the United States purchased from Mexico the Messilla Valley, about forty-five thousand square miles of southern Arizona, for $10,000,000. The purchase was arranged by Captain Gadsden, and is known as the Gadsden Purchase.

included, aggregated about 850,000 square miles,—more than the whole United States at the close of the Revolution.

Little did Mexico dream of the hidden wealth that lay beneath the surface of the lands she ceded to her great rival. Nine days before the treaty was signed the discovery of gold was made in California. Some years before this the enterprising Swiss, John A. Sutter, had settled in the beautiful valley of the Sacramento, had possessed himself of several thousand acres of land, and had built a fort, which he called after his own name. He owned many thousand head of sheep and cattle, had several hundred men in his employ, and was truly a prince in the western wilds. In the employ of Sutter was a carpenter from New Jersey named James Marshall, and it was he who first made the discovery. Marshall was superintending the building of a mill on a branch of the American River near the base of the Sierra Nevada Mountains, when he observed little shining particles in the mill race that proved to be gold. The news soon spread to the surrounding settlements, but the people were slow to believe.

At length, however, with the opening of spring, the conversion of the coast was complete. The village of San Francisco went wild over the great discovery. Many sold all their possessions and hastened to the gold fields. All other business came to a standstill. The judge abandoned the bench, and the physician his patients; the town council was broken up for want of a quorum; farms were left tenantless, and waving fields of grain were allowed to run to waste.[118]

The news that gold had been discovered in California spread slowly at first, as the railroad and the telegraph had not reached the remote regions west of the Rocky Moun-

[118] H. H. Bancroft, Vol. XXIII, p. 62.

tains; but at length it reached the East, spread across the Atlantic to Europe, and was published in all the leading newspapers of the world. Great was the excitement in every land, and ships from every clime were diverted from the channels of trade and headed for the Pacific Coast. Many came by way of Cape Horn; others braved the deadly climate of Panama, while thousands from every part of the Union crossed the western plains in moving wagons. Long trains of wagons wound their way across the plains and over the mountains toward the setting sun. Many were the perils of this long and weary journey—the wild animal and the wild Indian, exposure to the mountain snows, and, above all, the cholera. The cholera attacked these west-bound trains, and many a weary traveler never reached his El Dorado, but found a nameless grave, far from home and kindred, in the vast and trackless regions of the West. It was in the summer of 1849 that this tide of humanity from afar began to pour into the Sacramento Valley—a few to realize the dream of wealth, more to gain a modest competence, but the majority to meet disappointment, to return broken in health and spirits, or to fill an unknown grave in the wilderness.

California was peopled as no other colony or territory in the Western World had been, and in less than two years after the golden discovery, the number of inhabitants exceeded a hundred thousand; and it was this discovery that came to the rescue of Congress in deciding the great question involved in the Wilmot Proviso. But before disposing of the subject we must stop and note the election of a new President.

Strange as it may seem, the Democrats slowly lost in power during the Polk administration. A great movement usually wins friends as it proves its ability to succeed, but not so with the Mexican War. The reason of this change of heart was that many of the people lost interest in the war and in the party that had waged it, when they saw that the chief object was to humble a weak sister republic for the purpose of robbing her of her territory. Moreover, the slavery question played its part. The North feared that the newly acquired lands would, and the South feared that they would not, become slave territory; and for these opposite reasons the interest waned on both sides of Mason and Dixon's line. Much would depend on the next President. Who would he be? This was the absorbing question of the moment.

The Whigs were hopeful; their star was rising. From three prominent candidates they were to make their nomination—Henry Clay, "the same old coon," as the Democrats put it, and the two successful generals of the war. But Clay was rapidly growing old, the great questions with which he had been identified were now settled, and more than once he had led the party to defeat. His star was visibly waning, and no longer could the magic name of Clay awaken the enthusiasm of bygone years. Of the two military commanders, Taylor had a clear advantage over Scott. His achievements in Mexico were no greater than those of Scott; but he won his laurels while the war was still popular and the eyes of the country were riveted upon it. Scott's victories came later, when the people had begun to compare the war with a fight between a big bully and a child. Scott therefore never received the honor accorded Taylor. But the respective personalities of the two men had something to do with deciding the contest. Taylor was wanting in education and social polish; he refused to wear the uniform, and cared little for his personal appearance. He received the sobriquet of "Rough and Ready." These qualities appealed to the masses. Scott, on the other hand, was highly cultured, urbane, self-conscious, and dignified. He was exceedingly exact in his dress, speech, and actions. He was nick-named "Fuss and Feathers." Taylor had the further advantage of being new to fame, while Scott had been in the public eye for nearly forty years, and he was almost as much a politician as a soldier.

When Taylor was first informed that he was spoken of for the presidency he was astonished; then he laughed at the ridiculous idea. But as the months passed and the newspapers were full of the subject, he began to take it seriously. Clay wrote him suggesting that he withdraw his name, but this the old hero refused to do, and he entered the lists, determined to win if he could.

Taylor received the nomination at the Whig convention in Philadelphia. Clay was disappointed and refused to support him. Webster pronounced the nomination one "not fit to be made." Horace Greeley and Thurlow Weed held aloof till late in the fall, when they came into line. But Taylor had won the great popular heart. As Taylor was a resident of the South and a slaveholder, it was necessary to give the second place to a northern man, and Millard Fillmore of New York was nominated.

The Democrats met in Baltimore and nominated General Lewis Cass of Michigan for President, and William O. Butler of Kentucky for Vice President. Cass was a man with an interesting record. We first meet him in the War of 1812. He was a young officer under Hull at the surrender of Michigan, and rather than surrender his sword to the British officer, he broke it across a stone. After the war he became governor of Michigan Territory and held the post for eighteen years. Seeing that Detroit would grow into a city, he purchased a large farm just outside the village, and as the town expanded the farm grew in value until its owner became a millionaire.[119]   Next we find Cass in the Cabinet of Jackson, then minister to France, and finally in the United States Senate.   But Cass lacked one of the most essential qualities of the modern politician—he was, like General Scott, self-conscious, urbane, and he held himself aloof from the vulgar crowd.   Nevertheless Cass would probably have been elected but for the defection of his old enemy and rival, Martin Van Buren.   The Democrats of New York were divided into two factions, the Hunkers and the Barnburners. The latter were not in sympathy with the slave propagandists; they refused to support Cass, joined the Free-soilers, and nominated a third ticket with Van Buren at its head. Van Buren did not love Cass, nor had he forgiven the party for choosing Polk instead of himself four years before.   But at that time his great benefactor of Tennessee was still living, and this fact probably held the New Yorker in line with his party.   But now Jackson was dead, and Van Buren took the opportunity to take vengeance on the party.   He was quite successful.   His personal following in his own state was sufficient to split the party almost in the middle and to give the electors to Taylor; and New York was again a pivotal state and decided the election.

ZACHARY TAYLOR

Zachary Taylor was a soldier and only a soldier.   Of the wiles of the politician, of the wonderful machinery of party organization, he was as ignorant as a child.   Of the vast re-

---

[119] Had Cass been elected, he would be, thus far, our only millionaire President.   It is a significant fact, in this age of colossal fortunes, that we have never had a very rich President.

sponsibility of the presidency he knew almost nothing. But withal he was a rugged, powerful, honest personality. He loved his country above all things, and his motives were without a flaw. The son of a patriot who had fought in the Revolution, he was born in Virginia the year after General Clinton had evacuated New York. At an early age he entered the army and saw service through the War of 1812, and the Black Hawk and Seminole wars. Humbly he served his country for forty years, wholly unknown to fame until his sudden bound into prominence in the war with Mexico.

Scarcely was Taylor installed in the great office when the whole country turned to him for a solution of the momentous issue on which neither party had dared give expression in the campaign of the preceding year—that involved in the Wilmot Proviso. California was now knocking for admission into the Union—as a free state. As stated above, the discovery of gold had aided in settling the slavery question for the Southwest. The men who went to the mines were not slaveholders, though many were from the South. The slave owner must remain with his plantation and his family. The men who flocked to the coast were, for the most part, laborers, nor could they endure the thought of inviting the black bondsmen into their midst to become their comrades in the field of toil. When, therefore, the Californians, in the autumn of 1849, framed a state constitution, they excluded slavery from the soil by a unanimous vote. At this the South was deeply stirred. The war had been pressed to a finish by a southern President and by a Congress dominated by the South; the chief object had been to extend slave territory; and now to have the fairest portion of the newly acquired land snatched forever from their grasp was more than the slaveholders could bear. They turned with hopeful eyes to the new President. What would he do? He was a southern man, and he owned a large plantation and several hundred slaves in Louisiana. On this the hopes of the South were based, though Taylor had said that he would not be a sectional nor a partisan President. At length all doubts were set at rest when the President proved that his patriotism towered above his sectional or partisan feeling by recommending that California be admitted as a free state.

The slave power now became enraged; it demanded that California be divided in the middle and that the southern half be made a slave state, or that the Missouri Compromise line be extended beyond its original limits, the Louisiana Purchase, to the Pacific Ocean. Threats of destroying the Union began to spread through the South. Alexander H. Stephens wrote in December, 1849, that the feeling among the southern members for a dissolution of the Union was becoming far more general. Robert Toombs declared in the House that he did not hesitate "to avow before this House and the country, and in the presence of the living God, that if by your legislation you seek to drive us from the territories of California and New Mexico . . . I am for disunion." Calhoun, the greatest of southern leaders, had made artful efforts to unite all slaveholders in Congress to demand concessions from the North and to foster the spirit of disunion, if their demand was refused. Such was the condition of the country—California knocking for admission as a free state, the South demanding that it be divided in the middle, the North in equal turmoil, many of the people ready to yield to southern demands for the sake of peace, but a greater number declaring frantically that slavery should encroach no farther on free soil—such was the condition at the opening of that memorable year in American history—

From the time of the launching of the government under the new Constitution to the Civil War the darkest year of all was 1850. There could be no doubt that the threat of wholesale secession was serious. A convention of leading southern statesmen met at Nashville in June, 1850, and solemnly declared that a state had the abstract right to secede from the Union. Not one lone state, as in 1832, but most of the slave states seemed to contemplate taking the fatal step.[120] Had secession now been accomplished, our glorious Union would probably have perished. Jackson was in his grave and Lincoln was unknown; nor was there any great political party, as ten years later, pledged to the maintenance of its integrity.

While the country was in this state of unrest the Thirty-first Congress met. The House chose Howell Cobb of Georgia speaker, after a wrangle of three weeks. The Senate was the ablest that ever sat in Washington. Here for the last time was the great triumvirate,—Clay, Webster, and Calhoun,—all of whom had figured in every great governmental movement for forty years. Here, too, were Benton, serving his thirtieth year in the Senate, the stentorian Hale of New Hampshire, Stephen A. Douglas from Illinois, and Jefferson Davis of Mississippi; Seward of the Empire State, and the powerful pair from Ohio, Salmon P. Chase and Thomas Corwin. Early in the session Clay assumed the leadership, as always, and he brought forward a series of compromise measures which he hoped would restore harmony between the warring sections. These are

[120] Benton took the ground, however, and with some show of reason, that the bluster would subside, and that there was no serious danger to the Union.

known as the Compromise Measures of 1850, or the Omnibus Bill. In this famous bill were eight items, the most important being the first, which called for the admission of California as a free state; the sixth, which prohibited the slave trade in the District of Columbia; and the seventh, which called for a new fugitive-slave law. These measures absorbed the attention of Congress for more than eight months. The bill was eventually torn to pieces and passed in sections. Clay was the champion and leader throughout. He had passed his seventy-second year, and his health was broken; but the fire of his eloquence still glowed with the luster of former days. Clay was the most national, the broadest in his sympathies, of all men in Congress at this time. A resident of a border state and the owner of slaves, he was as truly a northern as a southern man. When Jefferson Davis declared in the Senate that the Missouri line must be extended to the Pacific, Clay's instant retort was that he could never agree to it, that the Southwest was free territory and must remain so, that we justly reproached our British ancestors for introducing slavery on this continent, and he was unwilling that the future inhabitants of California and New Mexico should reproach us for the same offense. Clay announced that on a certain day in February he would speak on his bill, and thousands of people, many from distant cities, came to hear this last great speech of this most magnetic of American orators.

In March three speeches of much historic importance were delivered in the Senate, by Calhoun, Webster, and Seward. Calhoun was slowly dying; but his unconquerable will fought down disease until he had prepared an elaborate speech on the compromise measures. Supported by two friends, he tottered into the senate chamber; but he was unable to read his speech, and this was done by another. The utmost attention was paid to this final word from the greatest of the living sons of the South. In front of the reader sat, with half-closed eyes, in rigid silence, the ghost-like form of the author. Calhoun was an honest man, and in this speech he gave expression to the honest convictions of his soul. He showed how the North, in his belief, had encroached on the rights of the South until the Union was in danger,—how the great Protestant churches had separated into northern and southern branches,—how one cord after another that bound the two sections of the country together had snapped, and soon there would be none remaining. He appealed to the North to consent to amend the Constitution so as to give the South the power to protect herself.[131] Thus ended the public career of the great South Carolinian. He died on the last day of March.

It is not true that Calhoun sought a dissolution of the Union. He probably loved his state and section more than the Union; and, believing that slavery was necessary to the welfare of his section, he espoused the cause of slavery. But as well say that Chatham, in defending the rights of the colonies, ceased to be a loyal Englishman, as that Calhoun no longer loved his country. And nothing in his life showed more conclusively that he still loved the flag than did this last great speech of his life, in which he pleads from the depths of his honest soul for the removal of the evils that in his judgment menaced the perpetuity of the Union.

[131] It was not then known to what Calhoun referred in this suggestion; but his posthumous papers explained that he would have the Constitution amended so as to elect two Presidents, one from the slave states, and one from the free states, each to have a veto on all national legislation.

Many and able were the other champions of the slave power during the generation preceding the Civil War; but Calhoun towers above them all. His prophetic vision exceeded that of any of his contemporaries. He saw the gathering storm, the implacable strife between the slave states and the free, long before it assumed threatening proportions. He saw, too, that the little, despised Abolition societies of the North would, by their unceasing cry against slavery, eventually mold the conscience of millions, and he called for their suppression by legislation. Calhoun was right in believing that if the moral consciousness of the nation opposed slavery, slavery must fall. But he made mistakes. He was wrong in believing that human legislation can govern the conscience of the people; wrong in predicting that the Union could not survive a bloody war; and strangest of all, he and all his brethren were wrong in their belief that social conditions in the South would be unendurable if the black man were given his freedom.

The next great speech of the month was made by Daniel Webster, but three days after that of Calhoun, and it is known as his "Seventh of March Speech." A voice from this great son of New England had been eagerly awaited. Since his reply to Hayne in 1830 Webster had easily held the palm as the greatest orator in America. As an intellectual giant Webster surpassed all men of his generation. As he stood before an audience the sweep of his eloquence, like a rushing river, bore everything before it. His mind grasped underlying principles, and these he made so clear that the unlearned man could readily comprehend them. Webster has often been compared to Edmund Burke; and the speeches of both have the rare distinction of holding a permanent place in the literature of their common language.

Twenty years had now passed since the mighty voice of Webster had spoken for nationality in tones that stirred the world. Old age was now creeping upon his frame and his powers were beginning to wane; but he roused himself like a Hercules for this one powerful final effort. The country was in deep agitation. The North had shown even greater inclination to rebel against the proposed Fugitive Slave Law than the South had done against free California. But all waited eagerly to hear from Webster, the greatest representative of the North. There was a feeling of uncertainty among his friends and not without reason. At various times Webster had shown his independence of party or sectional adherence. He had acted with the Democratic President in 1833; he had sided with the South in the Creole affair of 1841; and above all he had abandoned his party while a member of the Tyler Cabinet. But these episodes had only temporarily broken the magic spell in which he held the northern heart. It was left for this Seventh of March Speech to shatter the idol that the people had worshiped so long. The speech he made on this day was one of the greatest of his life. His constitutional discussion of the slavery question was learned and profound, and for the most part pleasing to his constituents. But his views on the Wilmot Proviso and the Fugitive Slave Law caused great offense. It was needless, he claimed, it was a "taunt and reproach" to the slaveholders to exclude slavery by law from California and New Mexico, as the laws of nature had already done this. "I would not take pains, uselessly to reaffirm an ordinance of nature, nor to reënact the will of God." He also declared that the North had lacked in its duty to the South in the matter of runaway slaves, that the South had just grounds of complaint; and he went out of his way to denounce the Abolition societies of his own section.

This oration of Webster created consternation throughout the North and brought the severest denunciations upon the head of its author. He was condemned on every side as a traitor to the cause of liberty. Giddings declared that the speech had struck a blow at freedom such as no southern arm could have given. Horace Mann said that Webster had played false to the North, that he was a fallen star, a Lucifer descending from heaven. Whittier, in the little poem "Ichabod," mourned the fall of one in whom honor and faith were dead. At a great meeting in Faneuil Hall Theodore Parker compared the action of Webster to that of Benedict Arnold, and declared that Webster was only seeking southern support for the presidency. In the course of a few months, this wave of indignation spent itself to some extent; but never again did Webster regain the popularity that he lost on this fatal day. It is difficult for us to understand at this day how Webster's apparently moderate statements could have raised such a storm, but it must be remembered that the country was greatly excited over this all-absorbing slavery question.

On the 11th of March Seward delivered in the Senate the third of the great speeches of the month. Seward had been twice governor of New York; his fame was national, and he was looked on as one of the leaders in political thought. His effort on this day fell far below that of Webster in rhetorical finish, but it made a profound impression upon the country; and from that moment Seward became the leader of northern thought on the great subject that disturbed the harmony between the two sections. This leadership continued to the opening of the Civil War, when a greater than Seward laid his hand upon the helm.

In this discourse of March 11 Seward took strong ground against the pending Fugitive Slave Law, declaring that public sentiment at the North would not support it, and that no government could change the moral convictions of the people by force. He also stated that there was a "higher law than the Constitution," and this maxim became the ground on which the people of the North resisted the law, afterwards enacted, for the capture of fugitive slaves. He further advanced the opinion that the fall of slavery in the United States was inevitable, evidently by peaceful means, as he disclaimed all belief in secession or disunion. By this speech Seward assumed the leadership that would have remained with Webster had the latter not taken a position at variance with the prevailing sentiment at the North.

The debates on these great measures continued for many months, sometimes reaching a state of extreme acrimony. In April Senator Benton almost came to blows with Senator Foote of Mississippi. Benton came from a slave state, but his views for the most part coincided with those of the North, and the southern members considered him a rene- gade and lost no opportunity to taunt him. Foote was making some caustic and insulting remarks about Benton, when the latter rose from his seat and advanced toward the speaker in a hostile attitude; whereupon Foote drew a loaded revolver. At this Benton became greatly excited and cried to his friends, who were attempting to restrain him: "I am not armed; I disdain to carry arms. Stand aside and let the assassin fire." A committee of investiga- tion afterward reported that no similar scene had ever be-

1800 — MILLARD FILLMORE — 1874.

From an enlargement of an original Brady negative in the possession of Frederick H. Meserve,
New York.

fore been witnessed in the Senate. But the matter was dropped and nothing further was done.

The measures under discussion were at length referred to a grand Senate committee of thirteen, with Clay as its chairman. This committee soon made its report, which differed little from Clay's compromise measures offered in January. President Taylor openly opposed the measures as a whole, and especially the Fugitive Slave Law and the offer to pay Texas a large sum of money for her claims on New Mexico. His sympathies were evidently with the northern Whigs. But his course was run. The hero of many battles at last met a foe that he could not conquer.

On the 4th of July the President attended a mass meeting at the laying of the corner stone of the Washington Monument, and he sat for several hours in the broiling sun. Partially overcome by heat, he returned to the White House, drank large draughts of iced milk and ate iced fruits. That evening he was taken ill with cholera morbus. In a few days it merged into typhoid fever, and on the 9th of July Zachary Taylor was dead. Sadly the funeral procession moved through the streets of the capital city, and not the least impressive feature was "Old Whitey," the faithful steed that General Taylor had ridden through the Mexican War, now led behind the casket, bearing an empty saddle. Thus for the second time the unfortunate Whig party had lost its President by death. The ultra-southerners received the news of the President's death with complacency; in the North the mourning was sincere and widespread. Strange too, for the dead President was a southern man and the incoming President a northern man. But the former was broad and national in his views; the latter was "a northern man with southern principles."

Millard Filmore, born in the wilderness of northern New York in 1800, was a self-made man in the fullest sense of the term. He picked up a meager education as best he could, became a leading lawyer of Buffalo and a member of his state legislature, and served for several years in the Lower House of Congress. As a member of the House he was noted for his conservatism and for painstaking industry. For several years he labored shoulder to shoulder with John Quincy Adams for the right of petition, and it was not until the higher honors of the presidency came to him that he became known as "a northern man with southern principles." Even then he was not a radical, and his favoring the compromise measures, contrary to the Whig sentiment of his own section, was doubtless based on an honest desire to do the best in his power for his country. The President tendered the position of secretary of state to Webster, who accepted it; and this fact, since it was known that Webster favored the compromise, and the further fact that four of the six other members of the Cabinet were from the South, revealed to the country that the new President held different views on the great questions of the day from those held by his predecessor. The advice of Seward, who had been the chief counselor of President Taylor, was now no longer sought. Seward men were removed from office and their places were filled with conservative Whigs, and it was plain that the administration intended to use its patronage wherever possible to unify the party on the compromise.

The great debates went on, and soon the fruit of the long toil began to appear. Before the end of August the Senate had passed the bill settling the boundary of Texas and giving that state $10,000,000 for the relinquishment of her claims on New Mexico,[122] also the bill admitting California, another organizing New Mexico as a territory without the Wilmot Proviso,[123] and, most important of all, the Fugitive Slave Law. The bill abolishing the slave trade in the District of Columbia passed the Senate in September. All these measures passed the House in September with little debate, and all were signed by the President.

From the foundation of the government there had seldom been a measure enacted into law of more far-reaching consequence than were some of the enactments of this Compromise of 1850. The measures were non-partisan; they were sectional. The Democrats and Whigs of the North joined in opposing the Fugitive Slave Act, while both parties at the South joined in opposing free California and the abolition of the slave trade in the District of Columbia. For some years the two great parties had grown nearer together, and now the chief cause of rivalry was based on a desire for supremacy.[124] The great questions of the times were sectional and not partisan, and the fact that the two great parties now stood on common ground and no longer represented opposing schools of thought explains in great part the dissolution of the one in the near future, for in the world of politics the coexistence of two of a kind is impossible. But this must be noticed later.

The compromise measures were on the whole favorable to the North rather than to the South.[125] Two items in this

[122] This act brought forth grave accusations of jobbery. Texas scrip, which had fallen to one sixth of its face value, now rose to par, and it was believed that many speculators in this scrip made fortunes by this act of Congress.

[123] A similar act concerning Utah had passed on the last day of July.

[124] Von Holst, Vol. III, p. 102.

[125] If we include the admission of California as part of the com-

famous mid-century legislation were of momentous interest to the nation. One, the admission of California as a free state, was deeply offensive to the South, but there it stood on the statutes, a permanent fact that could never be undone. The other, the Fugitive Slave Law, was equally offensive to the North; but it was not an abiding fact; it was a temporary measure, and its enforcement depended largely upon its individual reception by the people of the North. Moreover, it worked irretrievable injury to the slave power by awakening an antislavery sentiment in the North as nothing else could have done. The vicious law for the rendition of runaway slaves had been forced upon the North for other reasons than the desire to recover lost property.[136] It was not the border states, but the cotton states of the far South, from which few of their bondsmen escaped, that were most instrumental in placing this law upon the statutes. Their motive was to humble the North for having forced upon them the bitter medicine of free California. Neither section was pleased with the compromise. The great mass of conservatives was desirous that the agitation be stopped, but the radicals of both sections were again ready to throw down the gage of battle.[137] In Mississippi and South Carolina many of the leaders threatened secession. The Southern Rights Association held a convention at Charleston in May, 1851, and declared that South Carolina could no longer submit to the wrongs and aggressions of the federal government. But in an election to a secession Congress the following autumn the secession party was defeated. In

promise; but more strictly speaking it was not, as this item had previously been decided by the people of California.

[136] See Rhodes, "History of the United States from the Compromise of 1850," Vol. I, p. 187.

[137] Seward's Works," Vol. III, p. 446.

Mississippi a similar result was reached when Foote, who represented the Union sentiment, was elected governor over Jefferson Davis, who represented the radical party. In the North we find great discontent in the ultra-antislavery districts.[118]   Massachusetts rebuked Webster by placing Charles Sumner in his seat in the Senate, elected by Democrats and Free-soilers wholly on account of his antislavery position.   On the same ground Ohio sent the rugged, heroic Benjamin Wade to the Senate.   In Congress the southern radicals gave notice that all was not settled, that they must have Cuba and more territory from Mexico when needed, while the northern radicals, led by Seward, Sumner, and Giddings, declared that the Fugitive Slave Act could not be enforced.   Meantime the great body of conservatives fondly hoped that the compromise would be accepted as a finality and that the hated slavery question would trouble them no more for many years to come.   At length the southern leaders, with rare exceptions, came to this view: they agreed to accept the compromise as a finality, on the one condition that the North would honestly enforce the Fugitive Slave Law. The northern politicians would doubtless have agreed to this; but the enforcement of that law rested with the conscience of the people, not with the politicians, and it remains for us to notice

THE FUGITIVE SLAVE LAW IN OPERATION

It has been said, and truly said, that Millard Fillmore, when he signed the Fugitive Slave Law on September 18, 1850, signed his own death warrant as a national statesman.   By this little act he covered his name with dishonor, and no subsequent show of patriotism could redeem it; by

[118] *New York Tribune,* May 13, 1851.

this he offended the great section of the country to which he belonged, and for this he is remembered in American history.   Yet it is difficult to see how Fillmore could have done otherwise than he did, as the South had been so deeply offended over free California that a rejection of the Fugitive Slave Law would probably have brought immediate secession.

The Fugitive Slave Law was a vicious and inhuman measure, to say the least.   When captured by the pretended owner or his agent, the alleged runaway was carried before a magistrate or commissioner who should hear and determine the case.   The law was so framed as to work against the prisoner at every point.   The oath of the owner or agent (and the agents were often coarse, brutal men whose better instincts were smothered by years of slave driving) was usually sufficient to decide the matter.   The black man could not testify in his own behalf.   The benefit of a jury was denied him.   Even the commissioner was bribed by the law, for if he awarded the captive to his captor, he received ten dollars as his fee; if he set him free, he received but five.   The worst feature of the law was that it compelled any bystander to assist in making a capture, if summoned to do so by the slave catcher.   This was revolting to the average citizen of the free states, for the impulse was to aid the fleeing man in making his escape rather than to aid his pursuer.

Could such a law be enforced?   Thousands of people throughout the North believed that a man held in bondage for no crime—simply on account of the accident of his birth and the color of his skin—had a right to escape if he could. Conscience demanded that they aid him in his flight; the law demanded that they aid his pursuer; and many decided to obey the "higher law" of conscience rather than this law of their land. It is easy to see with what difficulty a law could be enforced when opposed by the moral consciousness of the people in the midst of whom it is expected to operate. From thousands of pulpits, from a large portion of the northern press, and from mass meetings held for the purpose, the Fugitive Slave Act was denounced as an unjust and wicked measure.[129] This feeling of the people was reflected in the state legislatures. Michigan, Wisconsin, and all the New England states passed personal liberty laws, for the protection of free blacks; and most of them made laws to regulate the business of the slave catcher, such as denying him the use of the jails and other public buildings, while a few states demanded a jury trial for the alleged fugitive.[130] These items show the general reception of the Fugitive Slave Law at the North, but this may be shown still more vividly by citing a few examples of its practical operation.

There were probably twenty thousand negroes in the free states who had at some past time escaped from slavery. Many of these were quiet, industrious people, earning an honest living for their families; all were liable to be dragged back to slavery by this law.[131] Scarcely had the law gone into effect, when many parts of the North were

[129] Wilson's "Rise and Fall of the Slave Power," Vol. II, p. 305. The conservatives also held meetings in the large cities of the North, and demanded that the compromise be accepted in good faith and that the Fugitive Slave Law be enforced.

[130] Vermont, Michigan, and Massachusetts demanded a jury trial. This was a practical nullification of the national law. Most of these laws were enacted after the passage of the Kansas-Nebraska Law in 1854.

[131] The law was retroactive, and it was denounced as unconstitutional by its enemies, who claimed that it was *ex post facto*.

overrun by man hunters. Many of the fugitives residing in the free states now hurried off to Canada, where the laws of England made them free; others remained in the hope of escaping detection. Sometimes the fugitive was caught and taken back to his former master; sometimes he was killed in the chase; but usually he made good his escape, owing to the aid and sympathy he received from the people of the North.

One of the first instances to attract attention was that of William Smith of Columbia, Pennsylvania. Many years before this law was passed Smith had escaped from slavery, had settled in this quiet town on the Susquehanna, and was now an industrious laborer, supporting a wife and family. He knew that he might be taken back to slavery at any moment under this law of 1850, but he hoped to remain undiscovered. One day while working on the streets he saw some slave hunters approaching him. He threw down his tools and started to run, but he was shot dead by his pursuers. Another instance in this same county (Lancaster, Pennsylvania) attracted far wider attention, and turned out very differently. Near the village of Christiana lived a colored man named William Parker, himself a fugitive, and his house became a place of refuge for other fleeing negroes. It was learned that he was harboring two men of his race who had escaped from their master, a Baltimore physician named Gorsuch. In September, 1851, Gorsuch, with a party of armed men, including his son, entered the town and demanded his property. The party surrounded the Parker house; the colored people of the neighborhood were summoned by the sound of a horn, and in the fusillade that ensued Gorsuch was killed, and his son severely wounded. This affair attracted the attention of the country. President Fillmore sent a body of marines from Philadelphia to the scene of the riot. Thirty-five persons were arrested,[188] but no jury could be found to convict them, and all were released. The two fugitives were never captured.

Another incident, known as the "Jerry rescue," that took place at Syracuse, New York, attracted much attention. Jerry McHenry, an industrious mechanic, who had worked at his trade for some years at Syracuse, was claimed under the Fugitive Slave Law, by a man from Missouri. Jerry was found and captured by the slave hunters. He was imprisoned to await trial the next day. Before morning a large party of men, led by Gerrit Smith, a wealthy member of Congress, and the Rev. Samuel May, went to the prison, battered down the door, rescued the prisoner, and, after concealing him for a few days, sent him off to Canada. The leaders of this rescue openly proclaimed their part in it, but none of them was punished.

Many of the runaway negroes did not go to Canada, but settled in the Northern states, as far as convenient from Mason and Dixon's line. At Young's Prairie, in Cass County, Michigan, a considerable colony had located, and here they lived in contentment in the little houses they had built. But the location was discovered by their various masters, and a party of thirty armed men rode from Kentucky to capture the fugitives at Young's Prairie. The party separated, and made several simultaneous attacks on the negro village at dead of night. Awakened suddenly from sleep, the blacks fought bravely for their liberty, but in a short time most of them were overpowered, fettered, and thrown into large wagons brought for the purpose. But one woman, while her husband was fighting in the only

[188] Siebert's "Underground Railroad," p. 280.

door of their cabin, escaped through a back window and gave the alarm to some white neighbors. In a few minutes a white man was galloping about the country on a fleet horse, giving a general alarm. By daylight the whole neighborhood was aroused, and a band of two hundred men, led by Bill Jones, a brawny-armed blacksmith, were dashing to the rescue of the blacks. They fell upon the Kentuckians, arrested them for kidnapping, and lodged them in the county jail to await trial. At the trial they were acquitted; but they returned to their homes empty-handed, after all their trouble and expense, for while the trial was pending, the colored colony was transferred to Canadian soil.[122]

Usually the slave hunter failed to secure his runaway; and, even when he succeeded, the expense was often so great as to render the undertaking unprofitable. The most famous case that came under this law was that of Anthony Burns, a colored waiter in a Boston hotel. He had escaped from his Virginia master, and he was now arrested as a fugitive. When the people of the city heard of the arrest, they were soon wrought up to a wild state of excitement. A great meeting held at Faneuil Hall was addressed by Wendell Phillips and Theodore Parker, and late at night it practically resolved itself into a mob and proceeded to the courthouse where Burns was confined, to attempt his rescue. Here was found another band of infuriated men, led by Thomas Wentworth Higginson, battering at the doors. The mob was driven back by troops called out by the mayor, one man was killed, several were arrested, and Burns was not rescued. A few days later he was remanded to slavery. The people made no further attempt to effect his rescue; but fifty thousand of them lined the streets hissing and jeering

[122] Coffin's "Reminiscences," p. 366.

as the negro was led to the revenue cutter in the harbor, guarded by the police force of the city and several thousand soldiers armed with muskets and artillery. The South had won its victory, but it was an expensive one, for public feeling against the Fugitive Slave Law was roused throughout the North as never before, and the *Richmond Enquirer* was led to say, "A few more such victories and the South is undone."[134]

Scarcely less than the excitement over Burns was that over the "Glover rescue" in Wisconsin in the spring of the same year. Joshua Glover was a black man who lived near Racine, Wisconsin. He was claimed by a man from St. Louis, and was captured, knocked down, bound, carried in a wagon to Milwaukee, and lodged in jail. The people of Racine soon heard of the proceedings, and held a mass meeting which declared the Fugitive Slave Law "disgraceful and repealed." About a hundred men then proceeded to Milwaukee and on arriving found the city in a wild tumult. The excitement gained in volume, and the authorities called on the militia to quell the riot, but the militia refused to respond. At length the crowd became dangerous, and when it surged upon the jail and demanded the prisoner, there was nothing to do but to give him up. Glover was soon landed in Canada, and the people returned quietly to their homes. Nearly every newspaper in the state applauded the Glover rescue, and the leaders of the riot, afterward arrested, were acquitted by a decision of the su-

[134] Siebert's "Underground Railroad," p. 331; Wilson's "Rise and Fall of the Slave Power," Vol. II, pp. 435-441. Burns was afterward purchased by friends at the North and sent to Oberlin College, in Ohio, but he died a few years later. The judge who awarded him to his captors was removed from the bench through a petition of the people.

preme court of the state on the ground that the Fugitive Slave Law was unconstitutional. The examples above mentioned are but a few of the most conspicuous out of hundreds. A half-witted person could have seen that the Fugitive Slave Law could not be enforced in most sections of the North; and any slaveholder could have seen, and most of them did see, that the law was doing irreparable harm to the institution of slavery by unifying the North against it.

THE UNDERGROUND RAILROAD

For more than half a century before the Civil War there was an ever increasing stream of slaves fleeing from their masters into the free states. In the years immediately preceding the war the number was estimated at about a thousand a year. It is true that many of the slaves were so well treated by their owners, or so grossly ignorant, that they had little or no desire to escape. But there were others, and their name was legion, in whose bosom burned a longing for liberty, so natural to the human heart. Especially was this true of those who had picked up the rudiments of an education. Many in the far South knew only that freedom lay in the direction of the North Star, that the distance was great, and that the way was fraught with unknown perils. The fugitives usually traveled by night and secreted themselves in the mountains or thickets during the day. Most of them came from the border states, and they comprised the most intelligent of their race. Some fled because of cruel treatment, but with the great majority it was the fear of the dreaded auction block that drove them to seek the land of liberty. However kind the master might be, however reluctant to part with his servants, his death or business reverses might at any time send them to the great cotton plantations or to the rice swamps of the far South, the most dreadful calamity that could come to a border-state slave. When once a slave was carried by a trader to the southern market, it was seldom that he was again seen or heard of by his friends and kindred.

The fleeing black man was often recaptured before reaching the free states, after which his condition was made worse than before. But thousands succeeded in crossing the border line and in breathing the air of freedom. But even then, after the Compromise of 1850, their chances of evading capture would have been very meager but for the aid rendered them by persons living along their route. There were hundreds of people in the free states, some colored, but most of them white, who were systematically engaged in giving aid, comfort, and advice to the fleeing slave. These lawbreakers were for the most part respectable and, in other respects, law-abiding citizens. They acted on principle: they believed in a higher law than any framed by human legislators; they believed that a man held in bondage by no fault of his own had a right to his freedom, if he desired it, and they felt it a duty to aid him in gaining it, if in their power. But, in addition to the pleasure of relieving the sufferings of the fleeing slave, there was in the business of aiding the runaway "the excitement of piracy, the secrecy of burglary, the daring of insurrection." [135] The work was carried on with the utmost secrecy and in the most systematic manner. The system was known as the Underground Railroad.

It consisted of many different routes across the free states. The "stations," twenty miles or more apart, were usually private homes in the garrets or cellars of which, or

[135] Hart's Introduction to Siebert's "Underground Railroad."

in nearby caves or haymows, the fugitives were kept and fed during the day, and from which they were sent on their way at nightfall. Many of those who engaged in the work did so at their own peril and often at great self-sacrifice, for the law was persistently against them. Mr. Rush Sloane of Sandusky, Ohio, paid $3000 in fines for assisting runaways to Canada; Thomas Garrett of Wilmington, Delaware, assisted twenty-seven hundred fugitives and paid $8000 in fines for violating the slave laws. Calvin Fairbank spent seventeen years in the penitentiary for similar offenses.[186]

One of the most active workers in connection with the Underground Railroad, and the reputed president of the system was Levi Coffin, a prosperous merchant who managed the station at Newport, Indiana, for twenty years. During this period he and his faithful wife, who were Quakers, harbored at least one hundred fugitives each year. The story in "Uncle Tom's Cabin" of the slave woman crossing the Ohio River on the floating ice with her child was a true story, and after this woman reached the home of the Coffins, Mrs. Coffin gave her the name "Eliza Harris," and Mrs. Stowe used this name in her novel.[187] The largest number ever harbored by Levi Coffin in one night was seventeen. For this he was arraigned before the grand jury. He was known to be a man of great probity, and nothing could lead him to speak falsely. When arraigned and asked under oath if he had harbored fugitive slaves, he answered that he had no legal knowledge that he had done so; he admitted having received and ministered unto certain persons who had come to his house destitute

[186] Siebert's "Underground Railroad," pp. 110, 159, 254, 277.
[187] Coffin's "Reminiscences," p. 113.

and homeless.   He had done this in obedience to the injunctions of the Bible.   These persons, it is true, had said they were fugitive slaves; but he had nothing but their word for it, and as the testimony of a slave could not be received in court there was no proof of his guilt.[138]   Mr. Coffin was released.

One of the most active of the underground workers was William Still, a free colored man of Philadelphia, who served for many years as chairman of the Vigilance Committee of that city, and who after the war published a large volume giving the experiences of the fugitives as related by themselves.   No career in the underground work was more picturesque and romantic than that of Harriet Tubman, herself a fugitive from Maryland.   She was almost white, was very religious and intelligent, and she earned the name of "The Moses of her People."   With Philadelphia as her headquarters she would collect money from sympathizers and make a journey to slave land.   After collecting a company of her people, she piloted them across the border and sometimes accompanied them to Canada.   She would quiet babies with drugs and have them carried in baskets. She is said to have made nineteen excursions into the slave states and to have abducted three hundred slaves without detection.[139]   Josiah Henson, also a fugitive, founded a colony and a school in Canada, and made various journeys to the South, abducting in all 118 slaves.[140]

[138] Coffin, p. 192.

[139] This woman was employed as a scout and spy in the Civil War. She is still living (1903) near Auburn, New York.

[140] It has been estimated that as many as sixty thousand or even seventy thousand colored people, a large majority of whom were fugitives, resided in Canada in 1860.   Many of them purchased small farms and built houses; others hired out as farm laborers, lumbermen,

One of the most powerful agencies in shaping the political conscience at the North during the decade preceding the war was "Uncle Tom's Cabin," by Harriet Beecher Stowe. This novel cannot be named among the greatest works of genius. The narrative shows much bias in the writer, and she is often unfair to the South; but as a series of pictures of slave life, colored with a profound human sympathy, the book attracted and held the attention of readers of every class. It sprung into immediate popularity; three hundred thousand copies were sold within the first year after publication; the sale soon exceeded a million; the book spread over England and her colonies, and was translated into twenty languages. The political effect of this novel did not appear at first, but it eventually became an important agent in the world of politics.[141]   The story appealed particularly to the young, and thousands of the boys who in the fifties laughed at Topsy, loved little Eva, wept over the fate of Uncle Tom, and became enraged at the brutal Legree, were voters in 1860; and their votes, as determined by that book, which led them to believe that slavery was wrong, became a powerful element in effecting the political revolution of that year.

SLAVE LIFE IN THE SOUTH

A hundred years ago the universal verdict of the American people was that slavery was an evil. Such leaders as Washington and Jefferson, themselves slaveholders, deplored the existence of the institution as long as they lived. In later years, when slavery became the chief political

etc. Family life soon became far more regular than in slavery, and the moral condition was greatly improved.

[141] Rhodes, Vol. I, p. 284.

issue, almost the entire South, following the lead of Calhoun, pronounced slavery in the United States a positive good. This change was partially due to conviction; but undoubtedly it arose in part from the fact that the slaveholder grew weary of defending what he confessed to be an evil, and, in answer to the cry of the Abolitionist, he veered around, took the offensive, and pronounced slavery a good thing. The question was also, as we have seen, an economic one. If slavery was an economic good, as the people of the South believed, it must also be a moral good; and if both, it ought to be defended and extended. In these latter days, since the institution is a thing of the past, the universal verdict is that which antedated the career of Calhoun—that slavery was an evil, an unmitigated evil.[142]

Nevertheless there were pleasant features in connection with slavery, especially in the border states, where it existed in a mild form. Many a slave was better kept by a humane master than he could have kept himself had he been free. In many a home the attachment between the owner and his slave was a sincere one; the slave was educated and taught religion, and was practically a member of the family. Many of this class had little desire for freedom. But the great majority of slaves were not of this class. Except the house servants, coachmen, and the like, the slaves of the cotton states were toilers in the field. They spent their lives in unrequited toil; and to one who had a spark of the consciousness of manhood or womanhood, what a dreary, cheerless, hopeless life it must have been!

[142] That slavery was a great drawback to the South, from an economic standpoint, is shown very forcibly, with many statistics, in the first chapter of Helper's "Impending Crisis." This book, written by a southerner and published in 1857, was an unanswerable arraignment of slavery.

On the great plantations the negroes lived in filth and wretchedness in villages of huts. Their clothing was made of "negro cloth," the cheapest and coarsest material that could be had; their food was almost exclusively corn meal, which they prepared in addition to the day's toil, often exceeding fifteen hours, in the field. Meat was occasionally allowed to those engaged in the most exhausting labor. And yet, where the conditions were at all favorable, the slave was a happy creature. This was due to the inherent quality of the race, and to the fact that he had no care of his own, no anxiety for the morrow. The chief punishment of the negro was flogging, and this was often administered with great severity, not only for insubordination, but for failure to perform the allotted task of labor. If a slave turned against his master, or attempted to escape, he was shot, or he received other punishment that often resulted in his death. There was no law against killing a slave for such provocation; but the willful murder of a negro was a crime in all the Southern states. If, however, a negro was killed by a white man, it often happened that there were no witnesses, or none but slaves, whose testimony was not good in law, and for this reason punishment seldom followed.

The slave lived in gross ignorance. Nearly all the cotton states forbade the teaching of slaves to read or write. In Virginia the owner alone was permitted to do this; in North Carolina the slaves might be taught arithmetic.[143] The Episcopal bishop of Louisiana, Leonidas Polk, who afterward became prominent in the Civil War, owned four hundred slaves, and he had them carefully trained in religion. But he was a rare exception. Many of the large

[143] Rhodes, Vol. I, p. 327.

slaveholders cared little for the moral training of their servants. In morals the average slave was utterly wanting. The women were without a vestige of womanly chastity, and the men were almost universally dishonest. This may have been partly due to the natural tendencies of the race; but it was in a great measure due to the evils of the system. A woman who felt herself owned absolutely by a master could hardly be expected to take an interest in herself, or to cherish a feeling of womanhood. A man who did not and could not own property, not even himself or his children, could not have much idea of the rights of property.[144]

The most revolting feature of slavery in America, one that the historian blushes to record (but history must deal with facts), was that too often the attractive slave woman was a prostitute to her master, that her children bore the stamp of his countenance; and yet according to the inflexible rule of the slave states, they shared the condition of the mother, and were sold by their own father. This evil was widespread at the South, as the mixed condition of the black race to-day will testify. A sister of President Madison declared that though the southern ladies were complimented with the name of wife, they were only the mistresses of seraglios. A leading southern lady declared to Harriet Martineau that the wife of many a planter was but the chief slave of his harem. Some slave owners, however, could not bear the thought of selling their own children, and they often planned for their ultimate freedom. But the death of the master often caused his plans to miscarry.

[144] Some humane masters, however, permitted their slaves to spend their leisure hours in earning money for themselves. Coffin reports that one man and wife saved $300, which they used in escaping to Canada and setting up a home.

An extreme example from Coffin will vividly illustrate this point.[146]

A Virginian owned a beautiful octoroon who became the mother of a son in whose veins flowed the blood of the master. No one could detect a trace of African blood in the child. When still a child the father sent him into another state to be educated and taught a useful trade. He grew to manhood, married a white woman, had a family of five children, and was a highly respected citizen. Neither he nor his friends had the remotest knowledge that he had been born of a slave woman. Meanwhile his father died, and the heirs in settling the estate remembered the beautiful white child that had been sent away many years before. Knowing that he was now a valuable piece of property, they resolved to find him, and did so after a long search. They sold him to a trader without his own knowledge. He had spent many vigilant nights at the bedside of a sick wife, but one night, as she seemed better, he entrusted her with friendly neighbors and retired for a much-needed rest. That night the trader with a gang of ruffians burst into the house, seized their victim while sleeping, and bound him. He demanded the cause of the seizure and was informed, for the first time in his life, that he was a slave. His captors took him from the neighborhood, and to make him look less like a white man, they washed his face in tanooze and tied him in the sun, and seared his hair with a hot iron to make it curly. He was sold to the far South, but some months later he made his escape and returned to his former home. His wife had died of the shock when informed of his capture, and his children were scattered. Again the slave catchers were on his trail, with bloodhounds. He eluded the keen-

[146] "Reminiscences," p. 28 *sq.*

1783 — WASHINGTON IRVING — 1859.

1849.

From an enlargement by Brady, of a daguerreotype by John Plumb, in the War
Department, Washington, D.C.

scented animals by wading through a mill pond and spending a night in the branches of a tree. He now sought counsel, and determined to make a legal fight for his freedom; but his health was broken from exposure, and he died before the next term of court. Such was one phase of slavery in America.

Another feature of the institution that brought it general condemnation was the interstate slave trade, with the evils that grew out of it. This did not exist in colonial days, when the African trade was open; it belonged wholly to a later period. The great cotton belt of the South and the rice swamps were always in want of more slaves, while the border states had more than they needed; and hence was established the interstate slave trade. This brought on two evils that must be condemned by every unbiased observer: the separation of families and the breeding of slaves for the market. It is no doubt true that the negro, especially while in bondage, did not experience in the same degree those intense family ties which are characteristic of our own race. But that the black race was not devoid of these finer feelings was shown by many heartrending scenes at the auction block.[146] To sell a man and his wife and children to different masters, living hundreds of miles apart, when there was no hope of their meeting again, was legalized cruelty that finds few parallels in history.

From this brief glance at slave life as it existed before the war any one can see why the national conscience was disturbed, why the voice of the Abolitionist arose from the North and increased more and more, and why that voice

[146] John Randolph, once asked to name the most eloquent speech he ever heard, answered that it was made by a slave woman, and her rostrum was the auction block. She was pleading for her children.

could not be stifled until the system itself was swept away. But, withal, it was the misfortune rather than the crime of the South that this baneful system had taken such a relentless hold upon its life.   While the conditions at the North were unfavorable to slavery and the institution in that section slowly loosened its hold and disappeared, it was otherwise with the South.   Here its roots had struck deeply into the soil; its branches had spread like the arms of an octopus until they embraced everything southern in their fatal grasp. From far back in colonial times the monster had been tightening its coils from year to year and from generation to generation.   And now at last this blighting institution had become so interwoven with the political and social fabric of the South that the South no longer had power to deliver itself from the cruel bonds.   While the leaders of the slave power cannot be held guiltless at the bar of history, it is certain that the South as a whole was the victim of this curse of slavery, bequeathed to it by former generations.

NOTES AND ANECDOTES

The Clayton-Bulwer Treaty. — This subject has been relegated to a note, not because it is of minor importance, but because it did not exactly fit in our slavery discussion.   John M. Clayton was secretary of state under President Taylor.   He arranged with Henry Lytton Bulwer, the British minister at Washington, the famous treaty that bears the name of both.   The object of this treaty was to facilitate and protect the construction of a canal at Nicaragua between the Atlantic and Pacific oceans.   By this treaty both countries pledged themselves never to obtain exclusive control over said proposed canal, nor to erect fortifications commanding it, nor to colonize or exercise dominion over any portion of Central America.   They further agreed to protect any company that should undertake the work, and to facilitate its construction, and they guaranteed the neutrality of such canal when completed.   But few years passed after the consummation of the treaty before it became the object of serious discussion, the provisions being differently construed in the two countries.   At length the canal question subsided, and for many years it attracted little attention. Meantime the Pacific Coast of the United States became filled with people, the relative interests of the two countries were greatly changed, and it was evident that the terms of the treaty were disadvantageous to the United States. After many years' negotiation, the Clayton-Bulwer Treaty was abrogated by a new treaty (1902), known as the Hay-Pauncefote Treaty, by which the United States secures full power to construct and to operate the proposed canal.

Louis Kossuth. — In that great year for revolutions in Europe, 1848, Hungary made a brave effort to cast off the Austrian yoke, and might have succeeded but for the interference of Russia. Louis Kossuth, the governor of Hungary, and one of the most remarkable men of his time, took refuge in Turkey, on the failure of the Hungarians to win their freedom. From Turkey he was conveyed in a United States war vessel to New York in 1851, and was received with demonstrations accorded to no other foreigner that ever visited America, except Lafayette. His reception by the administration and by both houses of Congress was extremely cordial. He traveled through the country and spoke in many cities, having an excellent command of the English language, and being possessed of extraordinary powers of eloquence. But on the whole his visit was a failure. His object was to secure the intervention of the United States in behalf of his downtrodden country. But the government could not see its way clear to suspend its traditional attitude of neutrality in European affairs. Kossuth then sought private contributions for the cause of his people, but even in this he was not very successful. He returned to Europe in July, 1852.

Anecdotes of Clay. — No man ever in public life in America had greater power in winning personal friends than Henry Clay. When John Randolph, who had been Clay's political enemy for many years, and with whom he had fought a duel, visited Washington in the last year of his life, he called on Clay. Clay received him very kindly, and asked about his health. Randolph replied, "I'm dying, Clay, I'm dying." —"Why, then," asked Clay, "do you venture so far from home? Why did you come here?"—"To see you," answered Randolph; "to see you and have one more talk with you."

When Clay made his famous farewell address to the Senate in 1846, he brought tears to every eye. At the close of his speech, as he was passing out of the chamber, he came face to face with Calhoun. They had been enemies, and had not spoken for five years, but at heart each really loved the other. Now, at this meeting, all animosity was forgotten, and without a word they fell into each other's arms and wept

silently. On one occasion when Clay was making a tour through the
South, there was on the same train a farmer, an old-school Democrat,
who was invited to step into the next car and meet Clay. "No," he
answered, "I would not be seen shaking hands with Henry Clay, the
old Whig." He was informed that his idol, Van Buren, had often done
so. The farmer declared that he did not believe it, that Van Buren
would never do such a mean thing. He offered to make a bet that he
was right and agreed to let Clay himself decide the bet. They came
to Clay's seat and stated the case. "Yes," answered Clay, "Van Buren
is a good friend of mine, and he made me a visit at my home in Lexington. Setting aside his bad politics, he is an agreeable gentleman
and a right clever little fellow." The man paid his bet, and went away
muttering that if that is the way the great men acted they might fight
their own battles hereafter, he didn't believe they were in earnest any-
how, only pretended to be so as to set others by the ears. See Sargent's
"Public Men and Events," Vol. II, p. 221.

Clay was a man of ready wit, and he often astonished his friends
by his answers. The following is a sample: One day while at a
Philadelphia hotel, he was called on by John W. Forney, editor of the
Press, in company with Forrest, the actor. It was just after the great
debates in the Senate on the Omnibus Bill, and these debates soon became the topic of conversation, especially the opposition Clay had encountered from Senator Soulé of Louisiana. Whereupon Clay exclaimed, "Soulé is no orator, he is nothing but an actor, a mere actor."
No sooner had he said this than he realized the presence of Forrest,
the actor, and turning to him, added, "I mean, my dear sir, a French
actor, a mere French actor." Forney's "Anecdotes of Public Men."

Anecdote of Cass. — General Lewis Cass was, as stated in the
text, a dignified, urbane man, who could brook no familiarity from his
inferiors. The following incident, given by Forney, will illustrate the
point: One of the leading hotels in Washington at this period was
Guy's Hotel, and here many of the leading government officials, including General Cass, stayed while at the Capital. It happened that General
Cass and Mr. Guy, the hotel keeper, both large, corpulent men, looked
very much alike, and each was often mistaken for the other. One day
a western man came to the hotel and met General Cass on the porch
and, taking him for Guy, slapped him on the shoulder and began,
"Here I am again, old fellow; last time I hung up my hat in your
shanty, they put me up on the fourth floor. Want a better room this
time. How about it, old man?" Cass braced himself up with great
dignity and answered: "Sir, you've committed a blunder, I'm General

Cass of Michigan," turned about, and walked off. The man stood and looked after him, dazed at his mistake. Presently Cass walked around that way again and the man again took him for Guy and exclaimed: "Here you are at last; I've just made a divil of a blunder. I met old Cass and took him for you, and I'm afraid the old Michigander has gone off mad." Just then Guy appeared on the scene.

Items of Interest. — The coming of Jenny Lind, the "Swedish Nightingale," in 1851, served, like the visit of Kossuth, to divert public attention from the all-absorbing slavery question. Her tour of the United States, Canada, and Mexico, managed by Mr. P. T. Barnum, was a brilliant success, the receipts exceeding $600,000.

The reduction of postal rates in 1851 was an event of historic interest. There had been two reductions before this, and at this time the rate for a letter weighing a half ounce or less was five cents for three hundred miles or less; over three hundred miles, ten cents, and to the Pacific Coast by way of Panama, forty cents. The rate was now made three cents for three thousand miles or less, and six cents for more than that distance. This act continued in force until 1883, when two cents was made the letter rate.

In 1849, and again in 1851, Narcisco Lopez led a filibustering expedition to Cuba for the purpose of rescuing the island from Spanish control. The expedition was supposed to be in the interests of the slave states with the annexation of Cuba to the United States for its ultimate object. But the Cubans did not join Lopez as the latter expected. His company was routed by the Spanish soldiers in 1851, and he himself was taken captive and was garroted in the public square in Havana.

CHAPTER XXVI

LITERATURE BEFORE THE CIVIL WAR—NATIONAL ERA

A HISTORY of the United States which includes our colonial childhood must necessarily give a prominence to the early settlements out of all proportion to their magnitude, as compared to the great movements of the population in later centuries. The Puritan migration of 2,000 a year for ten years was considered a movement of vast significance in the 17th century, whereas the present immigration of nearly a million Europeans a year to our shores attracts but a passing notice. The colonies are traced separately from their earliest beginnings, whereas the great states into which they have grown are scarcely noticed except in their connection with the Union.

The same is true of our literary history. The Cotton Mathers and Anne Bradstreets of our own times will not be remembered at all two centuries hence, and those of the early days are remembered only because they are the best the sparsely-settled country could afford. We have now to deal with a larger country, and in order to keep our chapters on literature within their intended limits we must leave unmentioned many writers who would come in for notice had they belonged to the earlier period.

IRVING, COOPER, POE AND HAWTHORNE

Imaginative literature in the United States had no existence before the opening of the 19th century. Works of earlier times, such as Bradford's and Winthrop's histories, Edwards's theology, and the works of the Revolutionary statesmen have a permanent value, but they are not pure literature nor were they intended as such by their respective authors.

The first American to produce imaginative literature that has a lasting place in the popular mind was Washington Irving. Born in New York in 1783, about the time George Washington entered the city on its evacuation by the British, Irving was one of the first to receive the name of the Father of his Country. Irving was the youngest of eleven children and this fact doubtless secured for him indulgences that he would not otherwise have enjoyed. Much of his boyhood was spent rambling at will along the lower Hudson amid the scenes that afterward became the subjects of some of his most vivid pen pictures. His education was irregular; he studied law, but chose not to practice his profession. At the age of twenty-one he made a tour of Europe covering two years, and was received in high social circles. Soon after his return he met with the great sorrow of his life— the death of the charming girl to whom he was engaged to be married. To this bereavement is supposed to be due the fact that he never married, and the further fact that there is a touch of melancholy throughout much of his writings.

Irving's first considerable book was his *History of New York,* by Diedrich Knickerbocker, a humorous account of early New York, an entertaining mixture of sense and nonsense. The success of the book was immediate, but this fact did not lead the author to adopt literature as a profession, and he and his brother launched into business. In a few years they failed and again our author turned to literature. From this time forth Irving was a man of letters. In 1819 he published his *Sketch Book,* a collection of short stories among which are *Rip Van Winkle* and the *Legend of Sleepy Hollow.* Soon after this followed *Bracebridge Hall* and the *Tales of a Traveler,* written while the author was in England. From England Irving went to Spain, in 1826, where he remained for some years, and as a result we have *The Alhambra,* the *Conquest of Granada,* the *Legends of the Conquest of Spain,* and the *Life of Columbus.* No other American had written books on Spanish subjects, and no others since have supplanted those of Irving.

After spending seventeen years abroad Irving returned to his native land and purchased a farm at Tarrytown on the Hudson which he named " Sunnyside." Here he lived for ten years, writing meantime various miscellaneous works. In 1842 he was appointed Minister to Spain, and returning, four years later, retired again to Sunnyside, where he spent the evening of his days writing his *Life of Washington, Life of Goldsmith,* and *Mahomet and His Successors.* He died in 1859 and was buried on a little hill overlooking Sleepy Hollow, which he had made famous.

The works of Washington Irving, though modeled to some extent after certain 18th century English writers, have an individuality truly his own, and they are quite equal to any English prose productions of the same period. Irving was not a profound thinker, he did not trouble himself with the great problems of human life; he had no special message for the world. He wrote with the apparent spontaneity of a singing bird, and there was no guttural note in his song. His writings are always charming, never powerful. His style is remarkably clear and musical, highly polished and romantic. His refined sense of humor is every-

1789 — JAMES FENIMORE COOPER — 1851.

From an enlargement by Brady of a daguerreotype, in the War Department, Washington, D.C.

where apparent; it is never coarse, ever spontaneous and peculiarly American. If there are two characteristics of the American people that distinguish them from all other peoples, they are a sense of humor and an unbounded optimism. Both are of post-revolutionary birth and the two were combined in Irving as in few other writers in our history.

James Fenimore Cooper and Washington Irving differed widely at almost every point. Irving was delicate of build, highly refined, companionable; Cooper was massive, rugged, quarrelsome. These qualities are clearly distinguishable in their respective writings.

Cooper was born in New Jersey in 1789, and a year after his birth his father, a member of Congress and a judge, moved to a large tract of land which he owned on the shore of Otsego Lake, in New York. Here in the wilds of the primeval forest, with hunters and trappers and Indians as his companions, the boy spent his early years. At the age of thirteen he was sent to Yale, but three years later he left his course unfinished and entered the navy. After a service of six years upon the sea he resigned his commission, married, and settled down to a quiet country life. Ten years passed and at the age of thirty Cooper had published nothing. One day as he was reading an English novel he remarked to his wife that he could write a better one himself. She suggested that he try. He did so and produced *Precaution,* a story of English social life of which the author knew almost nothing. The book was a failure, but this fact did not deter the author from trying again. The next year, 1821, he produced *The Spy,* a story of the Revolution.

The reception of *The Spy* was enthusiastic, not only in America, but in England and France. Cooper now determined to devote his life to literature, and he wrote novels year after year with astonishing rapidity. In 1823 came *The Pioneers,* the first of the "Leather Stocking Tales;" and the next year he published *The Pilot,* the first, and probably the best, of his stories of the sea. In the years following Cooper turned out a vast amount of fiction, much of which was worthless and has been forgotten. But probably a dozen of his novels are still read and are the best of their kind. Among these are the *Last of the Mohicans, Red Rover, The Prairie, The Pathfinder, The Deerslayer, Wept of the Wish-ton-Wish,* and *The Water Witch.*

James Fenimore Cooper died in 1851. In the last thirty years of his life he wrote thirty-two novels and many volumes of miscellaneous works, including a history of the Navy. He spent several years in Europe and on his return settled on his father's estate in New York, where he spent the remainder of his days. His later years were embittered by his controversies with various newspaper editors, whom he sued for slander because of their freedom in criticising his opinions.

In two fields of fiction Fenimore Cooper made what seems to be a permanent name for himself—in his novels of the sea and his novels of pioneer life—and in each of these he stands without a peer. Cooper is not without grave faults as a writer. We look in vain for the exquisitely finished style which characterizes Irving. His characters are artificial, their conversations and acts are too often strained and unnatural. He was not a delineator of character, not a psychological student; but in describing places and actions he was great. His writings are prolix and the long intervals between the intense scenes become rather provoking to the reader. And yet, a reader will seldom throw aside the book on this account, and when he reaches the best portions he feels amply repaid for having read the tedious preliminaries. Cooper has often been compared to Walter Scott, his chief model, who died in 1832, about twelve years after Cooper began writing. Cooper's style is more faulty than that of Scott, but his power of description is quite equal to Scott's. He clothed pioneer American life with a glamour of romance with a power scarcely inferior to that of Scott in writing of his native Scotland.

The most erratic genius, and in some respects the greatest, that America has yet produced was Edgar Allan Poe. In three fields of literature Poe made himself famous—as a literary critic, as a writer of short, fascinating, gruesome tales, and as a poet. His literary criticisms are forgotten; many of his tales are still read; his poetry, pointless though it is, is familiar to every civilized people. Poe was born in Boston in 1809. His parents, both of whom belonged to the theatrical profession, died ere the boy was three years old. He was then adopted by a wealthy Virginian named Allan. Poe was unstable of character; his education was irregular. He attended the University of Virginia, but did not finish his course. He was sent to West Point military school, but was dismissed for irregular habits. He quarreled with Mr. Allan, his godfather, left his home, and decided on a literary career. Before reaching his majority he published his first poems, *Al Aaraaf* and *Tamerlane*. This was before his final rupture with Mr. Allan. Soon after that event he achieved his first success in winning a prize of a hundred dollars in a newspaper competition. His contribution was *The Manuscript Found in a Bottle*. A successful career now seemed open to the young author, but his want of staying qualities rendered any high degree of success impossible.

On leaving the home of Mr. Allan, Poe made his home with his aunt in Baltimore. The young poet soon became passionately in love with his cousin, a daughter of this aunt, and they were married when she was scarcely fourteen. Poe's devotion to his child-wife was beautifully tender and after her death, some years later, he made her his *Annabel Lee*, in one of the most remarkably musical lyrics in the language.

> " For the moon never beams without bringing me dreams
>   Of the beautiful Annabel Lee.
> And the stars never rise, but I feel the bright eyes
>   Of the beautiful Annabel Lee;
> And so, all the night tide, I lie down by the side
> Of my darling—my darling—my life and my bride,
>   In the sepulcher there by the sea,
>   In her tomb by the sounding sea."

Poe became editor of a literary magazine in Richmond in 1835, but resigned the position two years later and went to New York. Here and later in Philadelphia he had similar experiences with other literary periodicals. After a brief service he would resign for no apparent cause, though his work was always successful and though poverty stared him in the face at every turn. Meantime he had gained a wide reputation as a writer of short stories, weird, grotesque tales, fascinating with all their horrors. But as a poet Poe was scarcely known until, at the age of thirty-six, he published *The Raven*, in 1845. This wonderful production, " with nothing in it," sounding the hopeless note of despair, was hailed throughout America and Europe as the work of a genius of the first order, and so it is regarded to this day.

Never was a man of genius more lop-sided, more disproportionately balanced than Edgar A. Poe. In addition to a most eccentric inherited temperament, he had to battle with the habit of using strong drink and opium. Repeatedly he attempted to reform, but time would weaken his resolution and strengthen his craving, until again he would fall. He was but forty years old when, one election day in Baltimore, he fell in with a crowd of political ruffians, election repeaters, who got him drunk and made him vote at many polling places about the city. At night he lay in the gutter drunk. He was borne to a hospital. In the morning he awoke. He uttered a prayer, " Lord help my poor soul," his last words, and he died soon afterward.

One writer has said, " Had Poe possessed a nature commensurate with his intellect, he would have been one of the greatest of the human race." The poetry of Poe is almost perfect in structure and workmanship; the range of his imagination was boundless; in his power as a rhythmist he excelled all men who ever wrote in the English tongue, save one—Algernon Charles Swineburne. But his poetry is woefully defective, nevertheless, and his field was very narrow. His verses are wanting in soul, in human sympathy, they never touch the deep life-notes.

Poetry is a union of truth and beauty, but to Edgar Poe it was only beauty. He wrote for dramatic effect; his work was not inspired; it was unspiritual. His works, prose and poetry, are destructive; they deal with despair and the grave, with lost reason and approaching horrors. But with all the fantastic horrors of his verse, its want of human sympathy and of spiritual revelation, a reader cannot help feeling that his strange, weird, unearthly music is fascinating, that his touch, as far as it went, was the touch of a master.

Poe's best known prose works are *The Gold Bug, Murders of the Rue Morgue,* and *The Mystery of Marie Roget.* His two poems, *The Raven* and *The Bells,* are of world-wide fame, while *Annabel Lee* and *Ulalume* and a few other lyrics are scarcely less known. Here follows *The Haunted Palace,* one of his most characteristic lyrics. The reader should remember that the " Palace " is a man, who at length loses his reason, probably through dissipation. In the " Banners, yellow, glorious, golden " we discern the waving hair; the " hideous throng " that " rush out " " through the pale door " are plainly the words of a madman. Some think that the poet made reference to himself in this poem, but there is no proof that he did so.

THE HAUNTED PALACE

In the greenest of our valleys
  By good angels tenanted,
Once a fair and stately palace—
  Radiant palace—reared its head.
In the monarch Thought's dominion—
  It stood there!
Never seraph spread a pinion
  Over fabric half so fair!

Banners yellow, glorious, golden,
  On its roof did float and flow
(This—all this—was in the olden Time
    long ago),
And every gentle air that dallied
  In that sweet day,

Along the ramparts plumed and pallid,
  A winged odor went away.
*   *   *   *   *   *
And all with pearl and ruby glowing
  Was the fair palace door,
Through which came flowing, flowing, flowing,
  And sparkling evermore,
A troop of Echoes, whose sweet duty
  Was but to sing,
In voices of surpassing beauty,
  The wit and wisdom of their king.

But evil things in robes of sorrow,
  Assailed the monarch's high estate.
Ah, let us mourn!—for never morrow
  Shall dawn upon him desolate!
And round about his home the glory
  That blushed and bloomed,
Is but a dim-remembered story
  Of the old time entombed.

And travelers, now, within that valley,
  Through the red-litten windows see
Vast forms, that move fantastically
  To a discordant melody,
While, like a ghastly rapid river,
  Through the pale door
A hideous throng rush out forever
  And laugh—but smile no more.

In this group of writers of imaginative prose Nathaniel Hawthorne must be classed, though in point of association he belongs to the next following group. Like Irving and Poe, Hawthorne was an artist, and he was the most original, the least imitative of the three. Descended from the earliest installment of Puritan immigrants, born in the old town of Salem, of witchcraft fame, in 1804, he was left fatherless at the age of four years. His father, a seafaring man, died of fever in a foreign land and his mother put on the weeds of widowhood, which she wore to the end of her life, forty years later. Nathaniel was a beautiful child, dreamy and solitary of habit, with dark, waving hair and deep, lustrous eyes. He was graduated at Bowdoin in 1825 in the class with Longfellow. Returning to his mother's home at Salem he spent twelve years, at the end of which he published *Twice Told Tales*, which made no impression on the public.

President Van Buren gave him a place in the Boston custom house, from which the spoils system removed him at the accession of the Whigs in 1841. Soon after this he married, moved to Concord and published *Mosses from an Old Manse*. Still he failed to reach the reading public, his family almost came to want, and again he accepted a government position. He wasted three valuable years as collector of the port at Salem, when another change of administration left him stranded, and, but for the meagre savings of his wife, penniless. " Now you can write your book," said his wife, as she placed his pen and paper before him,—and so he did, he wrote his masterpiece—*The Scarlet Letter*.

The good Whig President, Zachary Taylor, never knew what a service he did to American letters when he removed Nathaniel Hawthorne from the custom house at Salem. A weird and sombre tale is *The Scarlet Letter*, depicting Puritanism as no historian has ever done. But the book is less renowned for the story it tells than for the matchless

1809—EDGAR ALLAN POE—1849.

1844.

om an enlargement by Brady of a daguerreotype by John Plumb, in the War Department, Washington, D.C.

purity of its English. From this time the author was recognized in every civilized land as a first magnitude star in the literary sky. In 1851 he produced *The House of the Seven Gables.* When his old college friend, Franklin Pierce, became President of the United States, Hawthorne re-received the appointment as consul at Liverpool, England. He then took his family abroad, where they remained for several years, spending a brief period in Rome. While in Rome Hawthorne received the inspiration for his third great romance, *The Marble Faun,* written in 1859. In 1860 Hawthorne returned to the United States and again took up his residence at Concord. Four years later, at the age of sixty years, he died among the New Hampshire hills while on a driving tour with ex-President Pierce. In the writings of Hawthorne, especially in his three great romances, there is one central thought, namely, that sin, sooner or later, will bring its retribution. With Hawthorne's style no fault can be found. It seems more the work of nature than of art. The one fault to be found with his stories is that they lack sunshine, they are morbid and introspective; but, unlike the works of Poe, they do not sound a note of despair; there is always a gleam of heaven beyond.

In the characters of Hawthorne there is a strange supernatural something that eludes all attempts to describe. They are like the figures we meet in a dream; and the lonely, unfathomable life of the author reminds one of his own characters.

The circle of Hawthorne's readers is not very large. It comprises only persons of some refinement in literary taste. The ordinary novel reader who delights chiefly in plots and intrigues and love stories will find little to attract him in Hawthorne.

THE GREAT NEW ENGLAND MASTERS

In our brief chapters on literature it is not feasible to treat separately of the various schools—the idealists, the transcendentalists, and, after the Civil War, the realists, nor of idyllic, didactic, narrative poetry, and the like. It is preferable to notice our great writers as individuals, with an effort to point out the more prominent characteristics of each.

With the passing of Cotton Mather, as we have noticed, New England, or rather Massachusetts, suffered an eclipse as a literary center, and this continued for a hundred years, when there came an outburst of literary activity in the old Bay State that has not elsewhere been equaled in America. The beginning of the New England Renaissance was marked by the advent of William Cullen Bryant, who, though most of his life was spent in New York, was born in Massachusetts in 1794. He was the son of a country physician and his early boyhood was spent in the wild freedom of the forest, which deeply impressed his young life. He entered Williams College, but left the course unfinished owing to the poverty of his father, and, taking a course in law, entered the profession, and spent a few years as a village lawyer in western Massachusetts. But he was not fond of his profession; he longed for a literary career. In this he was encouraged by his father, who, in 1817, carried a few of his son's poems to Boston and submitted them to the editors of the North American Review, then lately founded. The editor to whom Mr. Bryant first read them was delighted; he took them to his colleague, who,

1804 — NATHANIEL HAWTHORNE — 1864.

1860.

From a photograph by Mayall, London.

on hearing them, replied, " Ah, you have been imposed upon; no one on this side of the Atlantic is capable of writing such verses."

The poems were printed in the Review, and among them was *Thanatopsis,* and thus American poetry was born. Vast quantities of verse had been written; but here, for the first time, was immortal poetry. Strange, too, the author had written this poem at the age of seventeen and had thrown it in his drawer where it lay for six years. In 1821 the youthful poet published his first book, which contained *Thanatopsis* and *To a Waterfowl.* He bounded into fame, and, strange to say, in all his long life he never rose above, never afterward even equaled, these youthful productions.

At the age of thirty-two Bryant became a citizen of New York and was soon editor of the Evening Post, and so continued for more than half a century. His appearance, as he grew old, was most patriarchal, with his deep, shaggy brows and his flowing, snow-white beard. His venerable figure was known to many thousands of the people and he was pointed out to the passing stranger as the most distinguished citizen of the metropolis. Abraham Lincoln declared that it was worth a journey east to see William Cullen Bryant. It was long after the Civil War when New York's Grand Old Man died of sunstroke at the age of eighty-four years.

Bryant was not a voluminous writer, nor was his range a wide one. He wrote no long poems. He is best known by *Thanatopsis,* by *A Waterfowl,* which a noted English critic pronounced the best short poem in the English language; by *The Death of the Flowers,* and other short poems of nature; by *The Flood of Years,* written at the age of eighty-two, and by his translation into English verse of Homer's Iliad and Odyssey.

Bryant was preëminently the poet of Nature. He gazed upon her "visible forms" and to him she spoke a "various language." He strolled through the deep and solemn wood, along the lonely shores of the lake, by the bubbling brook; these spoke to the poet's soul and he translated their message into human language; he embodied it into song. Though he drew his inspiration from Nature, the influence of the Greek masters is plainly visible in his writings. Bryant dwelt also with the eternities, with the vast harmonies of the Universe, with the music of the spheres. His poems are filled with religious awe; he stands as one inspired with the grandeur of creation, of which he seemed an admirer rather than an integral part. His limitations lay in the fact that his poems are cold and passionless; he never probes the human heart nor sounds its depths. From this fact he cannot be placed in the first rank among the great poets.

TO A WATERFOWL

Whither, midst falling dew,
While glow the heavens with the last steps of day;
Far, through their rosy depths, dost thou pursue
Thy solitary way?

Vainly the fowler's eye
Might mark thy distant flight to do thee wrong,
As, darkly seen against the crimson sky,
Thy figure floats along.

Seek'st thou the plashy brink
Of weedy lake, or marge of river wide,

Or where the rocking billows rise and sink
    On the chafed ocean side?

  There is a Power whose care
Teaches thy way along that pathless coast,—
The desert and illimitable air,—
    Lone wandering, but not lost.

  All day thy wings have fanned,
At that far height, the cold thin atmosphere,
Yet stoop not, weary, to the welcome land,
    Though the dark night is near.

  And soon that toil shall end;
Soon shalt thou find a summer home and rest,
And scream among thy fellows; reeds shall bend,
    Soon, o'er thy sheltered nest.

  Thou're gone, the abyss of heaven
Hath swallowed up thy form; yet, on my heart
Deeply hath sunk the lesson thou hast given,
    And shall not soon depart.

  He who, from zone to zone,
Guides through the boundless sky thy certain flight,
In the long way that I must tread alone,
    Will lead my steps aright.

Next to Bryant in point of time, among the New England
literati, was Henry Wadsworth Longfellow, the most popular of all our American poets. The son of a lawyer, Longfellow was born at Portland, Maine, in 1807, when Bryant
was a boy of thirteen years. He was graduated at Bowdoin
at the age of nineteen, and after an additional course of

three years in Europe, became professor of modern languages at his alma mater. From here, after six years' service, he was called to a similar position at Harvard, in which he continued for eighteen years. In 1854 he resigned his chair at Harvard in order to devote his whole time to literature. He died in 1882 at the age of seventy-five years.

Longfellow published several volumes of poetry, the first being *Voices of the Night* in 1839. His first long poem, *Evangeline,* was published in 1847. It is a story of the dispersion of the Acadians, delightfully told in hexameter verse. It became instantly popular, and has so remained. *Hiawatha* appeared in 1855. This poem, which is a setting in verse of old Indian legends, is written in a style unattempted in English before or since. After one becomes familiar with Hiawatha he sees the peculiar fitness of the form of verse to the primitive race described, and feels that the story could not have been told so well in any other form. *The Courtship of Miles Standish,* another of his long poems, is of the greater interest because of the fact that Longfellow was a descendant of John and Priscilla, leading characters of the story.

Longfellow's short poems, chiefly in lyrical form, are altogether too numerous to be mentioned separately here. Many of them, as *A Psalm of Life, Resignation, Building of the Ship, Paul Revere, The Rainy Day, Excelsior,* and others, are familiar to all classes of the people of America and Europe. As Bryant was the poet of Nature, Longfellow may be called the poet of literature. He was familiar with various modern languages and he gleaned freely from their treasures. Intellectually Longfellow was highly cultured and this fact is reflected in all his poetry. His verse is eminently correct. In point of technique he was a master.

1794 — WILLIAM CULLEN BRYANT — 1878.

1865.

From the original Brady negative in the War Department, Washington, D.C.

He was not a great creative poet; he was wanting in imagination and passion; he never reached sublime heights nor profound depths. He was preëminently the poet of the home; he evinced great skill in handling conventional themes, in inspiring anew with life and interest the most commonplace topics of everyday life. His verses are pure, inspiring, ennobling, and while they are readily comprehended by the masses, and even by children, they are not wanting in interest to the cultured. These qualities have endeared Longfellow to the American people, have given him the first place as our national poet, a position that he will probably hold for generations to come.

THE RAINY DAY

The day is cold, and dark, and dreary;
It rains, and the wind is never weary;
The vine still clings to the mouldering wall,
But at every gust the dead leaves fall,
    And the day is dark and dreary.

My life is cold, and dark, and dreary;
It rains, and the wind is never weary;
My thoughts still cling to the mouldering Past,
But the hopes of youth fall thick in the blast,
    And the days are dark and dreary.

Be still, sad heart! and cease repining;
Behind the clouds is the sun still shining;
Thy fate is the common fate of all,
Into each life some rain must fall,
    Some days must be dark and dreary.

With Longfellow one instinctively associates his life-long

contemporary, John Greenleaf Whittier, the " Quaker Poet," who was born in Massachusetts in 1807, when Longfellow was but a few months old. The genius of Whittier was perhaps hardly equal to that of Bryant or of Longfellow; but, like the former, he was a true poet of nature, and like the latter, he could write for the masses and clothe homely themes with a new and living interest. He was more passionate and less cultured than Longfellow or Bryant; more truly American than either, or indeed, than any other of our poets. Whittier was scarcely less a reformer than a poet; he espoused the cause of the slave and for thirty years before the Civil War wrote many short poems in the interests of the Abolitionists. This fact doubtless prevented his taking as high a place in the literary field as he otherwise might have taken. As a whole Whittier's poems are marked by their unstudied simplicity, their deeply religious reverence, their profound sympathy with suffering humanity and their idyllic, pastoral beauty.

Whittier was the son of a poor farmer. His early years were spent at work on the farm; he was literally the " barefoot boy " described in his verse. His education extended but little beyond that furnished by the country schools. At various times he was engaged in editorial work in Boston and Haverhill, but the greater portion of his life was spent amid the rural scenes of his childhood. His poems reflect the beauty of the rocks and hills of New England, the simple habits of the plain, country people, and the legends of their history.

A copy of Burns' poems early came into the possession of Whittier and his diligent study of it awakened his own powers. His earliest published verses were printed in a paper edited by the famous Abolitionist, William Lloyd

1807 — HENRY WADSWORTH LONGFELLOW — 1882.

1876.

From an original photograph by Gutekunst, Philadelphia.

Garrison, who drove fourteen miles across the country to meet the young poet. Finding the tall, uncultured lad of nineteen years in the field, barefoot, following a plow, Garrison soon made his acquaintance, and henceforth for many years the two were co-workers in the antislavery cause.

Whittier's *Voices of Freedom*, composed of antislavery poems, was published in 1849. He published many volumes at various times during his long career, the first being *Legends of New England*, in 1831, when he was twenty-four. *Snow Bound*, a charming picture of rural home-life in winter, published in 1866, is Whittier's masterpiece. *Maud Muller* was first issued in 1865. Many short poems of this author, as *Barbara Frietchie, The Barefoot Boy, Maud Muller*, and others, are well known and widely popular.

The three New England masters whom we have noticed —Bryant, Longfellow and Whittier—were purely poets; their prose writings were insignificant and need not be noticed. Three others remain—Emerson, Holmes, and Lowell—who were distinguished as poets, and also as prose writers. The first and greatest of these was Ralph Waldo Emerson (1803-82). Emerson's father was the pastor of the church that John Cotton had founded with the founding of Boston, and he himself, at the age of twenty-six, became successor of the famous Mathers as pastor of the Second Church of Boston. The rigid Calvinism of old Puritan days had merged into Unitarianism; but even this doctrine was too narrow for the youthful Boston divine, and in 1832, after a few years' service, he resigned his pastorate and became a lyceum lecturer and author.

After making a brief tour of Europe at the close of his pastorate, and meeting Thomas Carlyle, with whom he formed a life-long friendship, and other celebrated characters, Emerson returned to America and made his home at historic Concord, in the " Old Manse," which has been made famous by Hawthorne.

Emerson became head of the school of " Transcendentalism," that is, a realm of knowledge transcending the senses; but he preferred the term Idealism. He was long gaining a following. His essay on *Nature,* published in 1836, found few readers and after ten years scarcely five hundred copies had been sold. At length, however, the thinking world awoke to the fact that there was a true prophet in the old town of Concord. Before the close of his long life his home became the goal of pilgrims from every civilized country. Among American men of letters Emerson must be accorded first place. There is something in his writings, dealing with man's relations with the Infinite, that stamps them with permanency. The time may come when Bryant and Irving and Longfellow and Whittier will be forgotten; or when they will be remembered only as we remember the poetasters of colonial days; but Emerson is as sure of immortality as are Homer and Dante and Shakespeare. His writings are for all time and must be classed with the world's permanent literature.

Emerson's writings consist chiefly of short poems and essays. Aside from his *English Traits* and a few short effusions of a patriotic nature, as the *Concord Hymn,* his writings all deal with the same subject—man's moral relation to the Universe. He was a religious philosopher and nothing else. His religion was one of individualism. He had the supreme audacity to cast aside historic Christianity and to base his religion solely on inspiration from his own communion with God and Nature. He studied Plato and

Jesus and Paul and Luther, but evolved his philosophy from his own experience.   For Jesus the moral and religious teacher he had profound respect, but for Christ the Savior and Redeemer he had no use.   He believed that all men are inherently good and that all are capable of rising to the stature of Jesus.

Emerson did not seek to found a religious denomination or a school of philosophy.   He simply recorded his visions and sang his song, with little apparent concern whether the world heard and heeded or not.

Emerson's philosophy may be condensed to a few words: Nature is full of unfathomable truth; beyond human ken is an inexhaustible store of realities, more real than any material thing; God reveals himself equally to all men who seek him, no less in our own age than in ages past, and every man must go to the original fountain for his inspiration and for a revelation of truth.   This philosophy of life was not new with Emerson, but he put it in such a unique form as to make it truly his own.

In two respects Emerson's weakness is glaring: First, his reducing all divine revelation of the past to the level of the every-day inspiration of every man, which involved the rejection of the resurrection of Christ, the fundamental fact on which Christianity is based; and second, his ability to see but one side of human nature.   He could not understand that men are inclined to evil.   His own life, judged from a human standpoint, was without a flaw.   He had no apparent inclination to do wrong, and evil to him was only a matter of hearsay.   By his own standard he judged all men and saw no need of reformation and regeneration.   He lived in visions and dreams and recorded what he saw, and while much that he wrote is highly inspiring and ennobling, his prophecies are too limited in their scope to become a safe rule of life and practice.

In point of literary style, Emerson's poetry possesses a charm that leads one to read again and again, but too often it is obscure and vague and difficult to understand. His essays are smooth and easy to read; but the thoughts are disconnected and do not appear in logical sequence. But with all his defects of style, Emerson's originality was masterly. He was a great thinker, and his works sparkle with bright sayings, aphorisms, many of which have become embodied permanently in our language. The little poem *Each and All* is a fair sample of Emerson's poetry.

EACH AND ALL

Little thinks, in the field, yon red-cloaked clown,
Of thee from the hill-top looking down;
The heifer that lows in the upland farm,
Far-heard, lows not thine ear to charm;
The sexton, tolling his bell at noon,
Deems not that great Napoleon
Stops his horse, and lists with delight,
Whilst his files sweep round yon Alpine height;
Not knowest thou what argument
Thy life to thy neighbor's creed has lent.
All are needed by each one;
Nothing is fair or good alone.
I thought the sparrow's note from heaven,
Singing at dawn on the alder bough;
I brought him home, in his nest, at even;
He sings the song, but it pleases not now,
For I did not bring home the river and sky;—
He sang to my ear,—they sang to my eye.

1803 — RALPH WALDO EMERSON — 1882.

BY SAMUEL WORCESTER ROWSE, 1857.

From the original crayon drawing in possession of Professor Charles Eliot Norton,
Cambridge, Mass.

The delicate shells lay on the shore;
The bubbles of the latest wave
Fresh pearls to their enamel gave;
And the bellowing of the savage sea
Greeted their safe escape to me.
I wiped away the weeds and foam,
I fetched my sea-born treasures home;
But the poor, unsightly, noisome things
Had left their beauty on the shore,
With the sun and the sand and the wild uproar.
* * * * * * * *
Then I said, "I covet truth;
Beauty is unripe childhood's cheat;
I leave it behind with the games of youth."—
As I spoke, beneath my feet
The ground-pine curled its pretty wreath,
Running over the club-moss burrs;
I inhaled the violet's breath;
Around me stood the oaks and firs;
Pine-cones and acorns lay on the ground;
Over me soared the eternal sky,
Full of light and of deity,
Again I saw, again I heard,
The rolling river, the morning bird;—
Beauty through my senses stole;
I yielded myself to the perfect whole.

No two of our literary men present a greater contrast than Emerson and Oliver Wendell Holmes. Emerson was a dreamer, serious, deeply spiritual, an intense student of Nature; Holmes was a wit, a humorist, urban rather than rural in his tastes, practical and mundane, but capable of deep pathos. Oliver Wendell Holmes was born in Cambridge, Massachusetts, in 1809 and was graduated at Harvard in 1829. Choosing the medical profession, he went abroad and studied for some years. In 1839 he became professor of anatomy in Dartmouth College, but retained the chair only a year, when he returned to Boston, which was henceforth his home. In 1847 he was elected to the chair of anatomy in Harvard and filled it for forty-one years. His death occurred in 1894.

Holmes was America's first successful humorist. But he was more than a humorist. Entertaining indeed are his flashes of wit, but often they are mingled with maxims of wisdom or pathetic sentiment. For example, his reminiscent poem *Bill and Joe* is full of wit and entertainment; but here and there a serious note is struck. As in

> "A few swift years and who can show
> Which dust was Bill, and which was Joe?"

Most of Holmes's poems are "occasionals," written for celebrations of various sorts, especially those in connection with Harvard College. The author was a leader for half a century in the upper social circles of Boston and seldom did he disappoint the expectation that he would furnish, for high social occasions, a striking, characteristic bit of verse that would exactly fit the occasion for which it was written. Most of these occasional effusions will be forgotten; but much of his verse has a permanent value.

The old frigate Constitution, famous for the victory over the Guerriere, was about to be destroyed, when Holmes's *Old Ironsides* saved the precious relic from destruction. His comic humor is seen in such poems as *The One-Hoss Shay* and *The Height of the Ridiculous.* His serious reflections are found in portions of *The Last Leaf* and in *The Chambered Nautilus,*—the best two poems Holmes ever wrote.

As a prose writer Holmes made no mark till he was near fifty years old, when, in 1857, his *Autocrat of the Breakfast Table* came out in the Atlantic Monthly.   More delightfully entertaining prose had never been produced in this country, and it is still read with relish by all classes. *The Professor at the Breakfast Table* and *The Poet at the Breakfast Table* followed the Autocrat, but are scarcely equal to it.   In fiction Holmes wrote *Elsie Venner* and a few other novels.   He was not on the whole a great author, but as an entertainer through the medium of short, fitting effusions in verse he was inimitable.   The *Chambered Nautilus,* as here follows, though not in Holmes's usual vein, is a good, sound bit of poetry, with a tender and beautiful sentiment.

THE CHAMBERED NAUTILUS

This is the ship of pearl, which, poets feign,
    Sails the unshadowed main,—
    The venturous bark that flings
On the sweet summer wind its purpled wings
In gulfs enchanted, where the Siren sings,
    And coral reefs lie bare,
Where the cold sea-maids rise to sun their streaming hair.

Its webs of living gauze no more unfurl;
    Wrecked is the ship of pearl!
    And every chambered cell,
Where its dim dreaming life was wont to dwell,
As the frail tenant shaped his growing shell,
    Before thee lies revealed,—
Its irised ceiling rent, its sunless crypt unsealed!

Year after year beheld the silent toil
    That spread his lustrous coil;
    Still, as the spiral grew,
He left the past year's dwelling for the new,
Stole with soft step its shining archway through,
    Built up its idle door,
Stretched in his last-found home, and knew the old no more.

Thanks for the heavenly message brought by thee,
    Child of the wandering sea,
    Cast from her lap, forlorn!
From thy dead lips a clearer note is born
Than ever Triton blew from wreathed horn!
    While on mine ear it rings,
Through the deep caves of thought I hear a voice that sings.

Build thee more stately mansions, O my soul,
    As the swift seasons roll!
    Leave thy low-vaulted past!
Let each new temple, nobler than the last,
Shut thee from heaven with a dome more vast,
    Till thou at length art free,
Leaving thine outgrown shell by life's unresting sea!

The last of the great New England sextette is James Russell Lowell. Like Emerson and Holmes, Lowell (1819-91) was the son of a minister, an emancipated scion of the ascetic Puritanism of a bygone generation. Lowell succeeded Longfellow as professor of Harvard. In later years he entered the diplomatic service and became minister to Spain and later to England. Lowell was one of the most highly cultured men of his time, though his writings do not show the literary culture that we find in Longfellow. In humor Lowell stands second only to Holmes; in satire and literary criticism he stands first in the New England group.

In 1841, three years after his graduating at Harvard, Lowell published a small volume of verse entitled *A Year's Life,* which attracted but little attention. Three years later he put out another volume, and in 1848 still another. This year of 1848 was the banner year in Lowell's literary life, as it was the year of the publication of *The Biglow Papers* in book form, and *The Fable for Critics.*

The Biglow Papers, a witty satire dealing with the questions of the Mexican War, had appeared previously as a serial in the Boston Courier. It is written in New England Yankee dialect under the name of Hosea Biglow, a farmer, who opposes the war on principle. The poem is comic in the extreme and yet there are many serious touches and wise conclusions. When Lowell was discovered to be the author his fame was secure. The satire, as Stedman says, is "a positive addition to the serio-comic literature of the world." The following lines would indicate that the Yankee writer was opposed to war altogether:

> Ez fer war, I call it murder,—
>   There you hev it plain an' flat;
> I don't want to go no furder
>   Than my Testyment fer that;
> God hez sed so plump an' fairly,
>   It's ez long ez it is broad,
> 'An' you've gut to git up airly
>   Ef you want to take in God.
>
> 'Taint your eppyletts an' feathers
>   Make the thing a grain more right;

'Taint afollerin' your bell-wethers
     Will excuse ye in His sight;
Ef you take a sword an' dror it,
     An' go stick a feller thru,
Guv'ment aint to answer for it,
     God'll send the bill to you.

Another form in a later paper runs thus:

On'y look at the Demmercrats, see wut they've done
Jest simply by stickin' together like fun;
They've sucked us right into a mis'able war
Thet no one on airth aint responsible for;
They've run us a hundred cool millions in debt
(An' fer Demmercrat Horners ther's good plums left
          yet);

They talk agin tayriffs, but act fer a high one,
An' so coax all parties to build up their Zion;
To the people they're ollers ez slick ez molasses,
An' butter their bread on both sides with The Masses,
Half o' whom they've persuaded, by way of a joke,
Thet Washington's mantelpiece fell upon Polk.

Another series of Biglow Papers was issued by the same
author during the Civil War, satirizing public events, chiefly
at the expense of Great Britain and the South.

The Fable for Critics is a metrical sizing up of the various
well-known authors of the time, and although the rhythm
is often irregular, the rhyme far-fetched, and the sections
loosely united, the estimate of the author's contemporaries
is exceedingly clever. The satire, if such it may be called,
reminds one of Byron's English Bards and Scotch Review-

ers, but is free from the bitterness of the latter. Lowell was also the author of some excellent serious poetry, as *The Cathedral, Under the Willows, The Vision of Sir Launfal,* and many short poems on nature.

The fame of Lowell, however, will rest chiefly on the firmer basis of his prose works. His four volumes, *My Study Windows, Among My Books,* two volumes, and *Fireside Travels,* composed chiefly of high-grade literary criticism, are among the best prose works produced in this country.[148]

MINOR POETS

In addition to the "Masters" of the period we are treating there were many minor poets to whom, even in our brief study, a passing notice is necessary. First among these in point of ability was Fitz-Greene Halleck (1795-1867), whose meager output of verse leads his countrymen to regret that he did not write more. One of Halleck's short poems, *Marco Bozzaris,* is known to English-speaking people throughout the world. His *Red Jacket* is an excellent Indian portrait, and portions of his tribute to his dead friend, Joseph Rodman Drake, are tenderly beautiful.

Drake, born in the same year with Halleck, was a co-worker with the latter, but died young. His *Culprit Fay,* a story of some fairies supposed to haunt the Hudson Valley, was widely read at the time. His rather bombastic *American Eagle* is his only other poem that received much notice. Still another poet, born in the same year, James Gates Percival, received much attention in his day, but is now on the verge of oblivion.

[148] Another political humorist of the time, who ranks next to Lowell, but far below him, was Seba Smith, a native of Maine, who wrote the "Major Jack Downing" letters of Jackson's time.

Charles Sprague (1791-1875), who was born in Boston and spent his life there, was one of the shining lesser lights of the time. His ode to Shakespeare is one of the best written in honor of the bard of Avon; but his *Family Meeting* is much better known. Nathaniel P. Willis (1806-67) was still better known than Sprague, at least in polite society. He wrote much in prose and verse. He aimed to be striking and bizarre; he represented social caste and seemed to make no effort to do anything of an enduring character. His works are forgotten. Of greater strength than either Sprague or Willis was John G. Saxe, who was born in Vermont in 1816. Saxe was a humorist and he often set the country laughing. At least two of his effusions are still read—*Rhyme of the Rail,* and *The Proud Miss McBride.*

Women poets were not wanting at this period. Among them Hannah F. Gould (1789-1865) must be given the first place in point of ability. Her short poems dealing with quiet themes of home life are very numerous. *The Snow Flake,* her most popular lyric, possesses a charm that lingers long in the memory of the reader. Far more numerous were the writings of Mrs. Lydia H. Sigourney of Connecticut (1791-1865), who published a volume of prose or verse or of both every year for half a century. Her writings, however, have passed away with the generation that produced them. Mrs. Frances Sargent Osgood (1812-50), a native of Boston, wrote many short poems and was a power in the current literature of the time. But how such a master of verse as Edgar A. Poe should praise Mrs. Osgood's poetry so lavishly as he did is difficult to discover by a perusal of her work.

Other minor poets are remembered as "One-poem poets," that is, poets who are known solely by a single production which caught the public fancy and has thus far held its place. One of these is Francis Scott Key (1780-1843) of Maryland, whose patriotic song, *The Star Spangled Banner*, has been referred to on another page. Another was Samuel Woodworth (1785-1842) of Massachusetts, whose lyric, *The Old Oaken Bucket*, has always been remarkably popular with the masses, and shows no signs of being forgotten. To this class belongs John Howard Payne (1792-1852), a native of New York, an actor and playwright. In one of his plays is found the one little song, *Home Sweet Home*, which has made the author immortal. None of these three —*Star Spangled Banner, Old Oaken Bucket*, or *Home, Sweet Home*—is of a high order of literary merit, but each seems to have found a permanent place in the great popular heart. Among the poets of a single poem might also be named the Rev. Samuel F. Smith (1808-95), whose *America*, written in 1852, has come nearer becoming our accepted national anthem than any other ballad; George P. Morris, (1802-64), a native of Philadelphia, author of *Woodman, Spare that Tree;* and Coates Kinney, author of *Rain on the Roof.*

STATESMEN, ORATORS, AND HISTORIANS

We must here take leave, for a time, of the domain of pure literature. Most of the characters to be mentioned in this section have been noticed more fully in other departments of this work and will here be referred to with the utmost brevity. Among orators and statesmen of the period whose writings still live Daniel Webster (1782-1852) must be placed at the head. Webster reached the high-water mark in his famous reply to Hayne in the Senate in 1830. Scarcely inferior to this are his oration at the laying of the corner stone of the Bunker Hill Monument in 1825, his speech on the trial of a murderer before a jury at Salem, his Dartmouth College speech before the Federal Supreme Court, and his Seventh of March speech in 1850. Webster's power to stir his hearers is extended in a great measure to his readers. His work still lives for its literary value. But a careful student of Webster's English must be convinced that there is something artificial about it, which was common to the oratory of his day.

Henry Clay (1777-1852), a life-long political associate of Webster, had almost equal power with the latter in holding an audience. But Clay's speeches have little power to hold a reader, and are therefore useful only for their historic value. With these two John Caldwell Calhoun was associated, friend and foe, for forty years. He is also known to literature only through his public speeches, which, from the standpoint of literary merit, may be placed between those of Webster and Clay. The "Works" of these statesmen may be found in any good public library.

As writers on jurisprudence no others of this period can be named in the same class with John Marshall (1755-1835), and Joseph Story (1779-1845). Marshall's fame rests on his masterly decisions as chief justice of the Supreme Court. Story was the author of many books in line of his profession as associate justice of the Supreme Court and professor in the law school at Harvard. His greatest work is that on the Constitution of the United States, which has not been equaled by any other writer in the same field.

In the field of pure oratory Edward Everett (1794-1865) holds first place. Everett was a pulpit orator, editor of the North American Review, member of Congress, governor of Massachusetts, secretary of state, United States senator, minister to England, president of Harvard, and in 1860 candidate for the vice-presidency of the United States. He was the most cultured, finished orator in the country; his Orations and Speeches have been published in four volumes.

In the domain of forensic oratory Rufus Choate (1799-1859) held a foremost place. Many of Choate's speeches are to be found in book form, but some of his best efforts were not recorded. Choate was a pupil of the great Maryland lawyer, William Wirt (1772-1834), who was for twelve years attorney general of the United States and was candidate of the Anti-Masons for President in 1832. Wirt first drew public attention to himself at the trial of Aaron Burr, in 1807, and from that time to his death was one of the leading forensic orators in the country. In addition to his professional and official writings Wirt wrote the *British Spy, Life of Patrick Henry,* and other works, that give him a respectable place among men of letters.

The historians and their works are treated under Bibliography, Volume V. of this work. John Quincy Adams made no pretensions as an historian; his life was spent in the public service from boyhood to old age; but in his Diary, faithfully kept for many years, he left a work of great historic value. The career of Thomas H. Benton was somewhat similar to that of Adams. He was a statesman by profession, but he found time to write his *Thirty Years' View,* of Congress, and *An Abridgment of the Debates of Congress,* both of which are of much value to the student of history.

As a writer and editor of historical works Jared Sparks (1794-1866), takes perhaps the first place in point of the number of published works. He is best known by his

American Biography. Though Sparks produced nothing of permanent value in history, he was closely associated with America's first historian, who measures up to the standard of the best—William Hickling Prescott (1796-1859). Prescott was made blind, or nearly so, by an accident at college, and his life-work was thereby rendered very laborious. In 1837 he published his *Ferdinand and Isabella,* and in 1843 his *Conquest of Mexico.* These were followed by *Conquest of Peru* and by *Life of Philip II.* Prescott's style is somewhat florid, and less scholarly than the works of later writers; but on the whole his work stands among the classics in history writing.

The first volume of the monumental work of George Bancroft, which is noticed elsewhere, was published in 1834. Richard Hildreth during the same period wrote a *History of the United States* of about the same scope as that of Bancroft, while John G. Palfrey wrote an exhaustive *History of New England.*

John Lothrop Motley (1814-77) must be classed with Prescott as an historian of the first class; and the same is true of Francis Parkman (1823-93). Motley's *Rise of the Dutch Republic* (1856) and his *History of the United Netherlands* of a later date, and Parkman's delightful volumes on the *French and English in North America,* must all be classed among the greatest works in history in the English language. Parkman, America's greatest historian before the present generation, was a life-long invalid; but by dint of indomitable courage he succeeded in accomplishing the great work that he had planned in youth. His histories have few equals in their admirable blending of scholastic accuracy and romantic historic style.

MISCELLANEOUS WRITERS

One of the unique characters in American letters was Henry David Thoreau (1817-62), a native and life-long resident of Concord, Massachusetts. After graduating at Harvard in 1837, and a brief experience as a teacher and a surveyor, Thoreau betook himself to the solitudes of Nature, where he practically spent his life, observing her varied forms and recording his impressions. Having no family to support, he decided that he would not attempt to earn more than enough for his immediate wants. On one occasion he built a little cabin in the forest on the bank of a lake and lived alone in it for two years. The result was his book *Walden,* the best of his productions. In this book he describes Nature minutely and philosophically and with considerable originality. Thoreau was a silent, solitary, guileless man who studied and wrote in his own way and took no account of the progress of civilization. His other chief works are: *A Week on the Concord and Merrimac, Cape Cod, The Maine Woods,* and *The Yankee in Canada.*

Among the Concord group of Transcendentalists was the gifted woman, Margaret Fuller Ossoli (1810-50), a daughter of a Boston lawyer and member of Congress. An intimate associate of Emerson, a brilliant conversationalist and writer, Miss Fuller made an enviable name for herself. In 1846 she went to Italy and soon afterward married an Italian nobleman, Marquis Ossoli. In 1850 she and her husband embarked for the United States; when near the American coast the vessel was wrecked and all were lost. The works by which the Marchioness Ossoli is best known are her criticisms of Literature and Art and *Woman in the Nineteenth Century.*

Louise May Alcott (1832-88) was the daughter of an-

other of the Transcendental family, the erratic, eccentric
Bronson Alcott.   For this reason Miss Alcott is here mentioned, though her work belongs to a period subsequent to
that treated in this chapter.   Miss Alcott sprung into fame
in 1867 by the publication of *Little Women,* a realistic,
thinly-disguised history of her own childhood.   Her later
volumes, *The Old Fashioned Girl, Little Men,* etc., were
written in the same strain.

The great work of Mrs. Harriet Beecher Stowe (1811-
96), *Uncle Tom's Cabin,* has been noticed elsewhere.   The
other chief novels of this extraordinary woman are *The
Minister's Wooing, Old Town Folks,* and *Agnes of So-
rento.*   These, however, made no such impression as that
made by *Uncle Tom's Cabin.*   They are now seldom read.

The temporary reputation gained by Mrs. James Parton
(1811-72), a sister of Nathaniel P. Willis, under the pen
name of "Fanny Fern," was remarkable.   She wrote every
week for eighteen years for Mr. Robert Bonner's New
York Ledger, on all kinds of miscellaneous domestic subjects, at the rate of a hundred dollars a column.   Another
voluminous female writer was Mrs. Lydia Maria Child
(1802-80), whose works are chiefly on social topics and the
slavery question.

In this connection should also be mentioned Samuel G.
Goodrich (1793-1863) of Connecticut, who wrote school
books and children's books under the name of "Peter Par-
ley" to the astonishing number of 170 volumes.   More than
seven millions of these were sold during his lifetime.   But
this number seems meager compared to the number of sales
of Noah Webster's *Spelling Book,* which are said to have
reached the enormous total of sixty millions.   Webster
(1758-1843), who was also a Connecticut man and father-

in-law of Mr. Goodrich, made himself immortal as a lexicographer. His Dictionary was published in 1828, after twenty years' labor. It has been revised from time to time by other hands, always bearing the name of the original author, and is to this day one of the standard dictionaries of the language.

Webster's great rival was Joseph E. Worcester (1784-1865), a native of New Hampshire. He also labored for many years and in 1846 produced a dictionary of the English language almost if not fully equal to that of Webster.

Among scientific writers Alexander Wilson (1766-1813), the ornithologist, must take high rank. Wilson, who properly belongs to the preceding period, was born in Scotland and migrated to America when near thirty years of age. He settled in Philadelphia, and after reaching middle age his life-work was determined by an acquaintance with William Bartram, the well known Philadelphia naturalist. Wilson gave the remainder of his life to the study of birds, for which purpose he made long trips afoot to different parts of the country. His great work, *American Ornithology,* in nine volumes, was completed in 1808. The vivid descriptions in this work mark Mr. Wilson as a true man of letters, as well as an accurate scientist.

A most worthy successor of Wilson, and in some respects his superior, was John James Audubon (1780-1851) of Louisiana. Audubon spent his life studying birds in their native haunts. His descriptions are equal to, and his engravings better than, those of Wilson. His great work *The Birds of America,* containing 448 life size plates, was issued in ten volumes and sold for one thousand dollars.

In the field of mechanical science the mere mention of a

few names must suffice. Benjamin Silliman (1779-1864), "The Nestor of American Science," became widely known by his works on chemistry. Joseph Henry (1797-1878), long connected with the Smithsonian Institution, became known over the world as a scientific writer. Samuel F. B. Morse (1791-1872), inventor of the telegraph, has been noticed elsewhere. Alexander Dallas Bache, great-grandson of Benjamin Franklin, excelled in the United States Coast Survey and as a writer on scientific subjects. Robley Dunglison (1798-1869), achieved great success as an investigator and writer of books on medical science. Theological writers at this period were less powerful in governmental affairs than at earlier times, but the great religious denominations were not without strong leaders. Some of these attracted unusual attention by entering the lists in the long antislavery battle that preceded the Civil War.

Among the leading divines of the first sixty years of the nineteenth century were, in the Presbyterian Church, Archibald Alexander, his son Joseph Addison Alexander, Samuel Miller, and Charles Hodge, all of whom were professors in the Seminary at Princeton; William Ellery Channing, the leader of the Unitarian movement; Theodore Parker, who represented the rationalistic school of theology and was a vigorous antislavery advocate; Lyman Beecher, President of Lane Theological Seminary in Cincinnati, and his more distinguished son, Henry Ward Beecher, pastor of Plymouth Church, Brooklyn, and a famous antislavery lecturer; Charles Porterfield Krauth, a Lutheran theologian of extraordinary power as a writer, and Benjamin Kurtz of the same denomination; John W. Nevin, a leading theologian of the Reformed Church; Bishop George W. Doane and Samuel H. Turner of the Episcopal Church; Francis Way-

1755 — GILBERT STUART — 1828.

BY HIMSELF, 1790.

From the original portrait in the National Gallery, London.

land and Ira Chase, leading Baptist writers of their time; Alexander Campbell, the founder of the Disciple Church; Morris Jacob Raphall, the distinguished Jewish leader of New York; John P. Durbin, John McClintock, and Erastus O. Haven of the Methodist Episcopal Church; and among eminent Roman Catholic leaders, Archbishop Kenrick of Baltimore, Archbishop Hughes of New York, and Bishop England of Charleston, South Carolina.

CHAPTER XXVII

FIRST CENTURY AND A HALF OF AMERICAN ART [140]

BY CHARLES HENRY HART

THE genesis of art in a new land is more than interesting, it is important. Art is the companion of the highest cultivation: it therefore goes hand in hand with advancing civilization, and follows close in the wake of social development. To trace and follow the growth and progress of the fine arts in this country would be a work of the most profound interest and if treated, as it should be, from a philosophical standpoint, could not fail to teach most important lessons. Of course, such a discussion would require volumes where we have pages at our disposal, so it is not to be attempted here; but the rapid acquisition of immense wealth, in this free land of ours, has made our people known as the most lavish buyers of pictures in the world, and the bringing together of fine collections of paintings, in our midst, has generated a widespread taste for art and set our people, who are always first of all Americans, to look about them for American art and to inquire into its history, so that by understanding its traditions and recognizing its limitations, a better comprehension may be had of what we have done and what we have yet to do.

With this view in mind, it shall be my object to show briefly that we have had in this country a distinct school

[140] Reprinted by permission of Miss Florence N. Levy, from American Art Annual for 1898.

258

of American art. It will be admitted, without argument, that, since the Renaissance period, if not before, art has been an evolution and not a creation. Therefore, the school of American art cannot have distinctly different methods, of arriving at results, from other schools, but it can have its own distinctive qualities and did have them, clearly defined, until at least the end of the first half of the present century, which is the period I am to cover. I will show its beginning in Colonial days, as fully as the limited space at my command will permit, and then make mention of the artists who, up to 1850, helped to keep up the school of American art.

When we speak of American art, we do not mean the art of the aborigines, although it is far from being without interest, but it belongs to a study apart and distinct from the fine arts, which is the phase of American art we are to consider. We, the people of the United States, are apt, not unnaturally, to look to our mother country, England, as the giver of all of our most precious gifts of refinement and of culture. When it is to the fine arts we turn, we have heretofore felt sure it is the British Watson or Smibert who was the pioneer painter to limn the portraits of our forefathers on this side of the ocean. This is conclusively shown by the pages of Dunlap, Tuckerman, Benjamin, Clarence Cook and all who have written on the subject. It was left for the writer of the present article to discover that to Britain did not belong the honor of having planted the fine arts in this land and to place the crown upon the brow of a hitherto unknown son of Sweden.

It is true that Cotton Mather in his Magnalia mentions the fact that John Wilson, the organizer of the first church in Massachusetts, refused to sit for his portrait to a limner introduced for the purpose by Secretary Rawson; but "what

was his name or where his hame" no delving dry-as-dust
has yet discovered, so he must be dismissed with bare mention; only it serves to show that there was a portrait painter
here prior to 1667, when Wilson died. Desultory references
are made, in other New England writings of the seventeenth
century, to Joseph Allen and Thomas Child, as skilled in
limning, but as to how skilled we are unfortunately left in
the dark.

Therefore the first painter of recognized merit, known to
have practiced his art in the colonies, whose works have come
down to us, and who exerted any influence, by direct transmission, upon the fine arts of America, was Gustavus Hesselius,[140] who landed at Christina, now Wilmington, Delaware, in May 1711, and a few weeks later "Flyted," on account of his business, to Philadelphia. He was born at Fol-
karna, Dalarne, Sweden, in 1682, and died in Philadelphia,
May 25th, 1755. The earliest record of his art work that
we have is one of the most important items in the history of
art in America. On September 5, 1721, he received the
first public art commission known to have been given in
this country, "to draw ye history of our Blessed Saviour
and ye Twelve Apostles at ye last supper," for the altar of
St. Barnabas's Church, in Queen Anne Parish, Maryland.
The altar piece was completed, and its price, "£17," was paid
November 26, 1722. Unfortunately, the church building
was destroyed in 1773, and all trace of the painting has been
lost; but portraits painted by Gustavus Hesselius have come
down to us and are works of decided merit. Portraits
painted by his son and pupil, John Hesselius (1728-1778),
are quite familiar in Philadelphia and Maryland, while the

---

[140] The Earliest Painter in America. By Charles Henry Hart. Harper's Magazine, March, 1898.

works of John Hesselius's pupil, Charles Willson Peale
(1741-1827), who painted the first original portrait of
Washington that we have, and of Charles Willson Peale's
brother and pupil, James Peale (1749-1831) and of his son
and pupil, Rembrandt Peale (1778-1860), are known all
over the land and bring the teachings of Gustavus Hesselius
lineally to our own time.

So far as known, the next after Hesselius to come to practice limning here was John Watson, a native of Scotland,
who settled in Perth Amboy, New Jersey, in 1715, and
joined with his profession the business of money lender,
which he found the more profitable. His art has survived
only in several very creditable pencil portraits in little, and
his tombstone records that he died "August 22d, 1768, aged
83 years." Dunlap says that it was incidentally due to Watson's influence that he received the incentive that finally led
to his "History of the Arts of Design in the United States."

Up to the present time the best known of the early painters
in America has been John Smibert, who did not arrive here
until fourteen years after Watson and eighteen years after
Hesselius, but he was fortunate in being planted upon New
England soil, whose sons have always been loyal heralds
of their forebears. John Smibert, not "Smybert," as it is
commonly but incorrectly written, was one of the companions of Dean Berkeley, who is now chiefly remembered as
the author of the oft misquoted line, "Westward the course
of empire take its way," and before coming hither was favor-
ably known in Scotland as a painter of portraits. He accompanied Berkeley to America to become professor of the
fine arts, in the utopian university the future Bishop of
Cloyne contemplated founding in the Western Hemisphere.
The scheme failing, Berkeley returned to England, and

Smibert moved from Rhode Island to Boston, where he married, painted most of the noted persons of the town, and died in 1751, leaving several children, among them a son, Nathaniel, who adopted his father's calling, but survived him only five years. Smibert has enjoyed the distinction, heretofore, of having painted the first picture in America containing more than one figure, in his celebrated group of Dean Berkeley and family, in which the artist's own portrait is introduced, now one of the choice possessions of Yale University. This colossal canvas, 93x70, containing eight figures, is signed "Io. Smibert fecit 1729," which was eight years after Gustavus Hesselius painted his Last Supper with figures of Christ and the Twelve Apostles; so that Smibert is supplanted by Hesselius not only in the period of his coming, but also in being the author of the first composition painted here.

Contemporary with Smibert in Boston, and perhaps antedating him a few years, was Peter Pelham, who engraved in mezzotinto, as well as painted in oils, and died the same year with Smibert, leaving a successor in the arts in his son Henry Pelham, whose portrait has been handed down in his step-brother Copley's famous picture of the Boy and Squirrel. Pelham's chief distinction is having married the widow Copley, whereby he became the step-father of the future eminent painter, John Singleton Copley, whose early art training he undoubtedly guided. A close successor to Smibert, in Boston, if not a contemporary, was J. B. Blackburn, of whom nothing is known further than that he painted some very creditable portraits in whole length, and also family groups, much superior to those by Smibert and which served, with the works of Smibert and Pelham, to instill into Copley his taste for and knowledge of art.

The earliest known native American artist was James Claypoole, born in Philadelphia, January 22, 1720. Unfortunately, none of his paintings have been as yet identified; but he was the instructor of his nephew, Matthew Pratt, whose work shows that he was guided by a painter of no mean acquirements. Claypoole abandoned art for public life and was High Sheriff of Philadelphia during the Revolutionary war. The second native American painter we know was Robert Feke, born at Oyster Bay, Long Island, when Claypoole was five years old. He was wisely proud of his accomplishment and boldly signed and dated the portraits that he painted. But the first native American painter to have accomplished important work, which has come down to us, was Claypoole's nephew, Matthew Pratt,[150] who was born in Philadelphia September 23, 1734, and died in the city of his birth January 9, 1805. When thirty he accompanied his kinswoman, the fiancée of Benjamin West, to London, and after the wedding remained several months an inmate of West's home and became his first pupil. But Pratt before this had painted portraits of high merit, which show him to have been a careful draughtsman and a good colorist, with nice artistic feeling and a power in portraying the individual character of his sitters far beyond his master, West. Pratt's most important picture, "The School of American Painters," is in the Metropolitan Museum of Art, New York, and his whole length portrait of Cadwallader Colden belongs to the New York Chamber of Commerce.

Pratt's master, Benjamin West, was his junior by four years, having been born in Chester County, Pennsylvania, October 10, 1738. He received some instruction in art from

[150] "A Limner of Colonial Days." By Charles Henry Hart. Harper's Weekly, July 4, 1896.

one William Williams, about whom nothing is known beyond West's tribute, and began painting portraits at the age of eighteen; but candor requires it to be said they are utterly devoid of merit of any kind. When twenty-two, West went to Italy, and thence three years later to England, with which land his art is closely identified. He exerted, however, great influence over the development of art in this country, not only by his success and commanding position, but by his direct instruction, which was fortunately, as is not infrequently the case, much better than his work; the studio of Benjamin West having been, throughout his lifetime, the Mecca for all would-be American artists.

The brightest star, however, in the galaxy of early American painters was West's senior by one year, John Singleton Copley,[181] born in Boston, July 3, 1737, and the first native American painter to do work recognized as of highly meritorious quality, without European influence and study. Indeed, he is claimed by competent authority never to have surpassed some of his early portraits, and his own estimate was that his best pictures were painted in America. Thus, if New England is deprived of the honor of having the earliest painter in America, she is accorded the much higher distinction of having produced easily the first artist of distinguished ability in the American colonies.

Other men of this early period worthy of mention are Jeremiah Theus (circa 1760), of South Carolina, whose portraits are handed down as from the easel of Copley and serve to give local color to the unauthenticated tradition that Copley plied his pencil from Massachusetts to Georgia; John Woolaston (circa 1757), who came from England, and

[181] John Singleton Copley. A Review by Charles Henry Hart. American Architect. Vol. XI. p. 161.

painted chiefly in Virginia, where he limned the features
of the Widow Custis, before she became the wife of George
Washington; and Cosmo Alexander, a great-grandson of
George Jamesone, the Scottish Vandyke, who painted portraits from Rhode Island to South Carolina between 1770
and 1772, but is chiefly remembered as the first instructor
of Gilbert Stuart (1755-1828), the master painter of America, the bare mention of whose name is all-sufficient here.[182]
Ralph Earl (1751-1801), of Massachusetts, was one of the
best of our early portrait painters, and this is not meant to
be a damning with faint praise, while Robert Edge Pine [183]
(1730-1788) and James Sharples (1750-1811), both of
England, and Adolph Ulric Wertmuller (1750-1811),
Swedish by birth and French in art, have left some interesting works to show their ability.

Among artists to be noted in this résumé are Patience
Wright (1725-1786), the clever modeler in wax, and her
son, Joseph Wright (1756-1793), who painted as well as
modeled Washington more than once; John Trumbull
(1756-1843) and Edward Savage [184] (1761-1817), who
have each preserved for us the likenesses of many Revolutionary patriots; William Birch (1755-1834), the first and
best practitioner of enamel painting in this country; John
Ramage (circa 1775-1802), Robert Field (circa 1795-
1807), Benjamin Trott (circa 1795-1810), Joseph Wood
(circa 1796-1816) and Edward Greene Malbone (1777-

[182] Gilbert Stuart's Portraits of Women. By Charles Henry Hart.
The Century Magazine, 1897-1904.
[183] The Congress Voting Independence. A painting by Robert Edge
Pine. By Charles Henry Hart. Pennsylvania Magazine of History and
Biography, Vol. XXIX., p. 1.
[184] Edward Savage, Painter and Engraver. By Charles Henry Hart.
Proceedings Massachusetts Historical Society, January, 1905.

1807), all of whom painted excellent miniatures at the close of the last and opening of the present century, while Malbone is easily first in his art in this country and, at his best, the peer of any artist who ever painted in little.

Following these men came others of no mean importance and excellence. There was John Vanderlyn (1775-1852), whose "Marius" received a gold medal from the hand of Napoleon and whose "Ariadne" is the finest nude subject yet limned by a native-born American; Washington Allston (1779-1843), elected an Associate of the Royal Academy of Arts of Great Britain in 1818, and only failed of becoming an academician by his return to his native land; Matthew Harris Jouett [155] (1788-1827), of Kentucky, who for versatility and innate knowledge how to accomplish with the hand what the mind conceived, stands almost alone in the line of portrait painters, and whose work only requires to be better known to be appreciated; Thomas Sully (1783-1872), a charming delineator of fair women, and John Neagle (1796-1865), a true painter of strong men; Thomas Doughty (1793-1856), Asher Brown Durand (1796-1886), and Thomas Cole (1801-1848), the founders of landscape painting in America; Henry Inman (1801-1846), and William S. Mount 1807-1868), genre painters, who found their subjects in their own midst, painting American scenes with an American feeling; John F. Kensett (1816-1872) and Sandford R. Gifford (1823-1880), leaders in the open air school of landscapists, who saw the tenderness of atmospheric effect and fixed it to the canvas; George Fuller (1822-1884) and William M. Hunt (1824-1879), are all names not born to die.

Other painters who have a distinct place in the history of

[155] Kentucky's Master Painter. By Charles Henry Hart. Harper's Magazine, May, 1899.

American art, but not a very high place in art itself, are, among miniature painters, Henry Bembridge (1750-1820), Robert Fulton (1765-1815), Archibald Robertson (1765-1835), Anson Dickenson (1780-1847), Charles Fraser (1782-1860), Nathaniel Rogers (1788-1844), George Freeman (1789-1868), Anna Claypoole Peale (1791-1878), Hugh Bridport (1794-1832), George Catlin (1796-1872), Nathaniel Joscelyn (1796-1881), Thomas S. Cummings (1804-1894), George H. Cushman (1814-1876), and Richard M. Staigg (1817-1881); among portrait painters, Thomas Spence Duché (1763-1790), Jacob Eichholtz (1770-1842), John W. Jarvis (1780-1839), Samuel L. Waldo (1783-1861), Bass Otis (1784-1861), Charles B. King (1786-1862), William E. West (1788-1857), Chester Harding (1792-1866), Charles C. Ingham (1797-1863), Francis Alexander (1800-1880), James R. Lambdin (1807-1889), Charles L. Elliott (1812-1868), G. P. A. Healy (1813-1895), Samuel B. Waugh (1814-1885), Joseph Ames (1816-1872), Thomas Le Clear (1818-1882), George A. Baker (1821-1880), and Thomas Hicks (1823-1890); among history, genre, still life, marine and landscape painters, Raphaelle Peale (1774-1825), Joshua Shaw (1777-1860), Thomas Birch (1779-1851), John James Audubon (1780-1851), John Lewis Krimmell (1787-1821), Samuel F. B. Morse (1791-1872), Alvan Fisher (1792-1863), Robert W. Weir (1803-1889), John G. Chapman (1808-1889), George C. Bingham (1811-1879), William Page (1811-1885), James De Veaux (1812-1844), James G. Clonney (1812-1867), Cornelius Ver Byck (1813-1844), William Ranney (1813-1857), George L. Brown (1814-1889), Edwin White (1817-1877), T. P. Rossitter (1818-

1871), Henry Peters Gray (1819-1877), James Hamilton (1819-1878), F. O. C. Darley (1822-1888), Edward H. May (1824-1887), and Richard Caton Woodville (1825-1855).

Sculpture, architecture and engraving were not neglected. The first child of American parents, born within the United States, to carve in a resisting material was William Rush (1756-1833), of Philadelphia, and not John Frazee (1790-1852), of New Jersey, who claimed to be the first American-born sculptor.   These were followed by John H. I. Browere [300] (1792-1834), whose recently discovered busts from masks of the living face of Jefferson, Adams, and other national worthies place him in the front rank of the followers of the plastic art; Horatio Greenough (1805-1852), Hiram Powers (1805-1873), Joel T. Hart (1810-1877), Thomas Crawford (1814-1857), and Henry Kirke Brown (1814-1886).   In architecture we had notably Charles Bulfinch (1763-1844), Benjamin H. Latrobe (1764-1820), Robert Mills (1781-1855), Williams Strickland (1787-1854), John Haviland (1792-1852), Richard Upjohn (1802-1878), and Thomas U. Walter (1804-1887), while in engraving we have had David Edwin (1776-1841), the superior of Bartolozzi in the stipple manner; Asher Brown Durand (1796-1886), the peer of any European contemporary in line engraving, and John Cheney (1801-1885), without an equal in his time in the engraving of the female head.   Wood engraving and lithography were not neglected in the first century and a half of American art, but limited space forbids more than mere mention.   It

[300] Browere's Life Masks of Great Americans.   By Charles Henry Hart.   New York, 1899.

will be seen from this all too rapid survey what a mere skeleton of the subject is here presented and how rich a field is the history of American art.

CPSIA information can be obtained
at www.ICGtesting.com
Printed in the USA
BVHW071701061118

532319BV00011B/862/P

9 780483 420717